PHILOSOPHY BITES BACK

PHILOSOPHY BITES BACK

DAVID EDMONDS &
NIGEL WARBURTON

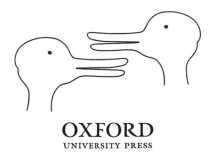

OXFORD
UNIVERSITY PRESS

OXFORD
UNIVERSITY PRESS

Great Clarendon Street, Oxford, OX2 6DP,
United Kingdom

Oxford University Press is a department of the University of Oxford.
It furthers the University's objective of excellence in research, scholarship,
and education by publishing worldwide. Oxford is a registered trade mark of
Oxford University Press in the UK and in certain other countries

First Edition published in 2012

Impression: 1

British Library Cataloguing in Publication Data

Data available

Library of Congress Cataloging in Publication Data

Data available

ISBN 978–0–19–969300–9

Printed in Great Britain by
Clays Ltd, St Ives plc

To Saul, Joshua, and Hannah

CONTENTS

CONTENTS

INTRODUCTION

W ho is the most important philosopher in history? Every now and again philosophers are asked about this in silly but enjoyable polls. A few names routinely crop up; no roll call could exclude Plato, Aristotle, Descartes, Hume, Kant, or Marx. But the philosophical canon is not fixed: it is a contested list, subject to argument and, occasionally, bitter disagreement. There was an outcry in Cambridge University in 1992, when the university authorities proposed to award the French thinker Jacques Derrida an honorary doctorate.

The following interviews are not meant to provide comprehensive coverage of the canon. There are notable philosophers whom you won't read about here, as well as some who aren't normally included on any core curriculum. Think of this list as more like an intellectual tasting-menu, an offering of morsels, packed, we hope, with philosophical nutrition. The contributors have made some suggestions for further reading which are included at the end of the book.

Philosophy now has over two and a half millennia of ideas from which to draw. Each generation rereads and reinterprets the significant figures from the past. We are fortunate to have spoken to some of today's leading exponents about some of yesteryear's most important thinkers.

The interviews began in oral form for *Philosophy Bites* (www. philosophybites.com), a popular podcast which as this book goes to print has had over 15 million downloads. When *Philosophy Bites* began, sceptics claimed there would be minimal interest in what they regarded as its esoteric material. But from all around the world, people have listened in to hear about Plato's views on love, Kant's synthetic a priori propositions, or Sartre's existentialism.

We are extremely grateful to the philosophers we've interviewed over the years: we've now had the privilege of hundreds of hours of free tutorials with some very clever and interesting people. We're especially thankful to those philosophers who appear in the book and who've granted permission for the interviews to be used in written form. All the interviews have been adapted so that they work as well as possible for the page. We'd like to thank our wives Anna and Liz, our agents, Caroline Dawnay and Veronique Baxter, and two institutions, London University's Institute of Philosophy and Oxford University's Uehiro Centre for Practical Ethics. The Institute of Philosophy has helped fund us, and provided us with a room in central London in which to conduct many of the interviews. Barry Smith and Shahrar Ali have provided constant encouragement, tips for interviewees, and the occasional glass of rather fine wine. We've also conducted several interviews at Oxford's Uehiro Centre for Practical Ethics and are grateful to the Centre's dynamic Director, Julian Savulescu, and also to the Centre's administrators, Miriam Wood and Deborah Sheehan.

Finally, thanks to our regular (unpaid) proofreader, Hannah Edmonds, to OUP's proofreader Javier Kalhat, and to our editors at OUP, Peter Momtchiloff, who commissioned this and our earlier *Philosophy Bites* book, and Eleanor Collins who saw it through production.

We dedicate this book to our children: Saul, Joshua, and Hannah.

David Edmonds and Nigel Warburton, April 2012
www.philosophybites.com

WHO IS YOUR FAVOURITE PHILOSOPHER?

For the past couple of years we've been asking the philosophers we've met a simple question, for which they were given no warning—who is their favourite philosopher and why? The eighteenth-century Scot, David Hume, came out first. That was no great surprise, though the extent of his lead was: he was the choice of more than 20 per cent of our sample. The other major philosophers always cited in the canon, Plato, Aristotle, Descartes, Kant, Mill, Nietzsche, Wittgenstein, were all well represented, but far behind.

Sarah Bakewell: *I'd have to go for two: Michel de Montaigne, who wrote essays about his life with a philosophical turn, because he is so much an ordinary human being; and also Friedrich Nietzsche because he also came at philosophy from completely unexpected angles. Like Montaigne, Nietzsche always looked for the underlying, unexpected angle to everything he wrote about.*

Helen Beebee: *My favourite philosopher is David Hume. His writings, particularly* A Treatise of Human Nature, *are a phenomenal intellectual achievement, and incredibly ahead of their time. He asked questions that others hadn't thought to ask. He challenged the orthodoxy when it came to religion and causation. I believe some of the things that Hume believed, but that's a side issue—I think a lot of philosophers have Hume as their favourite philosopher even if they don't really agree with what he says.*

Nick Bostrom: *That's putting me on the spot. I'm not sure I have one favourite philosopher. Contemporary philosophy, at least the way I'm doing it, is more like science in that many people have made significant contributions and you're* not so much following in the footsteps of one great individual but you're more drawing on the heritage of many people working over a long time.

Luc Bovens: *I very much enjoy reading Aristotle. When you read Aristotle, every letter, every word feels important. You have the feeling that he was writing in parchment. Every time I read Aristotle I see new things. At the London School of Economics we have an interest in philosophy being continuous with the sciences—this may be a controversial claim—and when you're reading Aristotle sometimes what you see is a proto-economist at work. You see a continuity between the style of argumentation that is used in philosophy and the style of argumentation used in the sciences. And deep down there is no distinction: that's what I find is so wonderful in Aristotle.*

Pascal Bruckner: *Well, as with every guy in my generation, when I was young it was Jean-Paul Sartre. I no longer have a favourite philosopher, but I have a big array of favourite philosophers going from John Locke to John Stuart Mill, Emmanuel Levinas, Karl Jaspers, Hannah Arendt. It's hard to pick just one and elect him or her as your master.*

Noël Carroll: *I guess my favourite philosopher is Aristotle. Perhaps the biographical reason is that I was trained a Catholic and I've had Thomism drilled into my bones since the early days. But I appreciate both his naturalist approach and, in reference to human affairs, the teleological approach.*

David Chalmers: *Lately, I've been very taken by the works of Rudolf Carnap who was a logical empiricist working in the 1920s, 30s, and 40s: his great work is* Der logische Aufbau der Welt (The Logical Structure of the World) *and right now I'm trying to work on a project that recapitulates some of Carnap's ideas and somehow tries to figure out the fundamental structure of descriptions of reality and where we can go from there. He's been an inspiration to me.*

Clare Chambers: *Well, I'm enormously impressed by the work of Catharine MacKinnon, who is a political philosopher and also an active legal scholar and practitioner. Her work is extremely significant both theoretically and practically.*

Pat Churchland: *My true, true love is David Hume: Saint David, as Simon Blackburn calls him. And that's because he was first of all tremendously dedicated to getting to the bottom of things. He was totally unswayed by fashion and the current ways of doing things; he zeroed in, in the most intelligent way, on the most difficult issues, and he got so much right.*

Tim Crane: *Descartes. Not because I think what he said was true, but because he was incredibly clear in his vision of things. He had an ambitious conception of the world that he wanted to fit everything into—and he did that in a very, very simple and clear way. And I like that.*

Alain de Botton: *Probably my favourite philosopher is Nietzsche because he has a fascinating metaphysical structure to his thought and at the same time writes beautifully, has a sense of humour, and is a genuine creative artist.*

Michael Dummett: *Gottlob Frege, because he was the first philosopher to give a clear analysis of the structure of sentences, and thereby of the thoughts that they express.*

Ronald Dworkin: *Well, I am very attracted to Immanuel Kant's work: it seems to me an endless source of interpretation and reinterpretation. One of the books that has given me most pleasure is a book sitting just there called* Kant et Dworkin. *And the pleasure is increased by the fact that I can't read it: it's in French.*

Cécile Fabre: *Oh my God. Can I have two? Yes. Well, my favourite philosopher in the English language is Thomas Hobbes. He writes with extraordinary beauty and in a way that is utterly compelling, even though his substantive conclusion, that is, that we should have an absolute monarch, is completely counterintuitive. My favourite philosopher in French is Rousseau, again because he writes very beautifully, very concisely. He has similarly counterintuitive views, but somehow writes about those views so compellingly that I keep being drawn back to his works, again and again.*

Kit Fine: *My favourite philosopher is Aristotle. He's one of the greatest geniuses of all time who wrote profoundly on a wide range of questions.*

Cynthia Freeland: *Aristotle. And that might surprise people because I am a feminist, and known as such, and he said so many misogynist things. But I think Aristotle was a philosopher who was grounded in biology and in trying to deal with the real world, and I'm an admirer of his respect for living organisms and also for his purchase on ethics: virtue ethics. So I find him very appealing.*

Raymond Geuss: *My favourite philosopher is Thucydides. And he's my favourite philosopher because nobody else thinks he's a philosopher, but I think he is.*

Jonathan Glover: *Socrates. Not because I accept many of his opinions, but because he invented the whole thing. I still teach, as does everyone in philosophy, by the methods Socrates invented. You ask people, 'what do you think about this, what's your opinion?', and then you press for maximum clarity and explicitness: 'do you mean this, or do you mean that?' When you've got it really clear, then there are counterexamples: 'Oh, that's your view, is it, but what about applying that principle to this case, surely you can't think this?' And this is the method of philosophy: it's a wonderful method. That's Socrates' first contribution. His second contribution was that he didn't shut himself off in some academy, but talked in the marketplace to people. He'd have been on Philosophy Bites, if he'd had the chance. Too many philosophers in my opinion treat philosophy as a kind of esoteric, technical thing, which isn't for the public. This is a huge loss.*

Alison Gopnik: *My favourite philosopher is David Hume. Partly because he's one of the few philosophers who you think would have been a really, really nice guy. But also because he was known not only as a father of philosophy but also of psychology, and he was someone who thought very profoundly about philosophical questions but also about empirical, psychological questions. And also because he was someone who appreciated the role of sentiment and emotion and everyday life in abstract logical argument.*

John Horton: *Probably my favourite philosopher is not a political philosopher at all. It's Ludwig Wittgenstein, who is simply the greatest philosopher that I've ever read: for his incredible rethinking of philosophy as an activity.*

Alan Howarth: *Well, my favourite philosopher would be a cross between Wittgenstein, John Stuart Mill, and Karl Marx: Wittgenstein for his careful, analytical approach to philosophy and his sensitivity to nuances of language; Mill for his liberal principles; and Marx for his socialist ideals and his general bolshiness.*

Frank Jackson: *That's a difficult question. I really have three favourite philosophers: Jack Smart, David Armstrong, and David Lewis. David Armstrong taught me when I was a student at Melbourne: he gave wonderful lectures, though I didn't believe much of what he said. I was a colleague of Jack Smart's for a year at Adelaide. And then I met David Lewis who seemed to me, as he did to so many people, to be something quite special: the sort of philosopher who only comes along every 50 or 100 years. If you were putting me on the spot, I'd have to put David Lewis at the top of that list.*

Sean Kelly: *I'd have to say Aristotle, but I don't read Aristotle in a traditional way. One of the things that I'm interested in in Aristotle is that he has a conception of what he calls the* phronimos. *The* phronimos *is something like the master of living a practical life. And what I'm interested in Aristotle's conception of the* phronimos *is that he thinks that the* phronimos *cultivates in himself the ability to recognize immediately, without deliberation or thought, what's demanded of him in a situation— and that seems to me a very important skill.*

Joshua Knobe: *I've always had this admiration for Friedrich Nietzsche. Maybe it was Nietzsche who first got me interested in philosophical questions. What I take from Nietzsche is the idea that we shouldn't simply be interested in understanding how people ordinarily think about certain kinds of questions, but that we should try to look deeper, and in some ways* *try to question these ordinary views that we have—and maybe rebel against the ways that we have ordinarily been thinking about them.*

Chandran Kukathas: *My favourite philosopher is David Hume. It's partly a matter of my own biography, since he was the first philosopher that I started working on systematically when I was a master's student many years ago. I find myself attracted to his common-sensical and humane attitudes. And I find myself attracted to his politics and also to his understanding of morality which is—how shall I put it—not nearly as stoical as the Germans, who are too stoical for me.*

Nicola Lacey: *I'm not a philosopher. I wrote a biography of a philosopher called H. L. A. Hart, and he engages my great interest as well as admiration. But if you were to ask me a slightly different question—which is: 'if you were a philosopher which philosopher would you really want to immerse yourself in and become expert in it?'—that would be Wittgenstein. To put this in the context of my work in both criminal law theory and on Hart: it's because I see Wittgenstein as analysing philosophical ideas in a way which is much more porous to an historical or a social-scientific approach, because of his idea that concepts find their form and texture within ways of life. That seems to me to invite more of an institutional analysis of criminal law which is what I'm really interested in.*

Melissa Lane: *My favourite philosopher, no surprise from my work, is the ancient Greek philosopher, Plato. And it's because in his thought we see all the fundamental questions of philosophy conjoined. So we see why, in order to think about ethics and politics, we need to think about psychology, about epistemology, about metaphysics—about how all of these questions are connected.*

Brian Leiter: *Oh Fred. Fred Nietzsche. I call him Fred. Well, because he's a great writer, and I think he's more right than wrong about most of the things he has views on.*

Tim Lewens: *I'm going to go for David Hume: because he's just right about most things.*

Guy Longworth: *René Descartes: because he gave us a set of philosophical issues of outstanding importance.*

Catharine MacKinnon: *Oh, the last woman I talked to, whoever she is.*

Simon May: *I would say, my favourite philosopher is Nietzsche. He was my second love, not my first love: sometimes your second love is even stronger than your first love. The reason is that he had the courage to look at the whole of western morality and critique it mercilessly. And I think that's what the job of philosophy is, and not to tinker round the edges or do too much conceptual slicing.*

Jeff McMahan: *My favourite philosopher is Derek Parfit who teaches at Oxford. His work combines imagination and insight and rigour and clarity in a way that's really unprecedented.*

Hugh Mellor: *My favourite philosopher is a fellow Cambridge philosopher, much more eminent and impressive than I am, called Frank Ramsey. He died in 1930, just before his 27th birthday, having created two branches of economics, a branch of mathematics, which was his job officially, and made contributions to metaphysics, to the philosophy of mind, the philosophy of action, the philosophy of language, the philosophy of probability, and decision theory, which have really not been matched since his day.*

Sue Mendus: *My favourite philosopher is John Stuart Mill: because he led a rich political life and worked out his philosophical theories in the political world; he was politically engaged. Although the myth doesn't tell you this, he was a very passionate man and a man with very great concern for those who were less well-off than he was. And I think he also had a sad life and struggled with his own personality, and with his own background. And he triumphed! So he's my favourite.*

John Mikhail: *I would mention two: David Hume and Jeremy Bentham. Hume was a phenomenal theorist of mental activity, absolutely exceptional in his subtle descriptions of our mental lives and in posing philosophical problems that have endured. And Bentham is a hero because of his moral* *and political outlook: the way in which he as a young person was scandalized by the corruption and the immorality around him in society, and set himself to change that, and he was really remarkably effective in doing so.*

David Miller: *I have two favourite philosophers, Hume and Wittgenstein. What I like about them both is that they've permanently inoculated me against a certain kind of scepticism. This is why, for example, I've never been in the slightest tempted by any form of postmodernism: because if you study these philosophers you'll see at once the self-defeating character of certain forms of sceptical reasoning.*

Tariq Modood: *My goodness. I've got a number of favourite philosophers. Socrates is a big hero. Probably the philosopher that I've been most influenced by is Wittgenstein. Wittgenstein's emphasis that philosophy is not about trying to establish an ideal language like mathematics, and that words are not imprecise—they do exactly what they're meant to do—but what they're meant to do is not necessarily the strain that philosophers put upon them. This emphasis on the fact that meaning lies in use is a very important concept for me. Another very important concept for me is 'family resemblance' because that helps me to understand how in my own field of multiculturalism those who try to get all groups to be like one particular model—of ethnicity or equality, or whatever—are not only pursuing what looks like a politically impossible task, but they're intellectually flawed. They're working with a conception of concepts that Wittgenstein exploded.*

A.W. Moore: *Kant, partly because of the incredible breadth of his philosophy and also because of something which in a way comes as a surprise in that context, which is the incredible unity of that philosophy.*

Stephen Neale: *Bertrand Russell. He clarified an aspect of the use of language with his Theory of Descriptions, the full ramifications of which have still not been entirely felt. It's such an important contribution. It's the contribution that Russell himself clung to his entire life: and when he was asked very late in life what was his most important contribution to philosophy, he said the Theory of Descriptions. And I'm inclined to agree.*

Susan Neiman: *Well, if I can only pick one then I'll pick Kant. He's actually the bravest of anyone. Kant's most important insight is that there's a huge gap between the way the world is and the way the world ought to be, and that both of those have equal value. And one needs to keep both of them constantly in mind. It's an extremely hard stance to take. It's very modern. It means a certain amount of living on the edge, a certain amount of permanent frustration. People tend to go in one direction or the other. Either they say, 'the way the world is, is all there is, and any sort of ideal is an illusion that you ought to grow out of'. Or they project some kind of illusion—this is where you get Stalinism or something similar—and they say, 'the way the world ought to be is the way the world is'. Living with both is extremely hard, and it means that you know that you will never realize entirely the ideals that you believe in. But I think it's the only way of being both honest and hopeful at the same time.*

Martha Nussbaum: *Well, that's a hard question, but I guess I would say John Stuart Mill, and part of the reason is that when I imagine meeting the great philosophers of the past and talking to them, I immediately imagine their likely reaction of disdain for a woman. And Mill is one of the few—perhaps the only—great philosopher of the past who actually thought of women as equals, and I think I could have a very good conversation with him.*

Onora O'Neill: *Well, I've worked on Immanuel Kant for more years than I'm going to tell you. And I think I've developed an unusual and broad reading of Kant's philosophy which is a good deal more sympathetic than some of the caricatures. So go there, it's worth it. Read it. Read some of the lesser works. And, of course I'm not alone in this now. Recent PhDs I've been in contact with cover Kant and environmental ethics, Kant and intellectual property. There's a lot in there when you get into the wider Kant.*

Philip Pettit: *Oh dear, oh dear, you should have given me some notice of that question. I'm a great enthusiast of Hobbes in so far as I think—I wrote a book about this a couple of years ago—that he's the one who first introduced a very important thesis: which is that we are pretty well like other animals except in so far as we chanced upon language. Now Hobbes devel-*

oped that in the absence of knowledge about evolutionary theory, but I think his views can be reworked consistently with what we know about Darwinian theory. Whether or not they're exactly right, it's such a wonderful idea. But, of course, I hate Hobbes when it comes to his political philosophy. So on that matter, I find Kant more appealing, though Kant in political philosophy troubles me too. I'd have to start mentioning more obscure figures, like Joseph Priestley, Richard Price, in the eighteenth century: these are really my heroes in political thinking.

Anne Phillips: *My favourite philosopher is Hannah Arendt. I don't really know why, but every time I start a new research project I find myself rereading Hannah Arendt and finding more interesting things about the world. I couldn't summarize her philosophy, but she seems to me to be one of the most original thinkers that there is.*

Nick Phillipson: *My favourite philosopher is still David Hume. There is something enormously sympathetic about David Hume. He is a sceptic, and not a dogmatic sceptic. He is very funny. He writes wonderful letters. And he was a good cook.*

Hanna Pickard: *My favourite philosopher is Hume, because I think he's wonderful to read and he takes emotion seriously, which in my view both moral philosophy and the philosophy of mind have failed to do, to the detriment of our understanding of human nature—and understanding human nature is what I would like philosophy to aim to do.*

Thomas Pogge: *I would have to say Kant. Why? For two reasons: one is that he was just so damn good. Kant is just inexhaustible. And I just love to read Kant, love to follow his thought, and every time I read his work I find new things. So this standard question—what would you take to a desert island if you could only take one book—it would definitely be the first Critique,* The Critique of Pure Reason, *even though I've read it many times before. The other thing is that I admire Kant's seriousness about philosophy. He was a man who, with regard to his moral philosophy, for example, was just incredibly careful and serious. He thought about moral philosophy as if what he* *thought really, really mattered and, of course, in the end it turned out that it did, if only over the course of centuries rather than years.*

Gideon Rosen: *Oh, that's a hard question. My children are always asking me 'who's my favourite this' and 'who's my favourite that', and I never have these lists in my head. I've been teaching Hume this week. And as of today, Hume is my favourite philosopher. Hume is a philosopher who was bemused by the limits of philosophy. Hume was an abstract thinker of the first order who turned his gaze on ordinary human thought and ordinary human practice and found that under close scrutiny it eats its own tail, it dissolves. But Hume thought that although human beings are rational animals and that this is an aspect of our nature that we should embrace and cannot deny—we are not just rational animals, we are also non-rational human animals—philosophical understanding of human life isn't designed to bring human life into line with philosophy, it's designed to bring philosophy into line with human life.*

Paul Russell: *Oh, that's a tough question. Can I cheat and have two? Historically, I'm a huge fan of David Hume: it reflects my Scottish background. I admire Hume's clarity and precision and his sense of what are important large issues. The other person I really admire, another prejudice of mine, is my supervisor Bernard Williams, who was a hugely influential and important philosopher of the twentieth century. I enormously admire his philosophical ability and insight, his range was terrific, and like Hume I felt he had a great sense for what were significant philosophical problems and issues. He offers a great critical insight into the nature of philosophy itself.*

Michael Sandel: *The philosopher I've found most challenging and exciting is Hegel. I suppose that's in part because Hegel—difficult though he is to understand—raised fundamental questions about the abstract morality of Kant, connecting morality with embodied ethical life. Hegel's challenge to Kant, philosophically for me, is one of the most exciting works in philosophy. So I nominate Hegel.*

Philip Schofield *My favourite philosopher is Jeremy Bentham. I got a job working at the Bentham project in 1984 and he's kept me fed and watered ever since.*

Peter Singer: *Henry Sidgwick is my favourite philosopher. He's the least well known of the founding fathers of utilitarianism—Bentham, Mill, and Sidgwick—but he's clearly the best as a philosopher. His masterpiece* The Methods of Ethics *is a wonderfully reasoned book: he thinks of many objections, he's scrupulously fair to his opponents. And he argues for what is essentially a utilitarian conclusion though he has to admit that he's not convinced that he's been able to defeat the egoist viewpoint. But there are so many questions that Sidgwick brings up and reasons about in a way that is still relevant and so often still right today that I think he is without peer as a careful, reflective philosopher.*

Barry Smith: *I guess my opinion has changed over time. Michael Dummett was the first favourite, but as I've grown older, Hume and Wittgenstein get a look in, and for his work on understanding language, Chomsky. If I had to pick one of them, it would be David Hume, the great Scot. I think he had a commanding understanding of every aspect of our lives: how the mind works, how we fit into the world, the nature of morality, our aesthetic judgements, politics. And he was really keen to understand exactly how we work as creatures: how our minds are built and how they are organized. And for that reason he didn't care whether he was called a philosopher or psychologist, or whatever. He just wanted to find things out—and he had a very good attempt at doing that.*

Richard Sorabji: *I don't really have a permanent favourite because I've changed my mind over time. At the moment, the two philosophers who excite me most are the later Stoics, starting with a Stoic called Panaetius who made moral philosophy very personal and original, and Mahatma Gandhi. But no doubt that's because it's my most recent book.*

Hillel Steiner: *Oh dear, you didn't forewarn me of this. Boringly, I'm going to have to opt for John Locke. Not merely or, indeed, especially for his* *political philosophy, which I find myself considerably in sympathy with, but more his place in history. He seems to me to have been an exemplary person.*

Dan Sterber: *Oh, that's a difficult one. I don't think I have one favourite philosopher. What I like in philosophy are precisely the disagreements, the dialogues, the ability to come with quite different points of view and exchange arguments.*

Robert Stern: *Well, it has to be Hegel. Because there's a complexity to the attempt to think through difficult issues and resolve them, which is an underused resource within contemporary philosophy, particularly within contemporary analytical philosophy. Most analytic philosophers have understandably been put off by the style, the language, and one thing and another, and not seen that often Hegel gives you options on the intellectual map that others haven't seen.*

Galen Strawson: *I think it's Immanuel Kant. Every time I hear the words* 'The Critique of Pure Reason', *I find myself involuntarily salivating. It's an absurd reaction, but it's just true: it's happening right now.*

Robert Talisse: *John Stuart Mill is my favourite philosopher: not because I agree with everything he says but I think that his main works, particularly* On Liberty, *is one of the most moving, well thought-out, accessible, and rigorously argued pieces of philosophy ever written.*

Tzvetan Todorov: *Maybe my favourite philosopher is Jean-Jacques Rousseau, because he is an extremely multifaceted author, a novelist, a drama writer, an autobiographer, a dreamer, an individualist, a socialist: he was extremely gifted, and probably an unbearable person, but happily enough we have the works.*

Alex Voorhoeve: *I think it would be David Hume. I like his approach as a naturalist, trying to figure out our psychology and where our moral and political judgements come from. I find him tremendously insightful and illuminating, and I'm always surprised at how discovering where your judge-*

xxiii

ments come from can influence your thoughts about whether they're any good.

Susan Wolf: *Living or dead? Well, Aristotle is the first person who comes to mind. He was wise and humane.*

Jonathan Wolff: *Probably Hume. The reason for this is that he wrote the* Treatise of Human Nature *when he was 26. And it's got probably thousands of completely original and new ideas in it: it seems to be a miracle that someone of such young years could have thought so much already. And also for his incredible economy of expression: on one page you might get three brilliant arguments. Most philosophers would have been quite satisfied with their life's work if they just produced the ideas on one page of Hume.*

1

MARY MARGARET McCABE ON
Socrates and the Socratic Method

David Edmonds: *According to the dictionary, a question is an*
expression of inquiry that invites a reply. No figure in the history of ideas
has been more associated with the question *than Socrates—one of the*
founders of western philosophy. He gives his name to a type of investiga-
tion through dialogue—the so-called Socratic method. His questions and
truth seeking so annoyed the Athenians that he was tried and found guilty
of corrupting young minds. His punishment—in 399 BC—was death
through drinking hemlock. Professor M. M. McCabe of King's College
London, submitted herself to a rigorous questioning by Philosophy Bites.

Nigel Warburton: *We're going to talk about Socratic method; that's*
the method of Socrates. But who was Socrates?

M. M. McCabe: Socrates lived in Athens in the fifth century
BC. He was ugly and disreputable to look at, but a striking and
compelling character—so much so that when he asked, people
answered: he commanded attention all the time from his
interlocutors. But this caused some difficulty in Athens
because the questions he asked were uncomfortable ones—
deep questions about why they did what they did, both
individually and collectively—and the Athenians didn't like

that much. They thought that somehow he was responsible for subversive elements in the state and in particular for some of the political difficulties in which Athens was embroiled at the end of the fifth century. So at the age of 70, in 399 BC, Socrates was executed: given hemlock to drink. He left a huge legacy to the rest of western philosophy.

NW: *And part of his legacy is the portrayal of Socrates in Plato's writing. Plato was one of his pupils and wrote superbly about Socrates.*

MMM: That's right. There are in fact several different sources for Socrates' life. There's a ribald play by Aristophanes, the *Clouds*; there's some rather hagiographic material by Xenophon; and there are other Socratic works. But the most important Socratic material is the collection of dialogues that Plato wrote in which Socrates was the main speaker: works about his life, his death, and his conversations with those luckless people who were trying to live their ordinary lives when Socrates called them to account.

NW: *But it's very important that we have these, because Socrates himself didn't write anything down.*

MMM: He wrote nothing; he was probably too busy talking. He supposed that what we should be doing is all the time asking questions of others and of ourselves about what it is we think, about what we're doing, and what it is to think about what we're doing: questions, that is to say, both about matters ethical and about matters epistemological. Let me give you an example: there was an Athenian called Euthyphro who was an expert on religion. Socrates meets him when they are both on their way to court: Socrates to defend himself against the charge of which he was convicted, Euthyphro to prosecute his own father for the manslaughter of one of his own slaves. Socrates says to Euthyphro: 'hang on a minute, are you sure you know what you're doing?' and Euthyphro says: 'yes, of course I know what I'm doing, I am an expert'. Socrates' investigation is in part about whether Euthyphro is right to think that what he's doing is right. But the most significant thing about his discussion with Euthyphro is his investigation about what it would be to know such a thing, what sorts of claims you make when you say, 'I know that prosecuting my father is the right thing to do'. So the discussion always works at that double level, both an account of the particular question at hand, and an account of what conditions there would be on answering it.

NW: *This kind of discussion is actually an example of what we call the Socratic method—where Socrates meets somebody, challenges their assumptions, and through asking difficult questions teases out just how little they know.*

MMM: Exactly. What he's trying to explain to us is not only how little they know but how little they understand about what it would be to know something. What we understand as the Socratic method is this business of continuous questioning; but we need to notice how complex that turns out to be. One has to think about the logic of the Socratic method as well; when he considers somebody's position in this sort of question and answer, what he is looking at is a collection of views that they hold, rather than investigating some single proposition and working out whether it's true or false. So Socrates is trying to see how everything that a person believes fits together. You can see how this makes the Socratic method a very complicated and deeply controversial process, because you're asking people the most extraordinarily impertinent questions about what they really think, and forcing them to face the exceedingly uncomfortable thought that what they think is somehow incoherent or inconsistent, or dismally incomplete.

NW: *And a lot of people found him intensely irritating because of that.*

MMM: Well they killed him; they had had enough of all of this, and so they bumped him off.

NW: *The person engaged in the Socratic method is not a thoughtful individual in a library: he's someone scrutinizing ideas in the marketplace, talking to people.*

MMM: That's exactly right; Socrates thinks that you can have a conversation with no holds barred and find things out that way. There's no suggestion that somehow or other we're stuck inside our own heads and can't do things collaboratively or collectively; he doesn't start from a position of scepticism about whether there are other minds, or suppose that I'm limited to my own subjective experience. Instead, Socrates thinks (or Plato shows us a Socrates who thinks) that these conversations are genuinely collaborative activities, that it is really possible to find things out together. And from our modern perspective we're inclined to think that's a bit overstated, that he's being ironical. People often say about Socrates: 'Oh, well, he *says* he wants to talk with his friends, but he doesn't really mean it, because he knows he's a clever-clogs and they're really stupid—all he is really doing is showing them up.' That seems to me to assume something about the tone of these discussions which may not be there. I think one should read what Plato has him say at face value and take Socrates to think that these question and answer sessions are *mutually* illuminating, both about the question in hand, and about what it would be to answer it.

NW: *Are these conversations good because they lead to knowledge or are they somehow intrinsically good because they're conversations?*

MMM: The first thing to remember here is that even when the conversations themselves end in impasse, in *aporia*, they don't fail to make any progress at all: often both the reader and the interlocutors find out a great deal en route about how thought and explanation and knowledge ought to work. Then, second, one might reflect a bit on what Socrates might be committed to in asking all of these questions: why it is worth doing at all? Why is this sort of uncomfortable conversation something we should care about, let alone die for? Some think that Socrates' interest in knowledge is practical—that we want to know so that we shall be good at getting things right, making accurate decisions, getting hold of whatever we need or want, arriving at satisfying our best interests. On such an account, Socrates would think that knowledge is worth having for instrumental reasons—for whatever goods it can provide us with, not for any value it might have in itself. But this picture of Socrates as seeking to calculate the best outcome, or to assemble the maximum amount of goods, sits ill, I think, both with the portrait we are given of a man careless of fame and fortune, and with his obsessive questioning, his constant interest in knowledge itself. Instead, the way to think about Socrates is by means of his own dictum—that the unexamined life is not worth living.

NW: *What does Socrates mean when he says the 'unexamined life is not worth living'?*

MMM: First of all think about it as a *life*. What Socrates is asking us to consider is a whole life, not a collection of goods that we might gather together one day or the next. So the focus is away from individual pieces of practical reasoning or the acquisition of particular goods, or even from the amassing of fortune, the searching for fame, and towards something that might have both the continuity and the structure of a life, centred on the person who lives it, rather than the things they acquire along the way. Secondly, think about what might be the objection to the *unexamined* life, or what might be the demand that we examine it. There might be two ways of understanding that demand: that we examine the life; or that we recommend the life of examining itself. If I am right that the Socratic method is as interested in the conditions for knowledge and understanding as it is in the answers to particular ethical questions, then we might conclude that what Socrates is interested in is the life of examining itself. So it would be that process of constant questioning, of making sure that your principles of reasoning and your processes of reasoning are honest and consistent, fit together and are things for which you're willing to be responsible, that characterizes, and even creates, the life that is worth living.

NW: *Does that then mean that all we need to do is go around questioning all the time to lead a good life?*

MMM: It might be depressing, mightn't it? Perhaps you would end up alone and friendless (not to mention the hemlock). And perhaps you would then be someone for whom the lives of others were nothing but the instruments to your own reflection, and the features of the lives that we think are ordinary would be of no account at all—all that would matter would be this sort of austere intellectualism: that would be all there is to life, morality, and everything. This goes down in the tradition as the question of whether the wise man (or the virtuous man) is happy on the rack. But it doesn't follow from what Socrates says about the examined life that the examination is *all there is* to a life; the examined life could be the central explanation or condition of what makes this a good life, without the examination's being all there is to it. So you can have friends, and love, and even do all sorts of frivolous things, and the life still counts as examined, if indeed you have the examination at its core. Socrates doesn't need to be committed to saying that the wise man is happy on the rack—he just needs to be committed to the view that if you've got two chaps on the rack, one wise and one not wise, the wise one's going to be better off.

NW: *That's really interesting because of this ancient injunction 'know thyself'. You might think the implication is you have to introspect, go into the wilderness, and think about your life away from other people. But for Socrates it's an essentially social activity.*

MMM: That's right. Supposing you try to work out what it is to be reflective; you might think, 'being reflective requires me to wander off into the wilderness, and worry'. I think that Socrates thinks being reflective is having a perspective on what you think that is detached—looking at, reflecting on the things that you think, as it were, from outside. But one of the ways in which you can do that best is in conversation, because what conversations do is to provide you with differences of perspective. And he might think, further, that one of the reasons to care about working out our lives like this, is that doing things together just matters, that social engagement is itself important, both for love and for knowledge.

NW: *Socrates claimed that he had nothing to teach; nevertheless, is there something we can learn from Socrates today?*

MMM: If Socrates thought we'd learnt something he would still not have thought he'd taught us. But I think he was right about something important. It seems to me that if we are involved in education—whether we're being educated or doing the educating, or, best of all, both at once—the Socratic method is a fundamental feature of the whole business. It doesn't constitute the whole of education, but it constitutes something at the core of what we might think education properly is: to discuss with others in this open-minded, open-ended way that allows them to reflect on what they think and us to reflect on what we think, without dictating, without dogma, without insistence, and without imperative. And what the interlocutors are asked to do, if you like, is to be true to themselves: to be sincere about their beliefs and to be honest about how their beliefs fit together and to have some respect for their companion. All of that, I think, is a lesson that we do rightly learn from Socrates.

NW: *What are the implications then for you as somebody inspired by Socrates' teaching within quite a constraining university curriculum?*

MMM: The standard ways that we have of teaching in universities are ways that Socrates wouldn't acknowledge as proper methods of coming to understand. For example, the lecture: it's actually impossible to lecture Socratically, since there is no conversation—Socrates complained all the time about 'long speeches', I think, because they just fail to engage with the other person in the right way. Socrates certainly wouldn't approve of examinations in the contemporary sense, because they suggest that there is a right answer and a wrong answer, and he wouldn't think about things in those terms. Although he doesn't deny that there is truth and falsehood, he thinks that knowledge and understanding don't come piecemeal like that, and are not checked by that kind of test. He wouldn't like bite-sized courses, modules, whatever one likes to call them. He wouldn't think you can start here and finish there, and get it right about metaphysics, for example—because he thinks that there are no lines of demarcation between one question and another. The Socratic method is demanding and extreme; but we can see that it is a model that one needs to bear in mind all the time. It keeps you honest just a little bit; it stops you from thinking, 'oh yeah it's easy, you know, I can go and give a few lectures and then I've done my job'. That's not what doing your job should look like—especially in philosophy.

NW: *Would you describe yourself as Socratic?*

MMM: I wish I could. I'd like to be. But it's very hard!

2

ANGIE HOBBS ON
Plato on Erotic Love

David Edmonds: *The scene: a drinking party, two and a half millennia ago. The revellers: a philosopher, a soldier-politician, a comic poet and a tragedian, a physician, a specialist in law. The subject of their discussion: love. To discuss one of Plato's most famous dialogues,* The Symposium, *and in particular the nature of erotic love, we spoke to Angie Hobbs, of Sheffield University.*

Nigel Warburton: *The topic we're talking about is Plato on love. We're talking about a specific kind of love, Eros. What does Plato mean by that?*

Angie Hobbs: The term means erotic love, and I've heard it beautifully described as 'whatever makes you tingle'. Traditionally, in Greek literature, erotic love was physical love for someone else's body, but what we're going to see Plato doing throughout his work, particularly in his great dialogue on love, the *Symposium*, is expanding the field of erotic love away from bodies. But the basic meaning of the term is erotic desire for one other human being.

NW: *You've mentioned* The Symposium. *What was that?*

AH: It's a sumptuous dialogue by Plato. It was written in about 385 BC, but mainly set in 416 BC, and it describes a probably apocryphal symposium, a drinking party, at the house of a tragedian called Agathon. Amongst the guests we have Socrates, the comic poet Aristophanes, a doctor, a student of rhetoric, and—probably the most famous man in Athens of his day—the glamorous, charismatic, general/statesman/bad boy/rock star figure, Alcibiades. And they all give their own views on what they think erotic love is: its definition and origins, its aims and objects, whether it's beneficial or harmful to mankind.

NW: *Let's start with Aristophanes. He's got a powerful speech about the nature of erotic love.*

AH: This is one of my favourite passages in western literature. In keeping with his profession, he gives us this fabulously inventive comic fantasy. Originally, he says, there were three different sexes of proto-human beings (though whether they can even be classed as proto-human is in fact disputed): male, female, and hermaphrodite (a mixture of male and female). And these beings were initially spherical. They were completely round, with four arms, four legs, two heads, two faces, and two sets of genitalia, and they rolled around the surfaces of the earth like acrobats. But this race got very uppity, they got above themselves, and the Greek gods, led by Zeus, wondered what to do about them. If they killed them all off, that would get rid of the threat but they would also lose all the libations and sacrifices. So the gods thought: what we'll do is cut them all in half. In so doing, we'll both weaken them, but also double the number of those offering libations. So Zeus orders Hephaestus—the blacksmith god—to cut these spherical beings in half to form creatures with two arms, two legs, one face, one set of genitalia (initially in the wrong place—we'll come back to this), and they mope around the world looking for their lost other half. And, Aristophanes says, this is what Eros is: it is the search for your literal other half; it is the desire to be reunited with this other half and thereby achieve your original state. It's the yearning and quest to regain what you've lost.

NW: *That's a powerful metaphor for sexual longing, but even in ancient Greek times it couldn't have been taken to be literally true?*

AH: No, but it's a very compelling way of evoking the notion of erotic desire for one other unique, particular, irreplaceable human being. Except, of course, there is an intriguing question about whether the missing other half is ever actually viewed by the questing lover as a whole human, or just as the lost half of him- or herself, something to be reabsorbed. Plato may be casting a very beady eye on what we now term 'romantic love' and forcing us to ask uncomfortable questions about the extent of egoism involved in this kind of love. And there are also complex questions concerning identity here. But there is no doubt about the fact that the search is a risky and potentially painful process: you may never bump into your other half. And even if you do, they could then die on you, and leave you with no adequate replacement: even if you form another attachment of some kind, you will always lack your other half. So the story conjures up all the longing and the intensity, and the passion of romantic love for one unique particular (whether viewed as a half or as a whole). But it also conjures up the risks and the dangers and the potential enslavement of that love.

NW: *What happens when you do meet up with your other half?*

AH: Well, initially in the myth it's all very frustrating, because the genitalia of these beings are in the wrong place, and they can't physically make love. So Zeus steps in and orders Hephaestus to remedy this: their genitalia are moved around and they can now make physical love. And then what Plato does with this myth gets really interesting, really intriguing. We are asked to imagine that these couples are physically intertwined in bed; they are in the midst of interpenetrative sex and, at this very moment, the blacksmith god, Hephaestus, arrives at their bedside—you would have thought an unwelcome and rather tactless visitor. And, interrupting them, Hephaestus asks: 'What do you really want? Do you want me to weld you together, not just in body, but also in soul, so you become one instead of two?' And they say, 'yes, yes, yes, that's what we want'. And Hephaestus says: 'Think carefully. Is this really, really what you want?' And they say, 'yes, yes, weld us, weld us!' And that's where the myth ends. They're going to be welded together in life—and I believe Hephaestus is envisaging a spiritual as well as a physical welding—and they will also be together in death. But the implication is that Plato, the author of this fantasy, through the character of Aristophanes, is asking us to think very hard about what we think romantic love is, and what we want from it. Because when you are together with your beloved, you can have that very intense physical and spiritual longing to be absolutely fused. But think what would happen if that actually occurred: could erotic love continue to exist? And I think Plato is raising some intriguing questions here, because he's saying: If you're defining love as a search for what you lack, then what happens if this search finds its object? Does erotic love tend towards its own annihilation? Because if you find what you're looking for, you've surely cancelled out the conditions that make erotic love possible. And do you want that? Are you ok with that?

NW: *That's Aristophanes. How does Socrates develop these ideas?*

AH: When it's Socrates' turn to talk, he says he's going to relay a conversation he had when young with a (probably fictional) priestess called Diotima, who—he mischievously says—taught him everything he knows about eroticism: lovely to have Socrates taught by an older woman. In the course of this conversation we are told that love is not love of one's other half, but only of the good: Aristophanes has got love wrong. You don't love something just because it's yours—if you have a toothache you want to get rid of the rotten tooth; you love something or someone because it or they are good.

NW: *So does that mean that lovers are in principle interchangeable for Socrates?*

AH: Yes, they can be. He says that the aim of love is to possess the good forever, which, of course, implies that we want some form of immortality. Now, in the *Symposium* there is no personal immortality available to us. Your particular personal life is going to come to an end when you die. So what we all do—in Freudian terminology, often unconsciously—is to seek various substitute forms of immortality, and Socrates says there are three of these, which he lists in ascending order of importance. First and least—in Socrates' eyes—you can have children; second, you can perform some glorious deed like Achilles, which will win you lasting fame; or third, and best, you can create enduring works of philosophy, literature, bodies of laws and education, and so on.

That's the way of achieving the good forever. But, says Socrates, the way we do any of these things is through a beautiful beloved, a beautiful love object. In the case of physical children, we physically fall in love with a beautiful beloved and use that beloved to create the children. In the case of honour and fame, or works of art and science, we use our love for a beautiful beloved as our inspiration—and in some cases, the education of the beloved is itself the creative work which will survive us. Now these beautiful beloveds, who are the means by which we achieve these various substitutes for immortality, are simply a representation or instantiation of what Diotima calls the Form of Beauty, which is an unchanging, non-sensible, eternal structure or principle—the perfect and transcendent principle of beauty. And every beautiful object in this phenomenal world—animate or inanimate—is simply an inevitably imperfect instantiation of the single form of beauty. The consequence of this is that each of the beloveds with whom we fall in love is individually replaceable. We're not attracted by their unique particularity as Aristophanes thought we were; we're attracted to them solely to the extent that they are a representation of the Form of Beauty and can help us towards our ultimate aim of possessing the good forever.

NW: *So the things that we tend to value most in life in terms of success, achievement, family—all those things are actually driven by a love of beauty?*

AH: Absolutely. To put it precisely: love is the desire to possess the good forever through begetting and bearing offspring by means of beauty. And it's no surprise to me whatsoever that Freud was hugely inspired by this particular speech in the *Symposium*. Freud says, yes, there is this basic stream of erotic energy which may then be channelled and diverted onto different objects. Freud, of course, calls this rechannelling, 'sublimation', and he believes that his theory of libidinal sublimation is profoundly indebted to Plato's theory of erotic rechannelling (though in fact there are also important differences as well as similarities between the two).

NW: *But for Plato love has a metaphysical aspect. It's connected to his whole notion of the Theory of Forms.*

AH: That's right. So far we've been concentrating on someone falling in love with a particular person, even if the reason they fall in love is only because that particular person instantiates the Form. What we now need to look at is the way Diotima uses this phenomenon of falling in love with an individual beautiful body and claims that, in fact, it's just the first rung of what she calls the ladder of love—and her account of this ladder is one of the most famous, powerful, and disturbing passages in western literature. She says: you start off being physically attracted to one other beautiful body. But then—anticipating the lyrics of Mick Jagger—you realize that the beauty of one body is akin to the beauty of all other bodies, so it's irrational not to be attracted to all of them. Next you come to understand that beauty is instantiated more fully in the soul than in the body, so you now start to fall in love with beautiful souls. And gradually you ascend this ladder which takes you further and further away from particular human bodies towards ever more abstract objects of desire. Because after human souls you turn your attention to human customs and institutions, and then to all the various branches of knowledge; and finally, revealed to you in all its glory at the top of the ladder, is the transcendent 'vision' of the Form of Beauty itself. It is in contemplating this perfect beauty, says Diotima, that life will be truly liveable. Because if you're in love with one beautiful person, you're enslaved to them, you're trapped (and, of course, your beloved could also die, or leave you): it's a painful, vulnerable existence. By contrast, the Form of Beauty is always going to be there for you, eternal and unchanging. But, interestingly, we may note that it's never going to love you back, either. The person dwelling with the Form of Beauty is in a state of bliss—and Plato uses extremely sexual language to describe the revelation of the form of beauty: it's an absolutely climactic vision—but the Form of Beauty, being perfect, is not the kind of entity that can love. As we've seen, in the *Symposium*, love stems from lack. So, in contrast to Christian notions of a loving God, contemplating the Form is a one-way experience. We may even want to ask whether Eros has transformed itself into something else at the very top of the ladder.

NW: *Alcibiades comes in at a certain point and one reading is that Plato illustrates Socrates' conception of Eros by the way Socrates reacts to Alcibiades.*

AH: Yes. It's interesting to look at the language with which Alcibiades' entrance is described. Alcibiades, remember, is this glamorous, charismatic, and ravishingly beautiful man—he was said to be the most physically beautiful person in Athens, male or female. And both males and females were in love with him. The one person who probably wasn't—despite his claims to the contrary—was Socrates. In fact, it was Alcibiades who fell in love with Socrates, turning on its head the normal Athenian upper class convention of the time, whereby an older man would have an erotic affair with a younger male lover in his teens. Anyway, this character, Alcibiades, arrives at our dinner party after Socrates has finished recounting his conversation with Diotima; so he's not heard any of the earlier speeches. He's drunk and supported by an *aulos*-girl— such girls often entertained in more ways than simply playing the *aulos*. He's wearing a wreath of violets and ivy which has tipped over his eye. Plato describes his entrance with the term 'suddenly': exactly the same term that he used of the revelation of the Form of Beauty. So it seems that we have to choose: do we want the Form of Beauty or a particular, beautiful, flawed human being? And when he finds out about the discussion, Alcibiades says, 'oh, I'll tell you all about love; but not a general account—I'm too drunk for that anyway— I'll just describe my particular love for Socrates.' And you get one of the most moving and powerful descriptions that I know about what it's like to be in love with one other, utterly unique, individual. In Alcibiades' case, it's a very painful experience because Socrates does not appear to return his love—he certainly won't allow any physical consummation. Alcibiades is disarmingly frank about the pain of rejection that he feels and his anger and jealousy towards Socrates. So, through Alcibiades, Plato lets us see both the good and the bad aspects of being in love with a particular individual, whom you view as unique and irreplaceable. He shows us the beauty and the romance, and the intensity, and the passion of such a love; he also shows us the vulnerability and the pain, the jealousy, and the anger. So even if Plato is ultimately saying, 'I think you should give all this up and ascend the ladder of love', he is also demonstrating to us that he does know what he's talking about. He does understand the fierce intensity and pull of what he's asking us to give up.

NW: *We've heard the three different positions. Which do you find the most attractive?*

AH: Well, I'm raised in the romantic tradition, so despite the pain, the fragility, the transience, I'd have to go with Aristophanes'.

3

TERENCE IRWIN ON
Aristotle's Ethics

David Edmonds: *Aristotle was a Renaissance man who lived almost two millennia before the Renaissance. He wrote on many, many subjects: politics, rhetoric, biology, logic, music, poetry, and much more. But none of his works attracts more interest than those on ethics. Terence Irwin has spent most of his career at Cornell University, and is now Professor of Ancient Philosophy at Oxford.*

Nigel Warburton: *The topic we're focusing on is Aristotle's ethics. Tell us a bit about who Aristotle was.*

Terence Irwin: A bare outline of Aristotle's life is this: He was born in 384 BC; he was the son of a doctor. He was a Macedonian, and hence, from the point of view of the Athenians, he was barely a Greek. He spent 20 years as a member of Plato's Academy, and then he left Athens after Plato's death in 347 BC. He travelled around the eastern Aegean, and, among other things, he engaged in natural history. He returned to Athens in 338 BC and set up his own philosophical school, the Lyceum. He organized an extensive programme of research, not only in philosophy, as we think of it now, but also in biology and in constitutional history, chronology, and many other things. He died in 322 BC, just a year after the death of Alexander the Great, whom Aristotle is supposed to have taught.

NW: *One of the things he taught at the Lyceum was ethics is how to live. What was his general approach to that question 'how should we live?'?*

TI: Maybe we could begin with the word. Aristotle was probably the first person to call this subject *êthika*, and that means, literally, the study of character. For Aristotle, this is part of political science. It's the most general aspect of political science in that it tries to discover the ultimate good for a human being. Aristotle argues that among the things we need in order to achieve that good is virtues of character. So that's why the work's called 'on character', or *êthika*. And these virtues involve the appropriate development and ordering of emotions and non-rational impulses.

These virtues of character are of two kinds. The first kind are self-regarding, concerned with one's own good. For instance, bravery involves the appropriate way of directing fear and confidence; temperance involves the appropriate direction of physical impulses. The second kind are other-regarding virtues. These concern one's own good in so far as it includes the good of others. Aristotle argues that since we have a social nature, our good includes friendship with other individuals, and more generally it includes links with the social and political community.

NW: *He believed that if we cultivate these virtues appropriately we will flourish as human beings. He has a lot to say about flourishing and about what it is to be human. He also thought that there was such a thing as human nature which gave rise to this flourishing.*

TI: Yes, maybe I can begin with human nature. Aristotle takes human nature to include both the physical and the mental, both the non-rational and the rational aspects of a person in so far as he or she is formed or permeated with or guided by rational thought. For Aristotle, the fulfilment of human nature involves the organization of the rational and non-rational aspects of human beings, so that they fulfil human capacities as a whole. That fulfilment is the condition that Aristotle describes as the human good, which he also calls *eudaimonia*. 'Eudaimonia' is usually translated into English by 'happiness', or, less appropriately, by 'flourishing'. 'Flourishing' is something that trees can do: but trees can't manage to be *eudaimon* according to Aristotle; only rational agents can do that.

So *eudaimonia* is like happiness, as we ordinarily understand it, in that it includes mental elements: pleasure, sense of well-being, satisfaction. But it's not confined to these mental elements. It requires pleasure and satisfaction in the activities that are appropriate for a rational agent. So, that's the way in which *eudaimonia* is similar to and dissimilar from what you might think of as happiness.

NW: *The virtues that give rise to* eudaimonia *have to be exercised according to the Doctrine of the Mean. What is the Doctrine of the Mean?*

TI: Its importance may have been exaggerated. Some people understand it as advice to aim at moderation in all things: that phrase is a mistranslation of a sentence of St Paul's, and it's also a misinterpretation of Aristotle. Aristotle means that virtue of character doesn't consist simply in expressing the impulses that one might acquire from nature or upbringing.

On the other hand, it is not simply an ascetic suppression of these impulses. It's something between the extremes of 'letting it all hang out' and repressing everything. In that respect, it's in the middle, an intermediate, or mean condition. This mean is the appropriate harmony of non-rational and rational impulses under the guidance of practical reason.

Take bravery as an illustration: the brave person doesn't try to suppress fear altogether. The brave person is the one who is afraid in the right conditions and for the right reasons, but not on the occasions when it would be interfering with acting appropriately. So that's how the general claim about the mean applies to this particular virtue.

NW: *Aristotle has been tremendously influential both in his own time and subsequently. Could you outline some of the ways in which his influence has been felt?*

TI: Perhaps I could mention two special periods of revival or renewal of Aristotle in ethics. The first can be dated roughly from the thirteenth to the seventeenth century, the so-called period of scholasticism. Contrary to the associations of the name, this is an extremely creative development and systematic working out of Aristotelian ethics by Christian philosophers and theologians: the period runs roughly from Aquinas in the middle of the thirteenth century to Francisco Suárez at the beginning of the seventeenth century.

The second period of renewal is in the nineteenth century, and the main figures are Hegel and Marx, and the British Hegelians especially, T. H. Green and F. H. Bradley. They looked to Aristotle to overcome some of the false assumptions, as they saw it, that were shared by moralists in the empiricist and rationalist traditions: Hume on the empiricist side and Kant on the rationalist side. Similarly, they looked to Aristotle to overcome the false political assumptions that they attributed to both conservative and liberal political theories of the eighteenth century.

NW: *Aristotle didn't just influence philosophers in these two periods: he's continuing to influence philosophers now.*

TI: Yes, and I can give a couple of examples of that. First, moral philosophers have shown renewed interest in the study of character and the virtues; these are the aspects of morality that involve *being* a certain way or living a certain kind of life rather than simply *acting* in certain ways. Second, some political philosophers have developed a communitarian critique of liberal political theory which clearly goes back to Hegel's critique of liberalism, but beyond that back to Aristotle.

NW: *Could you just expand on that? What is a communitarian approach, and how is it Aristotelian?*

TI: According to a liberal view, one ought to think of a state as a way of achieving and protecting the interests of individuals. A communitarian view goes back to Aristotle's claim that human beings are social and political in nature. According to this view, the appropriate aim of the state is to achieve the human good, and hence to design institutions and to train people so as to cultivate the kinds of virtues that Aristotle talks about. This view might have definite social and political consequences that would not follow from a liberal view. So, that's a debate in contemporary political theory that clearly has its inspiration in Aristotle.

NW: *You've devoted a lot of time to studying Aristotle's ethics: what did he get right in this area, and which aspects would you like to jettison?*

TI: The description of his position that I've been giving is meant to be sympathetic. I don't want to jettison him, but to correct him on certain points. Maybe I could pick two things. The most obvious is that Aristotle thinks only a few human beings are naturally equipped to achieve the sort of life that he takes to be the best life. We know enough about human beings and the social influences on them to know that he's wrong about that. So we need to understand Aristotle, to put it briefly, from an egalitarian point of view, and that's where Karl Marx's appropriation of Aristotle is especially important.

The second point is this. Aristotle thinks of practical reasoning in general, and moral reasoning in particular, as being ultimately concerned with one's own good or the good of the community in which one finds one's own good. He should have recognized that that's not all there is to practical reasoning. He should have recognized that people also have duties and rights that are distinct from those goods. To put it in technical terms, we need *deontological* as well as *teleological* practical reason; or, to put it in historical terms, we need Kant as well as Aristotle.

NW: *What does it mean in practice to say that we need Kant as well as Aristotle?*

TI: There are some things that we owe to people that we don't owe to them because that will make us better off or them better off or society as a whole better off. If, for instance, people are owed a certain degree of freedom of expression, if that's a right that they have, that's not something you need to justify by reference to anyone's good. That's a point you won't find in Aristotle; it's a point that Kant emphasises. That's what I mean by saying that one important aspect of morality is missing from Aristotle.

NW: *I could imagine somebody reading this, thinking that's all very interesting historically, but does a philosopher like Aristotle have any contemporary relevance? Why should I study Aristotle? What light does he shed on contemporary moral issues?*

TI: Moral philosophy has a practical point, but it doesn't necessarily tell you what to do here and now, or whom to vote for here and now. Those are questions sometimes for moral casuistry and sometimes for political thinking. But moral philosophy can provide principles that might guide us in formulating the right practical questions or help us evaluate acts or institutions or the design of a society. The provision of those sorts of principles is its practical point. Shall I say something about the questions to which those sorts of principles would be relevant?

NW: *Yes please.*

TI: Let me pick two questions that are connected with things I've been talking about. First question: what's education for and what should it include? For instance, should people merely be taught skills that will help them to function in the economy: is that all there is to education? Or should they learn to live a good life? Can they be taught to live a good life, and can they be taught to live it without indoctrination? Aristotle stands pretty strongly on the interventionist side of this debate. He thinks that learning to live a good life is something that can be taught and that it's an appropriate function for the state to undertake.

Second question: what is the right way to think about morality? In particular, should we try to train people to limit their pursuit of their own interest and to take account of other people?

Another way of putting this: should we learn to think of our own interest so that we recognize that we also pursue it in so far as we are also concerned for the good of others? That's a familiar way for people to think about their own interest in relation to others when they're thinking about members of their families or close friends. But is it sensible to think of this identification of one's own interest with other people's interest in relation to a much larger group of people, people you don't know? The Aristotelian answer to that question is certainly 'yes': the model of identification of interest and friendship extends to the larger group of people. If that's correct, it's a challenging way to look at morality and would affect the way that we think about such things as duties, self-sacrifice, and concern for others.

NW: *So according to Aristotle pursuing your own interest benefits other people?*

TI: It would be clearer to reverse that direction and say that in pursuing the interest of others you pursue your own interest, and that's why there's no conflict. That's not too hard to understand in the case of a parent doing something for their child. If you said, 'you're doing something for someone else (your child) and that's bad for you', the parent might say, 'That's ridiculous. What's good for the child is good for me too.' There's no conflict of interest in that case.

Aristotle's insight, or perhaps Aristotle's wishful thinking, is the claim that this pattern also explains other cases of concern for the interests of others. It fits not just relations between parent and child, or relations between friends, but also relations between fellow citizens, and even relations to people you don't know. Whether that's wishful thinking or an insight is a significant question about how we think about morality.

4

ANTHONY KENNY ON
Thomas Aquinas' Ethics

David Edmonds: *The most significant philosopher of the medieval period, Thomas Aquinas, was born in what in the thirteenth century was called the Kingdom of Sicily. He attended several universities, among them the University of Naples. After training as a priest, and joining the Dominican Order, he became a theologian. He wrote on a huge range of topics, including a detailed examination of several proofs for the existence of God. But here, Anthony Kenny, a leading specialist on Thomas Aquinas, discusses Aquinas' writings on ethics.*

Nigel Warburton: *The topic we're focusing on is Thomas Aquinas, and specifically his ethics. Can you first give a quick sketch of who Aquinas was?*

Anthony Kenny: Aquinas lived in the middle of the thirteenth century, which is the highest point of the high Middle Ages. He was a Dominican friar who spent most of his life in universities, such as the new University of Paris. Universities were new then, as were the begging friars and the preaching friars: the Franciscans and the Dominicans. Between them, they more or less shaped the intellectual life of the thirteenth century.

Aquinas' great contribution was the way in which he reconciled Aristotelian philosophy with Christian theology. At the beginning of his life, Aristotle was largely forbidden by the church authorities; by the end of his life, most of Aristotle's texts were obligatory material in the universities. And this change was mainly due to the genius of Aquinas.

NW: *What did Aquinas take from Aristotle's ethics?*

AK: Aristotle's ethics is based most of all on the concept of happiness, on what is the most worthwhile life for a human being. Aristotle thought that the most worthwhile life involved the exercise of virtues of various kinds. These included both ordinary virtues, such as courage and temperance, but also intellectual virtues, such as the pursuit of science and philosophy. He thought that in a full life people would achieve their happiness by doing well at what they were best.

If you think that happiness is the exercise of the different virtues then, of course, you have to explain what a virtue is, and why it will be enjoyable to pursue it. Many undergraduates, from many generations, have read Aristotle's *Nicomachean Ethics* and learned what Aristotle has to say about this.

Now, this is the main foundation of Aquinas' ethics, too. Aquinas' ethics is also based on happiness, it's 'Eudaimonistic'. But, of course, being a Christian, Aquinas adds an extra level of happiness. Whereas Aristotelian happiness is to be found principally, but not totally, in the present world, for Aquinas perfect happiness awaits the blessed in heaven. But he is very much in favour of Aristotle's account of the best way to spend your lifetime down here on Earth.

NW: *We should be absolutely clear about one point, though: for Aristotle, and presumably for Aquinas as well, happiness isn't a blissful mental state. It's not merely a sensation.*

AK: That's quite right. That's a major difference with most popular forms of ethics today. A very widespread form of ethics today is utilitarianism, which was founded by Jeremy Bentham, the late eighteenth-century, early nineteenth-century British philosopher. Bentham agrees with Aristotle that happiness is the fundamental concept—the thing on which all morality is to be based. In Bentham's case he writes that what is important is the greatest happiness of the greatest number. But Bentham has a very different view of happiness from Aristotle and Aquinas. Both Aristotle and Aquinas thought that happiness was an activity, not a feeling, and that the supreme happiness for rational beings was an intellectual activity. For Bentham, however, happiness is exactly the same as sensation: he draws no distinction between pleasure and happiness.

One big difference this makes concerns the kind of relationship you believe there is between human beings and other animals. For Aristotle and Aquinas, since happiness and virtue were the exercise of rational powers, only human beings belong inside the moral community. Whereas, if the fundamental principles of ethics depend on pleasure and pain, then animals must belong to the same moral community, since they too can feel these sensations.

It doesn't follow from the fact that Aristotle and Aquinas thought that animals weren't part of the moral community that you can mistreat animals. We can have obligations to creatures that aren't part of our own moral community. When

I say they're not part of our own moral community, I mean they don't have duties. For Aquinas, you can only have rights if you also have duties. Aquinas, of course, didn't think God was part of our moral community either. God was above it, in the way that animals were below it. But that doesn't mean that we don't have obligations to God, too.

NW: *How did Aquinas develop Aristotle's ideas?*

AK: Being a Christian, Aquinas has a number of extra virtues to add to the Pagan virtues of Aristotle. There's the famous triad from St Paul's Epistles: the triad of faith, hope, and charity. Faith—belief in the Christian revelation; hope—for the Christians, heaven; charity—love for God and our neighbour. He thinks these are in no way in conflict with the Aristotelian virtues, though they're something grander. They're built on top of other Aristotelian virtues but they don't supersede them.

NW: *In Christian theology, there are absolute commands about how you should behave—the Ten Commandments, obviously. Did Aquinas believe that there were absolute prohibitions on what we could do?*

AK: Yes he did. As did Aristotle. When Aristotle is expounding his Doctrine of the Mean, he says there are some things that don't have 'the right amount'. Any amount of murder or adultery, for example, is too much. But Aquinas is living in a context in which morality could be said to be founded on the Ten Commandments, on the notion of law. What Aquinas does is try to put together the Judeo-Christian notion of law as a basis of morality and the Aristotelian notion of virtue as the key element in morality. Later Christian thinkers emphasised law rather than virtue right up to and beyond the

Reformation. Immanuel Kant is the apotheosis of the notion of law—and duty—as the central concept of morality. In Aquinas, the proportion is quite different. He does discuss the law. He discusses the revealed law as well as the natural law—the latter, he thinks, God implanted in all our hearts—but much more of his ethical treatises are concerned with virtue than with law.

Let me return for a moment to Jeremy Bentham and utilitarianism. There's a big distinction between Bentham, on the one hand, and Aristotle, Aquinas, and Kant, on the other. Those last three all thought that there were some kinds of actions you should never do, no matter what the consequences. Whereas for Bentham and the utilitarian tradition, the consequences are the test of whether something is right or not. This important difference still survives in contemporary moral debate. There are some absolutists who say that there are certain things one should never do—many people would say torture and rape could never be justified. But if you're a thorough-going utilitarian you'll say, 'No, in certain circumstances, fortunately very rare, torture and rape may be justified.'

NW: *You mentioned that Aquinas' lower-level principles are actually quite extensive: can you give us a flavour of what they're like?*

AK: One important issue which he often discusses is the role of conscience, and the question of whether you should always obey your conscience. A lot of people have thought that, as long as you were obeying your conscience, everything was all right. Aquinas rejects this. Your conscience may well be ill-informed, and you have a duty to better inform it. If you disobey your conscience, he says, you're doing something wrong. But the mere fact that you're obeying your conscience doesn't necessarily mean that what you're doing is right. This is relevant to a number of contemporary issues. A lot of people believe that when the former British Prime Minister Tony Blair went to war in Iraq he was obeying his conscience. But Aquinas—and I agree with him about this—would say that this doesn't settle the question of whether Mr Blair acted rightly or not.

NW: *Aquinas is probably best known as a theologian. Is there a way of following Aquinas' philosophy without committing to Christianity?*

AK: Indeed. Some of the best recent writers on Aquinas haven't been Christians. Aquinas himself makes it easy to follow him without accepting the Christian premises.

In the history of philosophy, Aquinas was the first to make a sharp distinction between two kinds of theology: what he calls Revealed Theology and Natural Theology. Revealed Theology takes as its premises some sacred book or authoritative teaching of the church. But Aquinas says there's another kind of theology, a branch of philosophy, which avoids the use of those premises even if it thinks they're true. It starts only with things which can be proved by reason without any appeal to an alleged revelation.

He wrote a book, the *Summa Contra Gentiles*—the summary of teaching for the purpose of infidels. The *Summa Contra Gentiles* was expressly designed to be used in dialogue with Jews and Muslims. He says at the beginning of this book that when you're writing with Jews against Jews, of course you can quote the Hebrew bible. But we don't have any books that we share with the Muslims, and so the best thing to do, whether you're dealing with Jews or with

Muslims, is just to appeal to natural reason and common sense.

NW: *You sound quite sympathetic to Aquinas' approach—especially when contrasted with utilitarianism?*

AK: Yes, I am. First of all, I think that his general approach to ethics is correct, giving importance to happiness and virtue rather than law. I also think that, often, his treatment of particular lower-level issues is very sensitive. His style of writing is based on the medieval disputation: an academic exercise in which two graduate students would argue with each other, and then the professor would settle the debate between them—very much like the adversarial practice of the Common Law courts. And it's probably the courts that imitated the scholastics rather than the other way around.

This adversarial style of philosophy is rather a good style, and Aquinas always begins his treatment of a topic by setting out the position opposite to the one that he is going to defend and by presenting arguments for it. When you look up Aquinas to see 'Is there a God'? And the first thing you read is 'apparently not'. It's a very good intellectual discipline to think, 'Now, what's to be said on the other side?' His philosophical approach is wonderfully judicious. He's always trying to balance arguments from both sides. If he's arguing with somebody, he usually tries to make them emerge as well as they can, even if he's going to disagree with them.

Aquinas deserves to be treated by us in the way that he treated Aristotle. He learned a great deal from Aristotle; he was never afraid to contradict Aristotle, but did it in a civil way. We should behave towards Aquinas the way he behaved towards Aristotle.

NW: *Most students studying philosophy come across Aquinas in the theological context or in the philosophy of religion. Yet there are signs that he's becoming a more important philosopher today than he was 10 or 15 years ago.*

AK: I think that's right. This morning, I was reading a massive history of ethics by Professor Terence Irwin (of Oxford University), and I was very impressed to see that he devotes about twice as many pages to the ethics of Aquinas as he does to Aristotle's ethics. He is probably right to do so. But it would have been hard to imagine this happening 10 years ago.

5

QUENTIN SKINNER ON
Niccolò Machiavelli's *The Prince*

David Edmonds: *Niccolò Machiavelli, Italian diplomat and author of*
The Prince, *is in a select group of people—it includes Freud and
Kafka—who have had their name turned into an adjective. So what is it
to be a true Machiavellian? What approach to the running of a state did
Machiavelli advocate and why? There's no better person to ask than the
eminent historian of ideas, Quentin Skinner.*

Nigel Warburton: *The topic we're focusing on today is one of the
great books in the history of political thought, Machiavelli's* The Prince.
Could you explain who Machiavelli was?

Quentin Skinner: Machiavelli didn't initially expect to be
remembered as a political theorist at all. He began by
following a diplomatic career, but it was rudely interrupted in
1512, and it's between that date and his death in 1527 that he
composed all the works by which he is now known. He wrote
not merely as a political theorist but also as a poet and
playwright, and one of his plays—*Mandragola*, probably
written in 1518—still holds the stage nowadays. But we think
of him as the author above all of *Il Principe* [*The Prince*] which
was written in 1513, immediately after he lost his official

position with the change of regime in Florence in the previous year.

NW: *So he was working as a diplomat before he was a political theorist?*

QS: Yes, that's right. I think of his early life as coming in two halves. He's born in 1469, but almost nothing is known about him until 1498. We know that his father was a lawyer, who ensured that his son received a good humanist education, but essentially we don't hear about Machiavelli until he suddenly emerges to prominence in Florentine politics in 1498. That was the year in which the Papacy got fed up with Savonarola, who had effectively been running Florence since 1494 after the French invasion and the removal of the Medici. The Pope trumped up a charge of heresy, and Savonarola was burnt at the stake. That's the moment when Machiavelli suddenly appears on the scene, and one of his earliest extant letters is about the collapse of the Savonarolan regime. Machiavelli was only in his late twenties at the time, but when the new republican regime under Piero Soderini was set up in the spring of 1498, Machiavelli was at once appointed as Secretary to the Second Chancery.

NW: *In his role in the state there, what kinds of things will he be doing?*

QS: As Secretary to the Second Chancery he was also, and ex-officio, secretary to a committee known as the *Dieci* ('The Ten' or 'The Ten of War'). They were responsible for the diplomatic and foreign relations of the republic. Machiavelli was not an aristocrat, so he couldn't be an ambassador, but he acted as a secretary to numerous embassies. As early as 1500 he was sent to France, because the Florentines, who were traditional allies of the French, wanted to know what France's intentions were concerning Italy. Machiavelli had audiences with King Louis XII on several occasions during this trip. Two years later, it's he who's chosen to go to the court of Cesare Borgia, who had been granted lands in the Romagna by his father, Pope Alexander VI. Popes are not supposed to have sons but this one did. Florence was worried that Cesare might be going to march across their territories and possibly devastate them, and Machiavelli was sent to find out his plans and report back.

Then, in 1503 it's Machiavelli who is sent to cover the papal election in Rome. When Cardinal Rovere is elevated as Pope Julius II, it's Machiavelli who conveys the news to Florence. In 1507, he goes on an embassy to the court of the Holy Roman Emperor, Maximilian, whom he also meets. These embassies continue: in 1510 he's back in France, and again has an audience with Louis XII. So he's met the King of France, he's met the Pope, he's met the Emperor, and many of his reflections about these states-men go into *The Prince*.

If we now turn to *The Prince*, we find that Machiavelli thinks very poorly of these leaders. The King of France, as he explains in chapter 3, totally messed up the invasion of Italy. Of Maximilian he says in chapter 23 that nobody ever knows what he's going to do, least of all him: he announces that he's going to undertake some policy but then somebody else talks to him and he changes his mind immediately. He says of Pope Julius II in chapter 25 that, although he was successful, he was simply lucky: he was basically a warrior, which is what was needed at the time, but if other qualities had been appropriate, he would soon have come to grief. The only political leader of his age whom Machiavelli truly admires is Cesare Borgia, but as he points out in chapter 7 of *The Prince*, even Cesare failed ignominiously in the end.

NW: *How did Machiavelli come to write* The Prince? *How did he make the move from being a diplomat to being a writer?*

QS: He was forced to make the move shortly after Pope Julius II signed the ill-named 'Holy Alliance' in 1512, which had the effect of bringing Spanish troops into Italy. They quickly pushed the French out. The Florentines, traditional allies of the French, were then threatened with the sack of their territories, and caved in at once. The Medici returned, and many of those who had served the republic were dismissed. It's true that some survived: several of Machiavelli's aristocratic friends remained employed under the new regime. But Machiavelli had the misfortune to be mistakenly—so far as is known—identified as having taken part in an anti-Medicean plot immediately after their reassumption of power. So he's imprisoned and dreadfully tortured. Only at the beginning of 1513, when there's an amnesty—because a Medici becomes Pope—does Machiavelli get released. But he's then sent into internal exile. He has to go back to his farm, south of Florence, and he's left asking himself what he should do with his energies and his literary powers. It's then that he settles down, at the beginning of 1513, to write a book about what he has learned from his time as an observer of political life.

NW: *He imagines these conversations with the great thinkers of the past and the people that he's met as part of the process of writing?*

QS: Yes, that's fascinating. There's a celebrated letter of December 1513 to his friend Francesco Vettori in which he explains his writing practices. He wants to understand the secrets of statecraft known to the great moralists of Rome, Seneca and Cicero, and the great Roman historians, Livy, Sallust, and Tacitus. These are the authorities he is reading. But in order to talk to them, he says, he has to wait till the end of the day, go into his study, put on special robes, and then ask them questions which, under those circumstances, they feel able to answer.

NW: *The Prince is an unusual book for us, but it was within a recognized genre.*

QS: Absolutely. It's completely conventional in the way it's organized. When Machiavelli writes to Vettori, he tells him that he is composing a little book called *De Principatibus* (concerning principalities). It's interesting that he assigns it a Latin title, because one remarkable thing about the book is that it's in Italian and not in Latin. But, as you say, he is aligning his work with a well-recognized genre. Giovanni Pontano had recently written a book called *De Principe*, and Francesco Patrizi a similar book called *De rege*. Such works of admonition and advice to rulers were commonplace in Renaissance Italy, and Machiavelli's *The Prince* is simply another example of such a *speculum principis* or 'mirror for princes'.

NW: *So what was Machiavelli's main intellectual aim with* The Prince?

QS: Yes, a crucial question. He doesn't answer it specifically until the pre-penultimate chapter, chapter 24, when he says that he has been writing a book particularly for new princes, his aim being to make them appear to be old ones. By 'old' he simply means 'well-established' because, as he says at the beginning of the book, he believes that if you have inherited your principality, it would be very incompetent of you not to be able to sustain your position. The big problems arise when you are a new prince, and it's for rulers in that predicament that his advice is designed.

NW: *So if it's a kind of bluffer's guide for new princes it involves dissimulation: you have to pretend to be something that you're not. How important is that as a theme in the book?*

QS: It is in a way absolutely central. But I think one would first want to note that his guide for new princes is addressed more specifically to one particular family, the Medici. It's dedicated to Giuliano de Medici, one of the young princes restored in 1512. But he dies, and then Machiavelli revises the book in 1516 and rededicates it to the rather chinless Lorenzo de Medici. They were not very plausible candidates for greatness. Nevertheless, what Machiavelli says at the end of *The Prince* is that he believes they can attain what he calls *gloria duplicata*, double glory. This will be achieved, he says, if they succeed in founding a new state in Florence and then ornamenting it with good laws. Notice the emphasis on glory. The question for Machiavelli is always how princes can hope to appear not merely powerful but honourable and glorious at the same time. They should aim not just to seize and hold on to power but to display 'the power and the glory' to everyone.

NW: *One reading of this book, from what you've said, is that it was written very specifically for an individual, it had a target audience of one person.*

QS: That's a good way of putting it. Of course, Machiavelli believes that what he says applies generally to rulers who come to power without being legitimate. But you are right that he is particularly interested in one ruler. As has often been said of *The Prince*, it is, as it were, a job application. Machiavelli wants to get back into power himself, he wants to commend himself to the new regime in Florence. In the correspondence with his friend, Francesco Vettori, he's very anxious that his book should be presented to the Medici princes. Vettori reads it and is clearly horrified, and keeps putting him off. This is not perhaps surprising, for when you read the work, you'll see that—as has sometimes been said—it looks almost as if it's a satire designed to mislead princes, because the advice is so completely unconventional, although the format is so completely conventional. It's like a bomb in a prayer-book, as J. R. Hale once put it.

NW: *'Conventional' here would presumably be something like Christian morality.* The Prince *doesn't advocate straightforward compassion, kindness, the sorts of things which were prized by Christians.*

QS: Yes, that is right, but I would want to put it more exactly. As you begin to read the book, what you learn is that, although your ultimate goal as a prince is glory, you first have to know how to stabilize your state. One phrase that runs throughout *The Prince* speaks of the basic obligation of every ruler: *mantenere lo stato*. Not, of course, 'to maintain the state'—that would be an anachronism—but to maintain his state as a prince, to maintain his standing and position of power. You must know how to avoid what the French called a blow against your state, a *coup d'état*. You must ensure above all that you are not unhorsed.

NW: *How according to Machiavelli should a prince attain stability?*

QS: Any prince attempting to attain stability faces a dangerous enemy, an enemy he must learn to cope with. This foe is mentioned all through *The Prince*, and its name is *Fortuna*. Princes need to acknowledge that to achieve stability they've got to be fortunate. One of the deep points that Machiavelli wants to make is that there's no such thing as a successful politician who hasn't had phenomenally good luck. But he also believes—to cite the useful American idiom—that it is possible to 'get lucky'.

Fortune is the name of that force which is completely capricious. You can't rely on it, it's the opposite of reason, but you've got to reckon with it because misfortune can completely overthrow you—as happened to Cesare Borgia. Machiavelli says in chapter 7 that he offers Cesare as an example of everything that a prince should do to maintain his state and attain glory. However, Cesare fell desperately ill at the moment when his enemies were coming for him. Now, as Machiavelli adds, this was nothing more than an example of the extreme malignity of Fortune. But it meant that Cesare lost his state. So Fortune is the name of the force that can always crush you, however well you plan. But—and this Machiavelli takes from Livy—*Fortuna fortes adiuvat*, fortune favours the brave. You need to know how to get lucky, how to become the brave person who can hope to be fortunate.

NW: *So how do you become lucky in that sense?*

QS: This brings us to the moral heart of the book. What you need to do is to cultivate the quality that Machiavelli calls *virtù*. He is translating the Latin word *virtus*. *Virtus* is the quality of the *vir*. *Vir* in Latin means 'man', but there are two words in Latin for 'man'. One is *homo*, which means man or woman, a member of human kind. But the other is *vir*, denoting the manly man—the source of our word 'virile'. Machiavelli is saying that, to get lucky, what you have to be is that kind of man. The crucial notion is that of using *virtù* to master *Fortuna*.

So, for Machiavelli the question is: how can you hope, by means of manly qualities, to ally with *Fortuna* and even master her? His answer is that '*La Fortuna e una donna*', 'Fortune is a woman.' To master her, you must always be bold; like a young man seeking to conquer a woman (this is Machiavelli talking, not me). You must never hold back but always take action. He makes the point most explicitly in one of his late letters, presenting us with one of his best epigrams: 'it is always better to act and regret it than not to act and regret it'.

NW: *This 'manliness', it's not just a matter of being somebody who acts. You have to act in particular ways, surely.*

QS: Yes, that's right. There are two particular ways in which you must act, and here Machiavelli begins to polemicize against his classical authorities, and especially against the humanist understanding of the proper conduct of princes. About these writers he says that one thing they completely forget is that one key to success in politics is always to have a reservoir of force, of pure power, and be ready to use it. It's certainly remarkable how much that was *not* said in humanist political theory. For example, Erasmus' book of advice to Christian princes, written at almost exactly the same time, is a pacifist tract. He says that if you have to use force you would do better to give up being a prince altogether. For Machiavelli, that's the greatest heresy you could utter, as he makes clear in chapters 12 to 14 of *The Prince*, in which he demands that rulers should be military leaders as well. This was an unusual demand to make at this period, in which the use of professional mercenary armies had become the norm. But Machiavelli is vehemently opposed to this policy, and always insists that princes must also be commanders of their own citizen armies.

NW: *But the force isn't just directed outwards to potential threats from other armies but inwardly as well within the state?*

QS: That's right. But you should try at all costs to avoid using force against your own people. Instead you need to understand the second way in which you ought to act, which involves understanding what moral qualities are appropriate to a prince. The classical Roman writers, Cicero and Seneca above all, had given a very strong answer to that question. The first element of *virtus* in Seneca's account of princely rule is *clementia*, the quality of mercy. The second is *liberalitas* or generosity—as we might still say, 'princely' generosity. But most of all, a true prince is said to be someone who honours his word—who obeys *fides*, good faith. The pivotal moment in *The Prince* comes when Machiavelli suddenly informs us in chapter 15 that this entire account is wrong.

NW: *It's wrong because you should use what we would perhaps see as devious means to achieve your ends.*

QS: Yes, that's part of it, but it's wrong for two reasons, and one has been very little noticed by Machiavelli's commentators. One of the things he believes is that it may well be true that liberality (to which he turns in chapter 16) as well as clemency (which he discusses in chapter 17) are the names of admirable virtues. But he believes that we don't understand those virtues. Princes who give away huge sums of money think they are being liberal. They don't ask themselves where the money is coming from. But it's necessarily coming from the people, who have to be taxed heavily for such princely liberality to be possible. But this, Machiavelli says, is not true liberality: this is what he calls *suntuosità*, extravagance, which is not a virtue but a vice, and will cause you to be hated instead of admired.

Likewise with clemency: princes who value clemency think that the virtue consists in always forgiving your enemies. But Machiavelli thinks that the right way to be clement is to make an example of your enemies to begin with, so that you can then be more merciful later. He gives an example that would have shocked his original readers, for he criticizes a great classical hero, the Roman general Scipio, who was famous for having forgiven a mutiny. As a result, Machiavelli retorts, a second mutiny followed. Machiavelli insists that Scipio did not display true clemency, for his response was *troppo facile*, too easy-going altogether. And again, that quality is not a virtue but a vice, and one that will cause you to be viewed with contempt instead of admired.

You are absolutely right, however, that what Machiavelli mainly wants to say is that the ideal of the prince as someone who always keeps his word, who never uses devious means, is what is most profoundly mistaken. It is mistaken because the underlying ideal of manliness according to Machiavelli is not enough. Here he again turns against his Roman authorities. Cicero had laid it down in Book I of *De officiis* that there are two ways in which injustice can be done. One is by the use of force, the other by the use of fraud. Force, Cicero says, reduces us to the level of the lion, fraud to the level of the fox. They are beastly qualities, in other words, not manly ones, and have no place in civilized life.

Machiavelli answers in a celebrated and satirical moment in chapter 19 that, if you want to maintain your state, you will have to be prepared to act in beastly as well as in manly ways. So you had better learn which beasts to imitate. And those princes have done best, Machiavelli declares, who have learned to imitate both the lion and the fox. The classical ideal of manliness, in other words, is not enough. Machiavelli's hero among the Roman emperors is Septimius Severus, of whom he says in chapter 21 that he behaved like a ferocious lion and a very cunning fox, as a result of which he was feared and respected by everyone.

NW: *And the motivation for imitating these animals is that that's what's most likely to get you the results you want?*

QS: Exactly. Those are the qualities that will not only enable you to maintain your state but to obtain the glory you should be seeking as well. You should follow the manly virtues so far as possible, but you should know how to be brutal and beastly when, as Machiavelli puts it, this is dictated by necessity. So Machiavelli is telling the princes of his age that they basically need to know, as he puts it, how to turn and turn about, how to trim their sails to the winds of Fortune. Sometimes it will be best to keep your word, sometimes not; sometimes the virtues can be espoused, sometimes they will have to be ignored.

It may sound as if Machiavelli is celebrating thuggery, and this has often been said of him. But that, I think, is a mistake. In chapter 8 of *The Prince* he tells the story of Agathocles of Syracuse, of whom he says that he only ever used brutal methods, and that this enabled him successfully to maintain his state. But Machiavelli adds that by these means Agathocles gained *imperio ma non gloria*—power but not glory. The prince who aspires to achieve not just stability but glory must know when it is best to be cruel, miserly, and deceitful, but he must also know how to minimize the use of these vices, which Machiavelli never hesitates to stigmatize as evil. A successful prince will always try to be good, or at least try to *seem* good; it is just that he must also know how to make use of bad methods if this is necessary, as it often will be, for the maintenance of his state.

NW: *Would it be fair to say that Machiavelli was a consequentialist, that he judged acts on outcomes rather than the intentions with which they're performed?*

QS: That's exactly the right way to put it. He doesn't express the point as formally as you have done, but he certainly believes that you must sometimes be willing to do evil in order that good shall come of it. If the good in question is the preservation of your state and the attainment of glory for yourself and your *patria*, then you must be prepared to do anything to attain those ends.

NW: *Which presumably means that this isn't a philosophy for ordinary people.*

QS: That's a very interesting point. That's right; it is a philosophy for princes, it's for people who are leaders and it is probably not a book that you and I are meant to read.

NW: *But should our leaders read it? Is there something in Machiavelli that our present-day leaders might learn from?*

QS: Well, it depends on what you feel about consequentialist ethical theories. If you believe that there are goals for societies which are so important that they must be pursued at all costs, then you are a Machiavellian. It would also be fair to say, I think, that currently our rulers are in a Machiavellian mood. The basic aspiration of the liberal state has been to guarantee security for its citizens, and thereafter to leave them so far as possible to enjoy their liberties. But the current threat of terrorism has led to the curtailing of liberties, and also to the use of what many of us regard as immoral means—especially torture—in the name of trying to preserve security.

NW: *So politicians are behaving in that respect in a Machiavellian way?*

QS: Yes, that would be a fair way of putting it. They see the overriding goal as that of preserving the state, and they are urging us not to be too squeamish about the means that may be needed to preserve it. And that is the core of Machiavelli's political advice in *The Prince*.

6

SARAH BAKEWELL ON
Michel de Montaigne

David Edmonds: *Academics, writers, and journalists owe Michel de Montaigne a debt of gratitude, for Montaigne can claim to have invented the literary form known as the essay. Montaigne was born near Bordeaux in 1533 and died in 1592. In his essays, he addressed himself to a variety of subjects and drew on his own experiences: his reading, his travels, the people he'd met, his beliefs and feelings. The topics he discussed ranged from international affairs to his sex life, to his pet dog. Many great thinkers have been influenced by Montaigne and he retains a following today. His admirers include Sarah Bakewell, author of a book about Montaigne:* How to Live, or, A Life of Montaigne in One Question and Twenty Attempts at an Answer.

Nigel Warburton: *The topic today is Montaigne and how to live. Could you say a little bit about who Michel de Montaigne was?*

Sarah Bakewell: Michel de Montaigne was a wine grower and magistrate, mayor of Bordeaux, and various other things in the course of his not very long life. He lived in the area just outside Bordeaux, and had a fairly undistinguished, ordinary kind of career as a lawyer and administrator in the town. Then he decided to leave all that and reflect on his life, and after that came a book called the *Essays* which became an instant bestseller and still is today, well over 400 years later. It's never really lacked for readers and enthusiasts.

NW: *So what triggered that radical change in career?*

SB: The impression he gives is that he felt that he had reached the point in life where he wanted to retire from active duty and reflect on his experience. In an inscription he made on his wall celebrating his decision, he described himself as if he was almost at the end of his life or certainly well into a mid-life crisis; in fact he was about 37. His father had died recently which had meant that he inherited the family wine-growing estate—a lot of responsibility. So it was a combination of that and this desire to retreat into himself, which was a tradition he'd picked up from the ancient philosophers, particularly the Stoics. Seneca used to recommend a period of reflection and philosophy once you'd completed your contribution to the world of public affairs.

NW: *There he is in his study reflecting on himself and on his life; what kind of essays did he produce as a result?*

SB: When he first started, he wrote in a fairly conventional way: a page or two, on various themes, most of which he picked up from his favourite classical authors. So he loved to read Plutarch, Seneca, the historians, some of the poets. They gave him the idea of assembling different materials on particular themes, which is interesting enough. But if he'd just stopped there I don't think we would still be reading him today. Instead, after a while, he became more adventurous and started writing in a much more questioning way, particularly writing about himself and his own experience and the people that he'd talked to, and the things that he'd found when he looked into himself, his emotions, and his own reasonings.

NW: *One of those essays was focused on death which was a very poignant subject for him because he had had a very near-death experience.*

SB: He was already quite obsessed with death in what today seems a rather morbid way. Of course, he had lost some people close to him including his best friend, his father, and a brother. But he was released from some of this obsession with death after his own close brush with it. He was out riding one day when somebody crashed into him and he was sent flying from his horse. He was knocked unconscious and was quite badly bruised; he could easily have been killed. His friends carried him home, and he gradually began to come to, but for some time he was floating in a half-conscious state. He started to reflect on that experience afterwards because he felt he'd tasted death with his lips, he'd brushed close to death—he had all these wonderful ways of describing it. What he discovered was that there was really nothing to fear in that experience of which he had been so terrified before. He found it was actually just a voluptuous drifting, almost a pleasant sensation like when you're falling asleep. In fact, he was later told that while he was having this pleasant floating experience he'd been ripping at his clothes and vomiting blood, and looking as if he was in agony. So he thought, well, death might look like that from the outside, but from the inside, nature takes over and prepares the experience for you. It also changed his focus more towards life, and more towards philosophy and reflection.

NW: *Philosophy could have taken him to an obsession with death, anyway, couldn't it, because in the ancient tradition philosophers learn to die?*

SB: Well, yes, he took the idea that that's what philosophy is from the ancient philosophers: Cicero's 'To philosophize is to learn how to die' became the title of one of his essays. I think he came to the conclusion that if philosophizing was a kind of obsessing over your own death, it wasn't going to get you very far, and, if anything, it made dying and the process of coming to terms with death harder. He was probably more influenced by an idea taken partly from the Epicureans—that to philosophize is to learn how to *live*, more than to learn how to die.

NW: *There's also an element that ran throughout his thinking: that his own personal experience trumps any theorizing.*

SB: Yes, and his near-death experience and the philosophical thoughts he took out of it provide one of the absolutely essential examples of that. He was a great believer in experience as the main source of philosophical wisdom; one of his greatest essays is called 'Of Experience'. That's a huge essay that rambles on about all sorts of things, as many of his essays do. But it is all circling around the idea that you learn primarily through your own experience. This is also why he thought that peasants who had no book learning had more wisdom than the great philosophers, because they hadn't studied enough to clutter up their minds.

The irony, of course, is that Montaigne arrived at this view after a lifetime of reading about *other* people's experiences—reading, absolutely passionately and with deep attention, the

classical philosophers and historians, and everybody else.
I think his idea of personal experience has more to do with
his idea of nature and of human nature. Both his reading and
his own life led him to the thought that we really just need to
relax and rely on our own nature, rather than trying to
intellectualize or rationalize things. That's the feeling behind
it, rather than what we might see as anti-intellectualism.

NW: *There's also a tendency to contradict himself—which is discon-
certing in a philosopher.*

SB: It is, and he said, 'I may contradict myself but the truth
I never contradict.' He's saying that his self and his perceptions shift constantly, and he stays true to them. Thus he must
keep moving. His contradictions are a part of what make the
Essays fascinating reading: you have a sense of a mind thinking
in front of you as you read. Also, he kept adding to them over
a period of 20 years—and he did tend to add material rather
than going back and taking things out, or correcting them. So
you end up with this incredibly complex surface of the text
where different parts of it have been added at different stages,
and sometimes one sentence will contradict the one before.
But that is part of the sense of constant movement that you
get in his thought.

NW: *Sometimes Montaigne seems to suggest that subjective experience
is truth, that subjective experience is all that really matters.*

SB: Yes, but this is constantly offset, as well, by his
fascination with the world external to himself, which he
approaches both by just observing the physical world and
other creatures, other human beings, and by reading and
sharing the experience of countless other people. There's a

constant fascination with the richness and variety of the outside world, so you never get the feeling of a mind that's lost gazing into itself. The whole texture of the *Essays* is rich and varied, full of anecdotes and stories. He's got this one moment where he is watching his cat staring intently into a tree; then a bird falls out dead between the cat's paws, so Montaigne goes off wondering why this is, what's happening? There's a constant mixture between that kind of observation and looking into himself.

NW: *One of his lines is that you should come to philosophy almost by accident, not set out to philosophize. As a philosopher I find that slightly odd.*

SB: I find it odd as well, although I think in a way you have to come to almost everything in life by accident. But he said that, if he was a philosopher at all, he was an 'accidental philosopher'. What he meant by that was that he wrote so much, that every now and then one of his remarks was bound to coincide with something said by one of the great philosophers of the past.

He's not a systematic thinker: he didn't devote himself to philosophy in the sense of going on a quest to discover the truth about the world, or a rigorous interpretation of it. You do get a feeling of somebody who's just going on along with life and responding to it, but trying to always look for wiser or more philosophical ways of doing this.

NW: *You've already mentioned Stoicism and Epicureanism, and the other main school of the age in philosophy, Scepticism, was a major influence on him as well. So it's clear that he did have a classical education that affected the categories which he used in perceiving the world.*

SB: All of those philosophies were hugely important to him. The late Renaissance was a time when so much of that thought had been rediscovered. Scepticism, in particular, had a huge impact on his world, but then he also became the prime transmitter of Pyrrhonian scepticism, founded by Pyrrho and developed by Sextus Empiricus in the ancient world. He embodied it in so much of his thought and writing in the *Essays,* that he transmitted it to generations of thinkers after him.

It's almost impossible to imagine Descartes going through his process of radical doubt without his having come across the modernized version of sceptical doubt which Montaigne had picked up from the ancient world. Descartes doubted absolutely everything as a way of laying bare everything to the foundation so that he could build it all up from scratch again on a more secure basis. Montaigne, instead, accepted that everything was in doubt, but he seemed quite happy to live with that. The doubt *itself* gave him a foundation for a way of living that considered different perspectives on situations, that made it possible to avoid being too sure of one's self. So doubt, I think, became a way of life for Montaigne, whereas for Descartes it was just a stage to be gone through. Without Montaigne, I would almost go so far as to say that there could be no Descartes.

NW: *The connection between Montaigne and other philosophers is interesting because he's difficult to pigeonhole as a philosopher at all.*

SB: There's always been a debate about whether you can consider Montaigne a philosopher, and it's by no means certain that he considered himself one. He is a philosopher if you take quite a broad definition of philosophy, drawn from the ancient traditions he himself followed, according to which philosophy is practical. It's a pragmatic set of thought experiments, approaches, ideas: ways of being that enable you to live in a better way.

NW: *There's a sense in which you learn about how you might live through reading how he lived. So he's not didactic, he's not saying you ought to live as I did, but by engaging with his essays you are encouraged to think differently.*

SB: You could compare him more to novelists than to philosophers for that very reason. If you read a novel like *War and Peace* or *Pride and Prejudice*, and learn something from it that you can apply to your own life, it's because you're observing other people living their lives. You come out with more ideas than you had when you went in; you come out having shared somebody else's experience, and perhaps you are a little bit the wiser for it. Also, as an aside, a novel is entertaining; Montaigne is entertaining, and let's not underestimate the importance of that. He's fun, he's pleasurable to read.

For me, certainly, what I have learned from Montaigne is very much on that level. I've seen this sixteenth-century man coping with problems in his life or thinking about his life and reading in a way that I can understand and be part of. I can't understand all of it because there is a big historical gulf between us, but I can certainly share a part of that experience through his communication of it, and that's very much what a novel does. In Montaigne, it also becomes a form of philosophy because he does it overtly, and on a level that draws deliberately on philosophical traditions.

NW: *What sort of influence did he have on subsequent philosophers?*

SB: I mentioned he had an influence on Descartes which was not really acknowledged, but I think it was there. He had a tremendous influence on Pascal—another by no means professional philosopher. Pascal found Montaigne's scepticism very hard to take, and tried to rid himself of it. In later years—and, again, it tends to be people a bit on the fringes of philosophy—he had an influence on Voltaire. Rousseau was very much influenced by Montaigne. The whole project of writing an autobiography, or writing about yourself in this 'warts and all' honest way, was something Rousseau seems to have picked up from Montaigne, but he disowned that influence. In later years, Montaigne was certainly an influence on Nietzsche, so again we're talking about somebody on the fringes of the accepted mainstream of philosophy. Nietzsche thought that Montaigne was the person you should read in order to learn how to live.

NW: *You've spent about five years researching and writing this book, how did you start the project?*

SB: Well, I discovered Montaigne by accident. I'd heard of him, but didn't read him until I picked him up for a long train journey, in a shop where it was the only English language book—this was in Budapest. So it was a total accident, very suitable for an accidental philosopher. After that, I read him incessantly; he was a bedside companion for many years. I wasn't sure I could write about somebody I admired so much, somebody that seemed always to be one step ahead of me. Montaigne certainly is always one step ahead of anybody who writes about him, because he is so contradictory and so varied: whatever you think you can say about him, he's already said it about himself. But, gradually, I got the idea of trying to write, not just about him, but about all the people who've read him over the years and have made different Montaignes out of him. That, besides Montaigne himself and his biography, became the focus of my interest.

7

A. C. GRAYLING ON
René Descartes' *Cogito*

David Edmonds: *It's arguably the most famous phrase in philosophy:*
'Cogito ergo sum'. *And its author, René Descartes, is often described as
the founder of modern philosophy. Descartes was born in France, but
ceased both to think and to exist in Sweden where his death was probably
due to pneumonia (the Swedish queen Christina made him get up at five
a.m. to tutor her). Here, to discuss Descartes' famous phrase, is A. C.
Grayling, author of a recent biography of Descartes.*

Nigel Warburton: *The topic we're focusing on is Descartes'* Cogito.
*Before we get on to that, could you tell us a little about who Descartes
was, and the times in which he lived.*

A. C. Grayling: René Descartes is a significant figure in the
history of modern philosophy and, indeed, in the history of
modern thought in general. He was born in 1596; he died in
1650: so he lived in the first half of the seventeenth century,
which was an important time for the development of the
natural sciences and for what—owing largely to Descartes
himself—was a revolution in philosophy. He also lived through
a period of great tumult in Europe: the Thirty Years' War.
This was fundamentally a war of religion, an attempt by the

Catholic Habsburg dynasty to reclaim Europe from the Protestant states for the Catholic cause.

He was educated by Jesuits to whom he was loyal all his life. He was, I think, a sincere Catholic—certainly he didn't ever do anything that would get him into trouble with the Catholic Church. His great contribution is to have cut through all the jargon, technicality, and over-elaboration of Scholastic philosophy—which was philosophy that had become encrusted with all sorts of intellectual barnacles during and since the medieval period—and to refocus attention on a central question: What do we know and how can we know it with certainty? This question was especially important at the beginning of the scientific revolution, the period in which Descartes lived.

NW: *And he was a scientist, as well, wasn't he?*

ACG: He was a scientist and a mathematician. His contributions to mathematics are significant. We all know about Cartesian coordinates because we suffered from them at school: he came up with the idea while lying in bed watching a fly walking on the ceiling, and realizing that he could give you the location of that fly anywhere on the ceiling by using the edges of the walls as coordinates, and providing an X and Y axis reading.

NW: *But with his philosophy, epistemology, the theory of knowledge, was central. He wanted to know whether there was any belief he could be certain was true.*

ACG: Yes. Descartes says, in what is perhaps his most famous philosophical work, the *Meditations on First Philosophy*, that you have to begin by asking yourself the question: 'What can I know with certainty?' He tackles this question in the first and second of the six meditations, and does it in a very interesting way. He says, 'All the sceptical arguments that have been put forward in the past are insufficiently strong to enable me to set aside everything I thought I knew—to set aside everything that admits of the least taint of doubt. Neither scepticism about the senses nor the possibility that I'm dreaming are swingeing enough to allow me to do this. But suppose I hypothesize that there is an evil demon whose whole purpose in existence is to fool me about everything. If there were such a demon, is there anything it cannot fool me about? If there is, that is what I can be certain of.' And, according to Descartes, there is indeed one thing that you cannot be fooled about.

NW: *Before we get to that one thing, we should say a little bit about Cartesian Doubt: what was it?*

ACG: Descartes wasn't a sceptic; he uses sceptical doubt as a tool, an instrument for arriving at the point of certainty required as the bedrock for his inquiry. So he uses some of the traditional sceptical arguments: scepticism about the validity of what we learn through the senses; the possibility that we might be dreaming; or, most generally of all, the possibility that we are systematically deluded by everything we can be deluded about, by this evil demon, to set aside even our most assured beliefs, even our most foundational beliefs. If any belief admits of the least tincture of doubt, however absurd, that is the excuse he uses temporarily to set it aside in order to see what's left, what point of certainty remains.

NW: *So, I'm sitting here in front of you, I can't doubt that, can I?*

ACG: Well, yes, you can. You might be asleep and be having a nightmare that you're sitting here in front me, and that would be a reason for calling into question the truth of the proposition, 'I'm sitting here in front of you now.'

NW: *What argument does he use to get out of this scepticism?*

ACG: He says, the one thing I couldn't be fooled about even if there were an evil demon who was trying to fool me about everything, is that I exist. Or, to put it in the famous formulation that everybody knows (everybody also knows 'I drink therefore I am' on pub walls), he says, 'I'm thinking. That's something about which I simply cannot be in doubt, and I can't be thinking unless I exist. So, I exist.' This is the bedrock, the point of certainty. This, in the philosophical tradition is known as *the Cogito. Cogito ergo sum:* 'I think, therefore I am.'

NW: *So why does Descartes feel so certain that he exists? Surely he could be dreaming that he exists?*

ACG: Even if he's dreaming, he exists: he has to exist in order to dream. He has to exist to do anything: to work, to be in doubt, to be fooled by a demon. All these things are themselves proofs, in the moment, of the fact that he exists.

NW: *Some philosophers have pointed out that all the argument actually shows is that there are thoughts now. To say that 'I' exist implies something further than could be actually worked out from that argument.*

ACG: That is an interesting point and it was one to which Descartes was alert. Immediately after the *Cogito*, immediately after saying, 'The one thing I can't doubt is that I exist', he goes on to ask, 'What then am I? What is this thing that exists?' This, of course, is the root of the mind–body problem because he says, 'What I am is a thinking thing, and I might doubt that I have a body, I might doubt that there is an external physical word, but I can't doubt that there is this thinking thing that I am, and therefore that's *what* I am.'

NW: *And how does Descartes get beyond the simple* Cogito *argument? Because the* Cogito *itself is only going to give him a thinking thing: the conclusion that there's one thinking thing in the universe.*

ACG: Yes. This is where Descartes makes a key step, and this is to say, 'Right, so I know I exist. I've got all these beliefs about an external world, and what I need is a way of getting *from* what I think *to* that external world in a way that guarantees that my beliefs about it have a chance of being true. So I need a sort of magic ingredient X, the X-Factor, which will serve as a guarantor of the validity of my taking the beliefs in my mind to be true of something outside my mind.'

What would do such a thing? Well, if there is a good God—not merely a God but a *good* one who, because He is good, doesn't want to fool us—He doesn't want to give us intellectual equipment and five senses and then mislead us—then my beliefs about an external world have a chance of being true if I use my faculties responsibly. That, indeed, is the strategy Descartes adopts: he produces two arguments for the existence of God, and having got his God and a good God, he can be satisfied that there is a world and that most of his beliefs about it are true.

NW: *So one way of characterizing what Descartes does is to see the whole sweep of* The Meditations *as a U-shaped turn: at the very bottom is the* Cogito, *which is what he called his Archimedean point. Until that point, he's descending into scepticism. Then, from*

that point, he turns around, introduces God, and it's uphill all the
way, and he's back almost to the point from where he started.

ACG: That's a good description, yes. And he's using the
first-person pronoun, talking about his experience of sitting
down and trying to think about the structure on which his
knowledge is based; and by this first-person device gets the
reader to follow and be persuaded by him by in effect being
the 'I' of the meditations: 'I doubt this, but then I see that I
must exist, and then I see that I have in my mind an idea of a
perfect being. If there is such a being then I wouldn't be what I
am and have the faculties that I do unless I had the chance of
knowing the truth about the world' . . . and so on.

So that story allows the reader of the *Meditations* to follow
that path through doubt, down to the bedrock, which is the
Cogito, and then on to a reconstitution of everything that he
previously thought he knew.

NW: *How do you judge the argument of the* Cogito; *is it a good*
argument?

ACG: It's not even clear that it's an argument. Its status is a
controversial matter. If it were an argument, it would have
to have a major premise. It would be what's called an
enthymematic syllogism, with one of its premises assumed
and therefore not expressed. The Cogito says, 'I think
therefore I exist.' So that looks as though it's missing a major
premise stating, 'Everything that thinks exists.' But, of course,
at the level of scepticism which Descartes has reached at that
point, this premise is not available to him.

His critics said that it can't be a syllogism—so what is it?
Descartes never came up with a satisfying answer. Subsequent

philosophers have examined the possibility that it's some kind of *performative* utterance, as when you arrive at a party and say, 'I'm here!' which of course is true whenever you say it, but you've said it for the purpose of attracting attention on that occasion. Others have suggested that the *Cogito* is a 'presuppositional'—existing is a presupposition of anything else, including of course being able to think that one exists, so all Descartes is doing is pointing out a necessary condition of the truth of 'I think'.

Others have tried to argue that the *Cogito* is a logically degenerate statement, again of the form 'it's now' or 'I'm here' or 'I exist'. All these statements are self-verifying and therefore empty, just as 'I do not exist' or 'I'm not here' or 'it is not now' are self-refuting.

So there's controversy about the nature of the argument. But whatever one can say about its logical status, it remains undeniably true when anyone says it of himself or herself.

NW: *Is it fair to say that contemporary philosophers see the virtues of the downward slope of this argument up to the point of the* Cogito *and are fairly dismissive of the sorts of arguments he uses to build up from the other side?*

ACG: Yes, that's right. If you look at the history of epistemology since Descartes, the majority opinion, especially on the empiricists' side, is that scepticism shows us that we've got a job of work to do: we've got to get from the private data of consciousness to an external world. Now, how are we going to do that if we can't buy Descartes' story about a good deity? If you dispense with that as your security for getting from experience to the world, what's going to take its place? If you consider Locke, Berkeley, Hume, Mill, Russell, Price, and Ayer, major figures in the debate about epistemology, they all in their way focus on that question.

What's so interesting is what happened in the twentieth century in response to this issue, which was to say: 'Since we can't get from Descartes' starting point to an external world with any great security, perhaps we should recognize that it's the starting point which is at fault'—and that would be the greatest criticism of Descartes.

NW: *Having said that, the* Meditations *is superb as literature: this is a wonderfully clear piece of writing.*

ACG: This is one of the two significant things about Descartes' position in the history of philosophy. First, he identified the right question to be asking—what can we know and how?—right there in the early seventeenth century with the rise of modern science, junking all debate about how many angels can dance on the head of a pin, and cutting right to the chase.

Second, because he wasn't relying on jargon, on the apparatus that scholastic philosophy had generated, he was able to write in a way that was accessible to everybody. It's a piece of writing which is marvellously clear and lucid and accessible.

NW: *What do you think there is of value now for us in Descartes'* Meditations?

ACG: Apart from the pedagogical value—it's a book which is wonderful for beginning students because of its clarity and accessibility—it focuses a question in epistemology which has to be centre stage when you're thinking about the nature of knowledge and how we get it. We may disagree with

Descartes that the right place to start is with the private data of consciousness—if you look at Dewey, Wittgenstein, Heidegger, and others in the twentieth century, you see that all of them repudiate that Cartesian starting point. They all say: 'Don't start with private experience, start with the public world or public language. Anyway, start somewhere else because you will never be able to escape the mind otherwise.'

Nonetheless, Descartes' endeavour—to start from experience and get to a world—is a salutary one in the sense that if it's wrong, it's powerfully, interestingly, and importantly wrong, and it teaches us a great lesson. I don't think you can do epistemology in philosophy in a serious way unless you've engaged with Descartes, and thought through his way of thinking about these things.

8

Baruch de Spinoza on the Passions

David Edmonds: *Baruch de Spinoza died in 1677—the cause was a lung illness, probably due to his breathing in of glass dust: he'd spent much of his life as a lens grinder. Only after his death was his masterpiece, the* Ethics, *published. And so it was only posthumously that he earned a reputation as one of the great rationalists of the age. In the* Ethics—*a book written with the formal apparatus of geometry— definitions, axioms, and so on—he discusses a key concept in his philosophy—what he calls 'the passions'. What does Spinoza mean by the passions? Sue James is a Spinoza scholar and professor of philosophy at Birkbeck College.*

Nigel Warburton: *The topic I want to focus on is Spinoza on the passions. But before we get on to that, could you say a little bit about who Spinoza was?*

Susan James: The Dutch say that Spinoza is their top philosopher. He was the son of two Portuguese Jewish immigrants, who had come to Amsterdam a few years before Spinoza himself was born to escape religious persecution from the inquisition. They established themselves within the Amsterdam Jewish community, and that was the milieu in

which Spinoza grew up. When he was in his early twenties, his
father and older brother died. So Spinoza took over his father's
business and became a merchant, trading with Portugal in olive
oil and dried fruit. However, around this time he began to
express philosophical views that alarmed the rabbis of the
Amsterdam synagogue. He also started to broaden his
education, attending a school run by a colourful ex-Jesuit called
Franciscus van den Enden. Van den Enden taught Spinoza
Latin, and introduced him to a circle of radical intellectuals
including merchants, the director of the Amsterdam theatre,
and professionals of various kinds, several of whom became
his friends. Shortly after, for reasons that we don't fully
understand, Spinoza was excommunicated from the Amsterdam
synagogue and forbidden to associate with other members of
the Jewish community. At the age of twenty-three he gave up
his business and began to live as an independent philosopher
with no religious affiliation. He learned to grind the delicate
lenses needed by Dutch scientists for their telescopes and
microscopes, and started to write philosophy.

NW: *So what did he write?*

SJ: He began with some relatively brief works in which he
tried out various philosophical ideas that he would develop
later on. At this stage he was deeply influenced by the work of
Descartes, whose philosophy had created a great stir in the
United Provinces, and had given rise to a major split between
defenders of an orthodox Aristotelian approach and advocates
of the new Cartesianism. Spinoza publicly aligned himself
with the Dutch Cartesians when he wrote an exposition of the
first section of Descartes' major work *The Principles of
Philosophy*, and added an Appendix expounding some of his

own views. That was the first thing he published. So he became known as a philosopher broadly sympathetic to Descartes, and began to acquire an international reputation as someone who had really interesting and wide-ranging ideas about God, nature, human beings, and how we should live.

NW: *But it's his book, the* Ethics, *that's most studied now. It was written in this bizarre geometrical style. Why do you think he used that style?*

SJ: The geometrical style, which was modelled on Euclid's geometry, posited a series of axioms and postulates, and used them to deduce a sequence of theorems, each with its own consequences. This mode of demonstration was thought to have a unique epistemological status because it proved its conclusions with complete certainty, and this is partly why Spinoza uses it. But he is also drawing attention to the fact that—in the *Ethics*—he is doing Philosophy with a capital P. In his view, the geometrical method delivers incontrovertible conclusions of a sort that can only be arrived at in philosophy and mathematics. So it's quite distinct from the methods used in other types of enquiry such as history or theology.

NW: *Now he had really interesting things to say about the passions. But what does he mean by 'passions'?*

SJ: To understand that, we need to go back a bit to one of his most central ideas: that any individual thing, whether a stone or a human being, has the capacity to maintain itself as the thing it is. Spinoza calls this its conatus. The conatus of a relatively simple thing will be rather limited; for example, a stone has some power to resist being smashed when other things collide with it, but that's about all. By contrast, complex entities such as human beings can maintain themselves in all sorts of physiological and psychological ways—by breathing, training themselves to sleep better, fighting to the death, making friends, and so on. These are all ways of holding ourselves together or, as Spinoza puts it, of making ourselves more powerful. So the world, as he sees it, is full of individual things, each striving to persevere in its being; and when a particular individual interacts with another it may become more powerful, less powerful, or stay about the same. Spinoza claims that when human beings interact with other things they experience the resulting changes in their power as passions. Our fundamental striving to maintain ourselves manifests itself in our desires. We experience increases in our power as feelings of joy, and decreases as feelings of sadness. Within this basic schema, Spinoza then goes on to explain more specific passions. But his main claim is that, as we interact with other things, we're always striving to make ourselves more joyful and avoid sadness.

NW: *But the word 'passion' suggests something passive that happens to us rather than an action. Is that right?*

SJ: Yes it is. Spinoza maintains the classical idea that our passions register the ways that external things act on us. Here I am, surrounded by lots of other things that are causing various effects in me. For example, I am perceiving you, Nigel, sensing the warmth of the room, and so on. But these perceptions and sensations come with passions attached. As well as seeing you, I experience you as increasing or decreasing my power to maintain myself. So, if I experience you as acting on me in a way that increases my power, I'll feel some sort of joy; if the opposite, some sort of sadness.

NW: *In what sense, though, are they passive?*

SJ: The *passivity* lies in the idea that you're being acted *on* by something. Suppose, for the sake of argument, that sitting in this room is making me joyful. My passion or affect is partly the result of what the things in the room are like. But it's also partly the result of what I'm like and how I respond to the things around me. Spinoza thinks that the way we respond is partly determined by psychological processes of which we're largely unconscious, and over which we have very little control. For example, if this room is a bit like a different room where I once had a very enjoyable conversation, I'll associate the room I'm in now with a pleasant idea of the previous room, and this will cause me to feel pleasure now. But the whole associative process may well occur without my being conscious of the way it is affecting me. So, in this sense, I'm passive in the face of it. One of the ways Spinoza tries to capture this element of passivity is by describing the kind of idea that I have of an external thing, such as this room, as an *inadequate* idea. Part of what he means is that, because my idea of the room is the fruit of a particular interaction between it and me, it doesn't give me an accurate idea of what the room is really like. I only get an idea of the way it affects me. For that reason, passions tend to give us distorted or, as Spinoza sometimes says, mutilated ideas, and because they are mutilated or incomplete they may prompt us to act in self-destructive ways. We strive to empower ourselves; but when we do this on the basis of inadequate ideas we often fail.

NW: *That's intriguing because it sounds almost like psychoanalysis: the sense that I might be projecting things onto my relationship which may or may not be there in real life.*

SJ: That's right. Freud was very interested in Spinoza, and although they have completely different theories of the mind, they are trying to explain some of the same phenomena.

NW: *So if the passions just happen to us, could they ever be considered rational?*

SJ: Our passions both are and are not rational, depending on the standard you use to assess them. Judged by everyday standards, some passions are rational in the sense that they enable us to act in ways that maintain or increase our power. For example, it's not irrational to feel afraid of a tsunami and try to escape it. However, judged by these same standards, other passions *are* irrational. As we've seen, they often give us deeply confused ideas of ourselves and external things, and prompt us to pursue disempowering courses of action. So, if we use these everyday criteria, passions may either be rational or irrational. At the same time, Spinoza also appeals to a different standard of rationality, in relation to which all passions count as irrational. As we've seen, passions are inadequate ideas. They're incomplete and distorted, and don't give us a true understanding of what we and the world are like. To correct the errors that our inadequate ideas embody, Spinoza claims, we need to stand back from them and get a fuller grasp of their causes. Rather than just taking our loves and hatreds at face value, we need to work out how they arise. What causes me to feel joy at this moment? What causes it to seem that the room is the cause of the joy? And so on. As we extend our knowledge of the causes of our passions, our ideas of them become, as Spinoza puts it, increasingly reliable or adequate. And the more adequate our ideas become, the more we're able to think critically about the inadequate ideas from which we started. We become able to think about our passions in a new way, and are better placed to avoid the mistakes to which they would otherwise give rise. In Spinoza's view, learning to think in this more penetrating fashion amounts to becoming increasingly rational. To reason, he says, is just to think with adequate ideas. But since our passions are inadequate ideas, they are by definition irrational when judged by this standard.

NW: *Am I right to think that his philosophy is about coming to understand ourselves as much as the world?*

SJ: Yes. Those two have to go together. We have to understand ourselves in order to understand the world because we have to understand the way the world interacts with us. While Spinoza is interested in the scientific knowledge of the world that so preoccupies his contemporaries, he's much more concerned to discover how we can acquire the kind of moral knowledge that enables us to live well. That's really what he's all about. And that's why his *magnum opus* is called the *Ethics*.

NW: *And a major theme for him was freedom. How do the passions or emotions relate to freedom for him?*

SJ: Spinoza thinks that, in so far as you're passionate, you're in bondage and are unfree. Why, though, does he equate being passionate with being unfree? Here we come back to the passivity of the passions. The problem is that passionate people are continually being acted on in ways they cannot control. They are subject to the arbitrary effects of other things. The level of their power depends on how other things act on them. And this, according to Spinoza, is what it is to be unfree or enslaved. The project of becoming more free is then a matter of putting oneself in a position where one's capacity to maintain and increase one's power is less dependent on the arbitrary effects of other things, because one has more control over the way they affect one. For example, we can increase our freedom by learning to deal with passions such as grief or fear, rather than simply finding them overwhelming. At one level, this is a political project—a matter of creating circumstances in which people are protected from their own passions. But for Spinoza it is ultimately a matter of cultivating what he calls reasoning. As we just saw, reasoning is the process of acquiring more adequate ideas and using them to gain a true understanding of the causes and effects of things. It is, Spinoza says, a matter of becoming active by acquiring the ability to direct the course of one's own thoughts and actions. The more active you become, the less your ideas are determined by the way that things act on you. Or, to put the point another way, you become less enslaved and more free. By getting a better understanding of yourself and the world, you extend your power to deal actively with the situations in which you find yourself. And by empowering yourself in this way, you generate a sense of pleasure in your own activity which is, according to Spinoza, a source of unparalleled joy. So he has this fundamentally Stoic idea that understanding the world, understanding the causes of your own passions, understanding what sort of creature you are and what sort of environment you live in, will be a source of the most tremendous satisfaction and make you supremely happy.

NW: *This seems like an individualistic philosophy, but you alluded to the fact that he's got a view about how this relates to politics.*

SJ: It isn't really an individualistic philosophy, because becoming free is a collective project. Spinoza thinks of each human being as an extremely tiny part of nature, and thinks that each of us individually has an insignificant amount of power. So, although I can improve my lot by extending my rational understanding in the way I described, I won't get very far on my own. The only way we can effectively protect ourselves against the exigencies of our passions is by tackling the problem as a community, and Spinoza explores this task in two different registers. In the *Ethics* he talks about it as a project undertaken by a community of wise and virtuous people, who understand the importance of cultivating understanding and cooperate for this purpose. But in a different work, the *Tractatus Theologico-Politicus*, he discusses it as a project that can be undertaken by ordinary people who are mostly motivated by their passions. If people of this kind are to effectively increase their power, they first need to live in moderately propitious political circumstances. How, then, do you build a political community that will foster the growth of understanding, thus generating the greatest pleasure of which human beings are capable? Ideally, Spinoza argues, such a political community would be a democracy in which everyone plays a part in the cultivation of reason and becomes as free as they are able to. It has to be admitted that democracy, as Spinoza understands it, is by modern standards a very limited affair in which women, servants, the poor, and a number of other groups have no voice in political affairs. But, I think, nonetheless, that there is in Spinoza's philosophy a kind of urge or aspiration towards a maximally inclusive democracy. And in both his accounts, becoming more rational and learning to live well is a collective enterprise.

NW: *And what part does God play in all this?*

SJ: For Spinoza, God is everything there is. He eschews the idea that God exists apart from nature, as the creator of nature or anything of that sort. At one point in the *Ethics* he talks about 'God or nature', seeming to say that they're really the same thing. That isn't exactly right. But it is roughly right. If you think of all the causal power there is, that's the power of God. It follows that we are in some sense 'in' God, and our power is part of His power. I think Spinoza believes that, as we become more rational and active, we become better integrated into nature and a little more divine.

NW: *But, coming back to the passions, is there an appropriate emotional attitude that we should have towards God or nature?*

SJ: Yes, one that Spinoza describes as 'love', though love of a rather rarefied kind, very different from the erotic love or friendship that we feel for other people. Once we get a proper philosophical understanding of God we come to realize that He is the immanent cause of everything that exists, and that all our rational knowledge is knowledge of God. This knowledge is empowering; and love, Spinoza says in the *Ethics*, is a kind of joy that we feel when we experience things other than ourselves as empowering. So it's appropriate to love God, not merely in the sense of feeling a certain way about Him, but also in the more practical sense of devoting ourselves to knowing and loving Him better. That's what a wise or rational person does.

NW: *What do you think is the lasting impact of Spinoza's view of the passions?*

SJ: Spinoza is one of the first philosophers who really construed the passions as an integral part of social and political life. For many philosophers before him, the passions were dangerous states of mind that an individual had to learn to moderate and control for himself or herself. Spinoza not only defines passions as an aspect of our interactions with other people and things, thus making them fundamentally social. He also recognizes that the task of modifying them and limiting the damage they can do is largely a collective one, and is something that political communities have to grapple with. Surely, this is an important insight, relevant to contemporary political philosophers and moral psychologists, and, more broadly, to all of us.

9

JOHN DUNN ON
John Locke on Toleration

David Edmonds: *The late seventeenth-century philosopher John Locke is often described as the first of the British empiricists—all knowledge, he thought, came through experience. Locke made seminal contributions in many areas—in metaphysics, epistemology, and personal identity. He also wrote prolifically about politics and the justification for the state. Some of his most significant writings were produced in Holland: he'd been forced to flee into exile in 1683 after rumour of his involvement in a plot to assassinate King Charles II. This was a time when Europe was riven by religious conflict between Catholics and Protestants. Not surprisingly, Locke became preoccupied with the issue of religious toleration—the subject of this interview. Professor John Dunn is a John Locke scholar.*

Nigel Warburton: *We're going to focus on John Locke's ideas about toleration. Could you first say something about who Locke was?*

John Dunn: Locke was an Oxford don in seventeenth-century England who escaped from Oxford into politics and into cosmopolitan intellectual life and ended up writing some very important books.

NW: *He wrote several hugely influential letters on toleration.*

JD: Yes, that's right. He wrote about toleration over the whole of his intellectual life: it was his most consistent preoccupation. But he didn't publish anything until his late 50s, when he published three books in the same year: one, a great philosophical treatise, the *Essay Concerning Human Understanding*; the second, a very surreptitious book, the *Two Treatises of Government*; the third which chronologically was published first—and in Latin originally—was what we now call the *Letter on Toleration*.

NW: *What motivated Locke to write this* Letter on Toleration?

JD: The basis for demanding religious toleration and the scope over which it should extend were major intellectual interests of his throughout his life. But what moved him to write the *Letter on Toleration* while he was in exile in Holland in the 1680s was the overwhelming impact on European Protestantism of the revocation of the Edict of Nantes in 1685 by the French monarch Louis XIV. This was a more or less formal end to a period of effective practical toleration of Protestantism in France, admittedly on very grudging terms, and a prelude to all-out religious persecution. Locke was trying to defend the rights of European Protestants to practise their own religious beliefs.

NW: *So, for Locke, toleration is specifically religious toleration?*

JD: Yes, that's very important. The *Letter on Toleration* is a defence of freedom of conscience. In practice, what freedom of conscience meant was freedom of worship. It didn't unequivocally mean freedom of thought, and it didn't unequivocally mean freedom of speech, which are the two categories that most people think of today when they are thinking of toleration. He very specifically meant the freedom to worship God as you judge that God requires you to do.

NW: *That did not include freedom not to believe in God?*

JD: No, it certainly did not, and for very deep reasons from Locke's point of view. Of course, the primary reason was that Locke believed that there was a God, and that that God had some distinctive properties. What was most striking, and certainly perturbs people who read the *Letter on Toleration* today, is that Locke assumes that to fail to believe in God, to believe that there is no God, is a very serious practical danger to the lives of other human beings.

NW: *Why is that?*

JD: The fundamental reason is because Locke believed that it was only in so far as you recognize the threat of punishment in an afterlife, and to a rather lesser extent the promise of rewards in the afterlife, that you had sufficient reason to act in the way that you should.

NW: *So you might not keep your promises if you didn't believe in God?*

JD: He thought that you might do anything you felt like if you didn't believe in God, and that you might be quite reasonable in so doing. Unless you believed in the threats and promises of an afterlife, you couldn't reliably have good reason to behave as he thought you should.

NW: *What sort of arguments did Locke use to defend his idea that his contemporaries should have freedom of conscience?*

JD: The very simple argument he used was this: the most important interest that human beings have is discharging the duties that God assigns to them. It's the degree to which they succeed in doing that, that generates their prospects in the afterlife. The afterlife, *ex hypothesi*, is a setting in which you can guarantee that you will be over-punished or over-rewarded in relation to any rewards or punishments you might incur here in your natural life. So if you had a thrillingly gratifying but religiously deplorable life here, because of the afterlife, you could guarantee that that was a grievous practical error. If you had a thoroughly miserable but impressively devout life, you could guarantee that that would turn out tremendously well in the long run.

NW: *All this rests on Locke's basic premise then that there is such a God. If there is a God, then the risks of doing something that God did not want you to do are huge.*

JD: Yes, Locke thought that it was appropriate to forbid people to be atheists and to punish atheists very seriously, giving as his reason that the taking away of God, even only in thought, 'dissolveth all'. So, there goes freedom of thought.

NW: *That's interesting—because many of Locke's contemporaries would have used a belief in God as their justification for persecuting people of other faiths.*

JD: Yes. The big intellectual challenge that Locke faced in the *Letter on Toleration* was to refute the view that religious persecution was a religious duty. The most important intellectual innovation from Locke's own point of view was the construction of a rather rich theory of why that judgement was mistaken.

NW: *Could you give a flavour of that theory?*

JD: The key point about the theory was a distinction between the basis of membership on the part of a human being in two different sorts of society: first, a political society; second, a church or ecclesiastical society. The view that religious persecution was a religious duty incumbent on a political sovereign required the conflation of those two: it required identifying church and state. Locke very specifically distinguished the two conceptually. The basis of membership in a church had to be a sincere and personal choice and belief, whereas the basis of membership in a state, although at some point in the causal history of the state in question it had to pass through deliberate choice, couldn't, at any particular point in time, be simply a matter of personal choice because that would destroy the structure of the state. There couldn't be continuing political authority if it could be dissolved whenever anyone dissented from its requirements.

NW: *So, Locke separated the state from religious belief. How does he deal with the problem of the clash of different religions within a society?*

JD: The key step he makes is to remove from the state the possibility of its being the embodiment and judge of religious truth. He imposes on the state a particular duty—the duty to preserve the terrestrial rights of all its subjects. All citizens have a right to their own religious beliefs and they have the right to act on their own religious beliefs in so far as their action doesn't conflict with the civil rights of any of their fellow subjects. But no one has a right to act in a way which conflicts with the rights of any of their fellow subjects or citizens, and the role of the political sovereign is to monitor their interaction and ensure that interference in one another's rights is prevented or punished if it occurs.

NW: *He also had a pragmatic argument about why we shouldn't persecute some people for their beliefs.*

JD: He had a lot of arguments of different kinds about why religious persecution was a bad idea; he totted these arguments up, because religious persecution was in full swing at the time and he was eager to apply the brakes as drastically as he could. One idea was that religious persecution is futile because you can't alter people's beliefs by threatening them. Of course, that is a very strong argument if you're thinking about the impact of a threat at the moment at which you level the threat. I've never met anyone who can alter their beliefs merely because they are threatened. But the fact is that if you keep the threat up for two or three generations, you can have quite a dramatic effect on the content of people's beliefs.

He also has another sort of argument directed especially to Christians, which was that religious persecution was an intrinsically corrupting process spiritually for the persecutors. Some of his most eloquent writing was about that process of corruption. It wasn't really a formal argument, but it was an attempt to demonstrate imaginatively to members of his audience that many of their more self-righteous convictions clashed with other self-righteous convictions that they also held, and to encourage them to edit these self-righteous convictions so that they came out in a more reflective and imaginatively stable form.

NW: *Does the separation of church and state begin with Locke?*

JD: No, it doesn't begin with Locke. A lot of dissident Christian movements had argued for the desirability of this at different points beforehand. But Locke provided the most sophisticated and coherent theoretical account of it from inside Christianity, and no one has surpassed his account since.

NW: *We obviously live in an age where religious toleration is a live issue again: is there anything we can take from Locke for our present-day situation?*

JD: We can't take a practical recipe from Locke because it isn't a practical recipe. We can't take a very cheery and comforting message from him, either. But we can take from him a structure for thinking about the issue of personal freedom. The key distinction in Locke's theoretical account of the scope of religious toleration was the distinction between theoretical beliefs and practical beliefs. The reason why any interpretation of the requirements of Christianity, which did not itself entrench on the rights of other fellow citizens, was entitled to toleration, while atheism was not so entitled, was that, provided they didn't entrench on other people's practical rights, interpretations of the requirements of Christianity are purely theoretical beliefs. But because of his distinctive view about the structuring of reasons for action, atheism was a practical belief, because atheism is the belief that there's no reason why you shouldn't do whatever you're reasonably confident you can get away with, and of course that is an incredibly subversive belief.

There's religious belief about what to do in relation to God in order to save your own soul, which he saw as the central and most important content of religious belief. Then, there are concomitant inspirations about what you can permissibly do to one another. What we may do to one another falls within the space for which the political sovereign is responsible; it's within the space of human worldly

87

interaction, and it's not protected by religious inspiration. So, if I have the religious inspiration that I should now kill you, however sincere and authentic and motivating my inspiration may seem and feel to me, that isn't a matter of religious toleration; that's a matter of civic threat. On the other hand, supposing I believed that God was a very large green cheese, even if that was a pretty silly belief, it would be completely unjustifiable for you to do anything unpleasant to me apart from possibly sneer a bit because I held that belief, since I am entitled in that area to hold whatever inane beliefs I happen to hold. What I'm not entitled to do is to act practically in the world against anyone else's interest because of religious beliefs I happen to hold.

10

JOHN CAMPBELL ON
George Berkeley's Puzzle

David Edmonds:

There was a young man who said God
Must find it exceedingly odd,
To think that the tree should continue to be,
When there's no one about in the quad.

Dear Sir, your astonishment's odd.
I'm always about in the quad.
And that's why the tree will continue to be
Since observed by
Yours faithfully
God.

This rather succinct summary of the philosophy of George Berkeley was penned well after his death. Born in Ireland in 1685, Berkeley rose to become a bishop. But his fame rests on his metaphysics. He was an idealist, believing that reality consists only in minds and ideas, not in objects and things. According to John Campbell, from the University of California Berkeley, Berkeley's philosophy must be understood against the background of the seventeenth-century scientific revolution—a revolution whose influence continues to be felt today—which, in some way, says Professor Campbell, is most unfortunate...

Nigel Warburton: *We're going to focus on Berkeley's puzzle. What was Berkeley's Puzzle?*

John Campbell: Berkeley was working after Newton and Galileo, after the impact of the seventeenth-century scientific revolution in physics. If the physicists were right, if Newton was right, then the world that we live in was not a bit like we think it is. Newtonians were always pointing out that what the world consisted in was mostly empty space, occasionally interspersed with lonely clumps of atoms. The world we think we ordinarily encounter, the world of colours and smells and tastes, the world of other people, the world of tables and chairs—this world simply wasn't there. This was just a projection of the mind onto the alien universe that science describes.

In fact, things have deteriorated. The world as described by quantum mechanics is unimaginably alien. Most of us operate with a doublethink about this. Most of us just forget about it—and physicists, too, mostly forget about it when they're doing their shopping or making dinner, or whatever. But, really, our official view is that the world we actually live in is quite unlike the way our experience seems to show it as being. So that raised a question for Berkeley: 'How do we form a conception of such a world in the first place?'

NW: *You're saying that the physics of Berkeley's time described the world as consisting of lots of colourless molecule-like things. That's what we would call them, but they were called 'corpuscles' in his day. Any things such as colour, smell, taste were projected by the human observer and weren't really in the world out there.*

JC: Before the scientific revolution, it was possible to hold on to a common-sense picture where you encounter things the way they really are. This new physics pushed conscious experience back inside the head: it's just something generated by the brain.

NW: *So his puzzle is how we can say anything at all about the world outside us?*

JC: Yes, but Berkeley's puzzle comes quite deep in the argument. Because once you think that all that consciousness is, all that perceptual experience is, is a bunch of sensations generated in us, then we have the problem that it is on the basis of our conscious experience that we form our conception of what the world is. Berkeley quite rightly said that, if our starting point in forming our beliefs, our opinions about how the world is, is just blobs of sensation, then how can we so much as form the idea of an object independent of us? If all I've got to go on is this wall of sensation, how can I even frame the idea of something beyond that? His answer was: 'You can't, it's just an illusion.' So, although science is the starting point here, Berkeley says you kick away that ladder. Science itself turns out not to have the significance you think it does because all we can ever form the conception of is sensation itself. That is a very radical idea but there is something rigorous about the logic here.

NW: *So where does that leave us on Berkeley's picture of the world? How do we relate to anything?*

JC: It frankly leaves us in pretty bad shape. All we have are our ideas. Berkeley was a theist, so he thought he could have knowledge of God. But, of course, God simply has a bunch of ideas, too, and all you can ever form a conception of, according to Berkeley, is families of ideas. There is going to be structure in our sensations, there may be similarities between your sensations and mine, but we ourselves are not physical things. There is no coherent conception of matter; there is only the generation of ideas by souls. That's all you can form a conception of.

At this point, most of us feel that something has gone wrong, and you think, could we just go over the reasoning there and ask how we got to this position: isn't there a way out of here?

NW: *So is there a way out?*

JC: I think there is a way out, but you have to radically rethink the natural picture of what science is telling us about our relation to the world. For anyone who wants to hold on to the idea that there is a physical world and consciousness too, you've got to say at some point that science and talk about conscious experience describe the same world but at different levels. People always say 'at different levels'—and then they do this chopping motion with their hand, and then they say, 'Well, different levels!', as if that sorts it all out. But although it doesn't sort it all out, it must be the right starting point.

But once you have the idea that there are going to be different levels in the description of reality, you could have played that card right from the start. What I mean is, we usually take it that quantum mechanics is telling us there's nothing 'out there' but these basic particles, these basic forces, the colours, and so on, are projected by the mind. We didn't need to accept that. We could have said the colours are out there too, the smells and tastes are objective features of the world, it's just that they are describing the world at a different level, the level at which science describes it.

NW: *What about the obvious counterexamples there? An object looks different colours under different lights; a stick might look bent in water. The conclusion must be that there's no absolutely right way of describing the world independently of our perceptions of the world, mustn't it?*

JC: Well, if you just take the 'looks bent in water': whether the stick is bent or not seems to be a perfectly objective fact. It may look bent, but it's not. I take it just as plain common sense. So, although people can make mistakes about the way things are, or what colours things have, and so on, they do have the colours. When you're buying a shirt, you might say, 'Well, I know it looks yellow here but I just want to check this.' You take it for granted that things really have colours, that things really have shapes. Of course, we make mistakes, and sometimes they don't look the shapes they are, and so on, but that's perfectly consistent with saying that there really is a fact of the matter about all that.

NW: *Where does that leave us with hallucinations, though, because if somebody hallucinates something the relationship between the object and the experience of it is certainly not a straightforward one?*

JC: It's certainly possible to have a hallucination that you can't tell apart from perception of, let us say, a dagger. Philosophers sometimes seem to live in a world where these things are very common, but in fact they are quite unusual. Now, if you can't tell the difference between one thing and another, then sometimes that is because these two things are very similar. If you can't tell the difference between a real pearl and a cultured pearl, that may be because, chemically, they are very similar. But it's also possible that you can't tell the difference between one thing and another because you're just not very good at telling the difference between things of those sort.

Now, with sensation or experience, on Berkeley's picture, you have the same sensation whether or not you're having a hallucination. The sensation is intrinsically the same whether you're seeing a dagger or having a hallucination of a dagger. That's why you can't tell the difference between the two cases. I'm suggesting a quite different analysis. On this analysis, when you are seeing a dagger and when you are having a hallucination of a dagger, these are intrinsically quite different states. It's just that we're not very good at telling the difference between them. In the one state, there is no dagger as a component of your experience. In the other case, an actual dagger and its colour, texture, and so on really are involved. These are very different states, and it's possible that you'll not be able to tell the difference between them because of a limitation in your discriminative capacities.

NW: *So, you're saying Berkeley's starting point—that we couldn't separate the real qualities of the world from those which we project onto it—was just a fallacy?*

JC: That's right. It's something that's still with us today. I think that most educated people would take it for granted that colour is projected onto the world by the mind. But I think that that notion really is not well founded. All that science can tell you is that there is a level of description of the world at which we don't talk about colour; the colour drops out. That does not show that colour is the work of the mind. It just shows that we have to talk about different levels here.

Brain scientists hunt assiduously through the brain looking at this part of the neuron-firing or that part of the neuron-firing. They say, 'Now, where exactly is the sensation of colour? Where exactly are the sensations of the physical objects around us?', and these are nowhere to be found. That is very, very puzzling. People say, 'Well, maybe it's very, very complicated, and we need sophisticated mathematical analysis to find the sensation of colour', but of course there's a natural suspicion that no matter how complicated the mathematical analysis of the neuron-firing, there is still not going to be a sensation of colour to be found. What I'm suggesting is that that's because we are looking in the wrong place. The colour is where it seems to be, *the colour is in the world*, the colour is a characteristic of our surroundings, not a characteristic of our brains, and experience of colour is the relation that our brain puts us in to this stuff.

NW: *What you're saying sounds like common sense. The objects are out there, they've got qualities; I perceive them, they're more or less as they seem to be, and my conscious experience is simply a kind of mirroring of what's in front of me. Now, I know there are many philosophers who will listen to this and say, 'That's naïve, there is a huge contribution that the perceiving mind makes to our interpretation of objects—that is part of what conscious experience must be.'*

JC: You're right. First of all, it is common sense, and there's a sense in which it is naïve. It's trying to reinstate the picture of our relation to our surroundings that we could have had before the impact of science. What I disagree with is the idea that our brain makes a big contribution to our picture of the way the world is. We shouldn't think of it like that. If you think of it from an evolutionary point of view, the reason you have a brain is not to generate a whole bunch of sensations that have nothing to do with what's actually going on. Why would you want such a thing? The picture I'm suggesting is that all the stuff that we common-sensically take to be out there, really is out there, and the function of all the brain processing is just to make it visible to us. That does take a lot of brain processing, it's very important that we have brains. But their function is to reveal the world to us, not to generate a lot of random junk.

The scientific revolution seemed to take away the idea that there's a world that we all have in common, a world that we share. Because, after all, what's going on is that the world that's in common is this world of alien forces. All that is happening within me and within you is generating sensations in you, is generating sensations in me, and for all we know, they are completely different sensations. So, the scientific revolution really shut us off from each other. It gave us the present problem of other minds; it said, we shall never know what is going on in one another's minds. Now, if you reinstate the common-sense world, if you say the colours and so on are all there, that it's just a high-level description of the same world that science describes but is there independently of us, then what's happening in your experience is that you are encountering the very same qualitative world that I am encountering. So there isn't a problem about whether your experience is qualitatively the same as mine. Because it's the same qualitative world that we're all encountering.

11

PETER MILLICAN ON
David Hume's Significance

David Edmonds: *As David Hume lay dying, he distressed James Boswell by awaiting his death calmly while refusing to embrace either God or immortality. Hume is widely regarded as the most significant English-speaking philosopher of all time: philosophers still grapple with his ideas on causation, on induction, on morality. Whether he was an atheist, or merely an agnostic, is debatable. Peter Millican, a Hume specialist, believes that he toned down his critique of religion for reasons of prudence and so as not to alienate his friends. His views on religion, Millican argues, fit into a wider critique of human reason more generally. And it's in what Hume says about the limits of reason that his real significance lies.*

Nigel Warburton: *The topic we're focusing on is the significance of David Hume. For many people, he is the greatest philosopher. Could you say a bit about who he was and why his work is so significant?*

Peter Millican: David Hume was one of the great philosophers of the Early Modern period, the seventeenth and eighteenth centuries. He's standardly thought of as one of the big three British empiricists, along with Locke and Berkeley. But I think Hume has a significance greater than that. He stands apart from all of the philosophers of the period as the first really modern thinker who developed a view of human reason which belongs far more naturally with Darwin than with Descartes or Aristotle, or any of the previous thinkers.

NW: *What did come before Hume and what was he reacting against?*

PM: What you had in the whole Early Modern period was a reaction against the medieval world, which had been largely built on Aristotle. Aristotle's theory of the world was based on the idea that everything that happens is fundamentally intelligible in terms of purposes. You can understand the way that things work in the world in not only God's purposes, but purposes within things as well. So, if you ask why a stone falls to the ground when you let it go, the answer is that it's striving to reach the centre of the universe. Why do heavenly bodies move in circles? They strive to move in circles to imitate as closely as possible the divine perfection and so forth.

Now, what happened in the Early Modern period as science developed, and in particular as the theory of the heavens that was associated with Aristotle got overthrown (Galileo's telescopic observations played a major role here), this picture became displaced by a view of the world based on mechanical science. People like Galileo and Descartes, instead of seeing the way things behaved as being determined by purposes or strivings, saw nature as fundamentally *causal*, and *mechanically* causal. Why does something move? Well, because it is caused to move by something else bashing into it, or pushing it, or whatever.

That was taken further in Britain by people like Robert Boyle, John Locke, and Isaac Newton. They saw this as a huge advance on Aristotle because, instead of having occult interactions between things—the mysterious idea that matter might strive to reach a certain position or anything like that—nature becomes intelligible in terms of mechanical laws.

NW: *So, where does Hume come in here?*

PM: What Hume did was to take this notion of intelligibility and say, 'Actually, guys, you don't really understand why anything works the way it does.' At the time, people used to point to things like gravity and say, 'Gravity is a real problem. How do we explain how things can attract each other from a distance? Mechanical causation, billiard balls—that's fine, but gravity's far more problematic. How can a planet be attracted to the sun? It would have to know where the sun was in order to accelerate in the right direction, and that looks suspiciously like the sort of occult striving that everyone now rejects.' So people considered gravity a real puzzle.

Now, what Hume did was to say, 'No, actually, the same kind of puzzle that you have about that, you ought to have even about the interaction of billiard balls. When one billiard ball bashes into another, you think you understand why it causes the other one to move. You think it's intelligible, but really it isn't.'

NW: *Ok, let's take that example of billiard balls colliding. I hit the white one, it hits the red one, the red one moves: the motion is somehow transferred from one to the other. I can see the cause of the effect.*

PM: It is very hard to pull yourself away from this natural way of looking at things. Hume has a lovely thought experiment for making his point clear. He asks us to imagine Adam, the first man, created by God with perfect human cognitive faculties: he's got perfect sight, his senses all work well, etc. So suppose that God's just created Adam, and in front of him, Adam sees one billiard ball moving towards another. God says to him, 'Adam, what do you think is going to happen when that ball reaches the other one?'

How could Adam even start to work out what was going to happen? Maybe the ball will stop, maybe the second one will move, maybe the first one will bounce off it in some direction, maybe the second one will turn into a frog. How can he know, without prior experience to call on, what's going to happen when the two balls collide? He can't. And the message is that whenever we make an inference like that about what's going to happen, we are always drawing on past experience. Then the big question is, what right do we have to do that?

NW: *What right do we have to do that? It seems quite reasonable to think about what's happened in the past and assume it will carry on along similar lines in the future.*

PM: Hume wouldn't deny that, in a sense, it's perfectly reasonable. But the point he wants to focus on is this: we have no insight into the nature of things that leads us to make that supposition. It's a very natural supposition to make—we do naturally take for granted that what's happened in the past will broadly continue in the future. But, again, Hume has a very nice argument. He asks: 'What ground could we give for extrapolating from the past to the future?' It's not self-evident: you can coherently imagine it not continuing into the future in the same way. Likewise, you can't give any sort of deductive proof that it will continue because it's perfectly coherent that it shouldn't continue. And nothing that you sense about objects—for example, when you perceive the billiard ball—

nothing that you learn directly through your senses tells you about how it will behave in the future, as we've seen in the case of Adam. So what other recourse do we have? The only other recourse is an appeal to experience. But appealing to experience is what we're trying to justify. So when you try to produce any justification, any argument, any reason for extrapolating from the past to the future, you can't.

NW: *So you're saying that, for Hume, trying to justify the idea that the future will be like the past (by saying that the future has always been like the past in the past) is almost like pulling yourself up by your bootstraps: it's not a satisfactory way of justifying what's known as induction.*

PM: Exactly. That sort of justification would only work if you're already persuaded that induction is a rational method of inference.

NW: *Presumably, Hume is going to say that we are just relying on some kind of natural tendency to see the future as carrying on in the same way as the past.*

PM: Yes, that's right. Again, Hume doesn't want to say that it's wrong that we should do that. The point he's making is that when we do extrapolate in that way, we are relying on this brute animal instinct that leads us to expect the same in the future as we've experienced in the past. He's not saying we shouldn't do that, but let us be aware that its basis is an assumption, an animal instinct; it's not founded on any kind of God-like insight into why things behave as they do.

NW: *That idea that we have to see human beings as part of the animal kingdom must have been quite radical in the eighteenth century.*

PM: Very much so. We were talking earlier about how the mechanical view of the world became very popular in the seventeenth and eighteenth centuries. But man was always excluded. So Descartes, for example, thought of animals as just material machines, but he famously drew a very radical distinction between mind and matter. And a very prominent bogey in the seventeenth century was the materialist Thomas Hobbes, who denied that there was an immaterial world; he said that *everything* was material, which was anathema in the seventeenth century. People were even criticized for denying the existence of witches and such things because it was very important to the world view that, although the physical world could be understood causally and mechanically, there was also another world, a spiritual world, a world of mind, which is quite distinct from the physical world, and we humans partake in that.

NW: *Another important related aspect of Hume's work is his attack—I can't put it any other way—on some of the standard arguments for God's existence.*

PM: Yes, although for many years people actually thought of this as not being central to Hume's philosophical mission, I think that's quite wrong; indeed, Hume wrote more on philosophy of religion than any other area of philosophy. In the early stuff, he tended towards self-censorship; he removed from the *Treatise of Human Nature* his discussion of miracles, for example. Then in his later work in the *Enquiry*, he comes back to religion and is very critical about it, arguing that it doesn't stand up to rational scrutiny. Now it can actually seem very puzzling that Hume takes this line because many people think of him as an irrationalist. As we've seen, he is indeed sceptical about the pretensions of reason, but in fact, he is at the same time very pro-science and anti-superstition, which is quite a delicate balance. We've seen that Hume reduces the basis of scientific reasoning to an animal instinct—the instinct for expecting the future to resemble the past. But then he wants to advocate such reasoning and say that this is how we *ought* to reason about the world because it provides the only basis we have for learning from experience.

NW: *How does that apply to particular arguments about God's existence?*

PM: Perhaps the clearest example, and it's a very elegant example, is the discussion of miracles in Hume's *Enquiry concerning Human Understanding*. Imagine that you're a religious believer who founds his belief on stories of miracles. Imagine that you say, 'So and so told me a miracle and I believe it.' What Hume does is to reply, 'Hang on a minute, why do you believe what they say?' The answer has to be that you believe what so and so says because they tend to tell the truth. Then Hume points out here that you yourself are relying on induction, you yourself are relying on the assumption that because so and so has generally told the truth in the past, that's good reason for supposing that they will tell the truth in the future. But, in that case, you ought to be consistent. If you're going to use induction as your basis for belief, then you ought to apply induction also to your understanding of how things behave.

But you've never experienced (let's say) a statue crying. So, if this person told you that they saw a statue crying, you've got a conflict. On the one hand, you've got inductive evidence that they tend to report the truth, which tells in favour of the statue crying. On the other hand, you've got your own experience of statues which tells you they don't cry. So, the religious believer ends up in a conflict between two inductive arguments, and what Hume says—roughly—is that the argument based on the uniformity of nature about the statue will always beat the other one because we know from experience that people do make mistakes, they are subject to illusion, and they also lie.

NW: *Is there any place for God in Hume's account of the world?*

PM: No, I think that Hume is to all intents and purposes an atheist.

NW: *That's interesting because a lot of people have read his work closely and think of him not as an atheist but as a very sceptical agnostic.*

PM: Hume is quite difficult to pin down on the question of God's existence. That's entirely understandable, given the time in which he wrote—you could be prosecuted for infidelity at the time and it certainly would have alienated a lot of his friends if he'd come out explicitly as an atheist. So, it requires some reading between the lines of Hume's texts. He tends, for example, to write pieces in which the first and/or the last paragraph imply that he's a believer. But then when you look at all the arguments in between, they point in the opposite direction. This was actually a very common trick at that time; it's been called 'theological lying'. Hume's essay on the immortality of the soul is a perfect example, but even though its first and last paragraphs appeal to faith to justify life after death, it was considered too dangerous to publish during his lifetime. When he was dying, he told James Boswell that he thought the belief in immortality ridiculous, and Boswell's dismay illustrates why Hume had to be so careful.

NW: *To sum up: Hume's significance is that he attacked the idea that we have this faculty of reason that allows the world to be intelligible to us in a transparent way, and also that he removed God from the picture.*

PM: Yes, that's right. These are two sides of the same coin. Prior to Hume, people thought of the world as designed by a divine intelligence and saw our own intelligence, our minds, as given by God so as to enable us to understand the intricacy of his creation. So the two somewhat go together. What Hume does is to take out the divine creator, and he says we've got no reason to suppose that the world was created by a perfect being. He also, perhaps inevitably, displaces us from any ambition of being above nature, so that we shouldn't think of our reason as being some faint copy of a divine faculty, and instead ought to see it as an augmented and very powerful instance of an animal faculty. Rather than aspiring to any sort of God-like point of view, we should accept that we're just clever animals, and adjust our expectations accordingly. We can still aspire to find out how the world works—by observation and experiment—but we can't expect any ultimate insight into *why* it works that way. And exactly the same lesson applies to our understanding of ourselves: we too are fully part of the empirical world, not some separate world of spirits.

12

Adam Smith on What Human Beings Are Like

David Edmonds: *Adam Smith is the most famous of all economists. His contribution to philosophy is less well known. A key figure of the eighteenth-century Scottish Enlightenment, Smith taught moral philosophy at Glasgow University, and was a close friend of David Hume. His first book,* The Theory of Moral Sentiments, *is now rarely read by philosophers, but perhaps it should be. We would know much more about Smith if he hadn't ordered his executors to destroy his papers. But Nick Phillipson, now retired from the University of Edinburgh, pieced together the remaining evidence to write an acclaimed life of Smith. Who better, then, to give an account of Smith, the philosopher of sympathy, than his sympathetic biographer?*

Nigel Warburton: *We're talking about Adam Smith and his ideas about what human beings are like. Smith is world renowned as an economist, but he's not generally known as a philosopher. Yet you think he was a great philosopher.*

Nick Phillipson: He was a great philosopher, but his philosophy has sunk to the bottom of the pool, and he has become, over the years, a one-book man: the author of *The Wealth of Nations* and the author of a particular economic theory. Actually, at the end of his life, he said he preferred his first book, his *Theory of Moral Sentiments*, to *The Wealth of Nations*.

NW: *In that book, Smith took a similar approach to David Hume, a great friend of his.*

NP: Yes, he did. Hume and Smith met in the late 1740s when Smith was in his 20s. Smith laid out his philosophical stall in the next ten years in lecture courses on rhetoric, moral philosophy, and jurisprudence. He also tagged his first thoughts about economics on to the jurisprudence course. The question for historians is: what's he up to, what's the game?

NW: *So what is the game?*

NP: Well, the game was about the biggest game in the Enlightenment league: it was to construct a science of man—a science which would explain how human beings come to be the people they are, how civilizations have taken the shape that they have, and how human beings and their governments ought to behave in the circumstances in which they found themselves. To answer all this you had to start by defining what human beings are.

NW: *His philosophical predecessors saw human beings as pushy, selfish, egotistical entities, atomized individuals in a society where they tear each other apart. Thomas Hobbes, for instance, was famous for taking such a view. What did Smith think?*

NP: Smith wasn't worried about human beings tearing *each other* apart; he was worried about human beings been torn apart by the wild beasts at the dawn of creation. In the notes that his students took of his lectures there is a fascinating account of the beginnings of human society. It's a speculative, or what he called a 'conjectural', account. Human beings are the weakest of all animals, Smith said. They are physically weak; as individuals, they can't compete with any of the other animals: they can't run, they can't fight, they have no hair (he's wrong about that, actually), so they will freeze. To put it bluntly, they will die unless they learn to cooperate. In his early account of where human beings come from, there's the notion that to cooperate you have to exchange, and that means inventing some sort of language. To start with, this was probably a matter of using signs and sounds—warning someone that there was a tiger behind the tree. In time, it becomes more sophisticated. Out of this, Smith develops a theory of language to explain how we have come to be language users, using a language and a grammar capable of expressing complex abstract thoughts. And this matters, because the more we use language and the more we increase our language skills, the easier it is to communicate and cooperate with others, and the more sociable we become. And so his account continues: a closely intermeshed study of how human beings exchange goods, services, sentiments with each other.

NW: *Hobbes in his 'state of nature' has people giving up their natural rights for security. Hobbes recognized the fragility of life in the state of nature: as soon as you go to sleep, no matter how strong you are, some weak person could come along and kill you. How different is Smith's account of the state of nature from that?*

NP: Smith doesn't think that human beings are necessarily as predatory as that: wild beasts are more fearsome than other human beings. However, it is undoubtedly true that there are predatory human beings, and some human beings have to be treated with great caution. We are likely to learn this lesson when we start to tamper with other people's possessions. In other words, it's not likely that someone is going to try and kill me for the love of killing me—let's forget about the psychopaths in the primitive world. What's much more likely is that they are going to try and pinch my spear. This may not matter too much in primitive societies in which so many goods are shared in common. What does matter is when we find that we are living in a world in which there is scarcity and competition for the things around us. That's when we start to think of things like a piece of land as 'mine'. Once this happens, we become aggressive and the reason we become aggressive, in protecting what we feel is 'my property', is not necessarily because of its utility value. It's because we now start to see an attempt to seize 'my property' as an attack on me. In this world of exchange and in a world in which the supply of goods is restricted, the notions of property and person have become identified.

And what is being knit together is a world in which people engage in complicated deals—partly to do with honour, partly to do with things—about rights to property. And when that happens, you immediately think of that right as something that needs to be protected. And this calls for a governor of some sort who will enforce that right. Political society is born.

NW: *One of Smith's and Hume's contemporaries, Jean-Jacques Rousseau, saw the process of civilization as corrupting something pure that had existed in the natural world. Is that how Smith saw it?*

NP: Yes, it is. This is one of the most fascinating aspects of Smith's moral philosophy. The story goes back to his student days at Glasgow University in 1736–1740 when he was introduced to the work of the British philosopher Bernard Mandeville (1670–1733), one of the most hilarious philosophers you could read and someone who had a big influence on Rousseau. Mandeville wanted to explain how human beings, who were the naturally most selfish of animals, were turned into docile, tractable social animals. He had wonderful fun talking about educational processes and the tricks our nurses, teachers, and governors play in order to flatter and bully us into a state of sociable servility. Smith read Rousseau when he was working on the text of the *Theory of Moral Sentiments*, and was struck by the way in which Rousseau had tweaked Mandeville's theory by starting off from the premise that human beings were naturally a simple and pure species who were corrupted by society and turned into creatures who had become quite unrecognizable to themselves. Smith didn't dispute that the effects of the civilizing process would change us out of all recognition, but he didn't agree with Rousseau that this was a form of corruption—and I regard his *Theory of Moral Sentiments* as a sustained reply to Rousseau.

He thinks Rousseau is absolutely right to say that social education does have the effect of turning us into someone else. But that isn't the end of the story. Socialization is a much more complex process than Rousseau and Mandeville realize. Of course, it begins by us doing the pretty contemptible thing of trying to behave in ways that will please others, but it doesn't take long to realize that we can't please everyone all the time. So what happens then? We do something very simple and natural, but something that no one has thought about theoretically. We turn away from the crowd. We turn inwards on ourselves and have interior conversations with ourselves. Smith describes this as having a conversation with a fictitious person—a fictitious person he calls an impartial spectator. In fact, in time, our respect for the opinions of this fictitious man in the breast is likely to become so powerful that we fear his disapproval more than the disapproval of real people. Smith thinks that this everyday practice is of immense importance in shaping our personalities. It's a practice that becomes habitual, which teaches us self-reliance, and gives us a conscience. It's a self-reliance we come to value for its own sake as well as for the admiration other people often have for it. And so the paradox is that we *do* become unrecognizable to our former selves, as Rousseau said, but we become the person we think we would like to be.

NW: *Does Smith actually have a story about where this impartial spectator comes from? Because it seems mysterious. Does our conscience come from a God-given soul?*

NP: No. Smith is, after all, the closest disciple that Hume ever had, and Hume was one of the most famous infidels in Europe, and determined to produce a philosophy which didn't depend at any point on religious hypotheses. Hume and Smith were both convinced that all scientific and philosophical systems, all human thought in fact, has its roots in the imagination. In the last resort, the impartial spectator is a figment of the imagination, a fiction, and the paradox is that we come to value the approval and disapproval of this fictional entity more than that of real people.

NW: *Now, my limited knowledge of Smith's economic theory is all about the hidden hand, the way that capitalism provides the best solution to all kinds of complex negotiations. We should let selfish individuals fight out the best price in the marketplace and that will benefit all of us more than any organized system.*

NP: That is the take that we all have. The idea of an invisible hand which reconciles private and public interest is always said to be the most powerful of Smith's ideas—and it certainly is polemically powerful. This is a boring thing to say, but it isn't actually peculiar to Smith as a theorist of trade. Smith the economist should be seen in his historical context as a man arguing against a whole culture of restricting the workings of the land, labour, and capital markets in the belief that this was the best way of increasing the wealth and security of a kingdom. Smith wanted to prove that this system wouldn't increase the GDP or work in the long-term interest of land owners, merchants, and workers. What people often forget is that Smith was a realist in matters concerning the liberalization of the market. He knew perfectly well that many vested interests would see liberalization as harmful to their interests, and he knew better than most that this could lead to serious and dangerous political trouble. What he wanted was cautious, piecemeal liberalizing improvements. In fact, it's worth remembering that Smith may have been a great philosopher but he was also a very modest one. He didn't think that economics or philosophy could ever be an exact science because no science can be. On the other hand, that's not what his disciples felt. And one of the sad stories about the fate of *The Wealth of Nations* is the attempt to turn his principles into the basis of a hard science.

NW: *But would it be fair to say that Smith saw commerce as a civilizing force?*

NP: Yes. Commerce allowed you to deploy your goods and resources to increase what he called your individual 'comfort and conveniences'. This was a liberalizing process, which would increase communication between people. The more people were encouraged to exchange goods, services, and sentiments, the more they would come to trust each other and the better place society would be. So, overall, commerce has an ameliorating effect on social behaviour. But he didn't deny that commerce would turn up some pretty ghastly people who think that greed is good. Indeed, one of the things that's often forgotten about Smith is that he thought that one of the tasks of the governments of his day was to keep an eye on the 'greed is good' brigade. In those days, this brigade was made up not so much of bankers as merchants. He didn't doubt that we need these people: but they certainly needed to be watched.

NW: *Everybody knows there are things to be learned from Adam Smith's economic theory, but what should we take away from his philosophy?*

NP: That's a very interesting question, and not one I've ever been asked before. My students consistently get more out of *The Theory of Moral Sentiments* than *The Wealth of Nations*. I think the reason is that human behaviour is inherently interesting. Smith encourages us to think about the ways in which people interact in society, about the way in which they judge other people, and about the ways in which we judge themselves. He wants us to think that ethics and social psychology go hand in hand, and that it's all a matter of thinking carefully about the things that we all do anyway. He's bringing philosophy to common life. He's giving us a complicated but convincing account of how we try to live decently at ease with ourselves and with those around us. He's making us all philosophers.

13

MELISSA LANE ON
Jean-Jacques Rousseau on Modern Society

David Edmonds: *Karl Marx saw the industrial revolution and its injustices as an inevitable stage on the way to a communist utopia. But, before Marx, there had been another searing critic of so-called 'progress'. Jean-Jacques Rousseau was an intellectual celebrity: a philosopher, novelist, musicologist, educationalist, polemicist, and author of arguably history's most influential autobiography—his* Confessions. *He was born in Geneva in 1712, and died in 1778. The industrial revolution was still to come, but his Parisian friends—who mostly became ex-friends—were joyful participants in the advances in arts and sciences. Rousseau, however, railed against modern society and the idea of progress in the arts and sciences; he warned against the cities, and their 'black vapours'; he eulogized nature. Melissa Lane is a historian of ideas and political theorist at Princeton University . . .*

Nigel Warburton: *We're going to focus on Rousseau and his critique of modern society. Could you say a little bit about who Rousseau was?*

Melissa Lane: Yes. Jean-Jacques Rousseau was a citizen of Geneva in Switzerland in the eighteenth century. In later life, he would make much of that because part of his critique of modern society was a critique of the French, where he made his career. He celebrated and idealized the purer republican values of Geneva. Rousseau led a very interesting itinerant life as a secretary in households of the great, such as the French ambassador to Venice. At the same time, he led a less reputable life, fathering five children out of wedlock with a mistress. In the younger and middle parts of his life, he was a friend and companion to the men of the *Encyclopaedia*. The enormous *Encyclopédie* project was celebrating all of the advances of the arts and sciences. Diderot and Voltaire were two of the great names associated with it.

NW: *Before we get on to his critique, what were the ideals of the Enlightenment?*

ML: Well, certain strands of the Enlightenment celebrated advances in arts and sciences and in particular the development of what we've come to call commercial society. Commercial society was driven by people's wants as well as by their needs. The celebration of commercial society grew out of a critique of republican politics that depended on a notion of people being virtuous and self-controlled and limiting their desires in order to maintain their civic dedication. In the commercial society, it was said, we can be more prosperous and more peaceful, if we trade with each other; the private vices of people consuming luxuries can bring society together in a new way. It will have peace and order and growth built on trade and interaction.

NW: *Rousseau was part of this movement—at what point did he turn against it?*

ML: There was a particular moment. In 1749, he was on his way to Vincennes in France to visit Diderot, who was imprisoned there for violating the censorship. And he spotted the subject of a prized essay that had been set by the Académie of Dijon. The subject was whether the restoration of the arts and sciences had contributed to the improvement of mankind. Later in the *Confessions*, his autobiography, he said that at that moment, he was visited by a kind of illumination which led him to say 'no'. And all of his critique of modern society flows from that moment.

NW: *What kind of societies were the French philosophers contrasting their notion of modern society with?*

ML: The context was the coming to grips with the discovery of the new world: America and then Australia. This confronted Europeans with a question about the status of the peoples there. The Scottish Enlightenment thinkers would develop a four-stage theory of history: people start at the primitive stage; then comes a hunting stage, then a pastoral or agricultural stage, and finally the stage of commercial society. This was seen as a form of progress: for example, Adam Smith and David Hume both write that, if we contrast a king among the Indians in North America with a peasant or a worker in Scotland, we see that the peasant or worker is better off—and that's due to the progress of civilization. Hume was Rousseau's contemporary and erstwhile friend until Rousseau believed that he had turned against him.

NW: *So what was it that Rousseau objected to about modern society?*

ML: He expresses his illumination in his *First Discourse* published in 1750 on the sciences and the arts. He says our psychology and our morals have been corrupted by this progress of social development and it's made us unhappy and estranged us from ourselves. He develops a kind of speculative anthropology to describe what man was like in a state of nature and how human sentiments and emotions then developed. His view was that this progress of social development brings with it a kind of dependence on the opinion of others: modern society is all about the need for pride and esteem that has to come from others.

He draws a contrast between *amour de soi*, self-preservation sentiment, self-love in the benign sense of just trying to keep myself alive with what he calls *amour-propre*. *Amour-propre* is my self-esteem, my vanity, my sense of how others see me.

In civilization, we become entirely driven by our *amour-propre*. This is always leading us to be in a competition with others and we can never be truly satisfied. The terrible paradox of civilization for Rousseau was that we're in a society of plenty and yet we are less happy than when we wandered naked in the glades of some barbaric past. Our desires start to outstrip what we can do for ourselves and we become completely dependent on other people and how they view us. We become locked into a kind of rat race of competitive esteem-seeking which none of us can ever win; we're all going to be miserable.

It was crucial for Rousseau that the king or the aristocrat in this order was as miserable as the peasant: in fact you're even worse off to the extent that you're even more dependent on other people's esteem.

This is the genesis of the psychology of the master–slave dialectic in Hegel, of the critique of bourgeois civilization in Marx, and on to Freud. All of this has one key origin—in Rousseau.

NW: *For Hobbes, life outside society is pretty grim—with driven egoists competing for scarce resources. Is that how Rousseau sees what's called the state of nature?*

ML: Not at all. This was a point on which Rousseau fundamentally challenged Hobbes, although in other ways his politics was greatly indebted to Hobbes. In the true state of nature, Rousseau had an image of people as being very solitary creatures who wander around peacefully and only occasionally meet for sexual congress. They're independent and self-sufficient.

NW: *Do you think to some extent this is a reflection of Rousseau's own desire to be alone?*

ML: Well, that's a very interesting thought. Rousseau didn't think the scrabbling-for-acorns stage was actually a stage that we should, in itself, idolize, because he sees that many of our best human capacities also develop gradually and through interaction. So he had a notion of perfectibility that wasn't entirely negative. But he thought that we could try to arrest social development at the level of the village or the hut, where we've graduated to the stage of family. In this stage, we have true familial affection, and not just occasional meetings for sex, and we have a very limited social life. But we're still living in a kind of primitive agricultural way: we're yeomen tilling the soil, and our desires and our competitive instincts haven't been fully awakened yet. In that stage, we achieve the same kind of self-sufficiency that we had in the acorn-grubbing stage. To come on to your point about his own personal desire for isolation, in his *Reveries of a Solitary Walker*, one of his very last works, he describes an affair that he had and the kind of perfect mutual understanding that he shared 'as like being alone'. So I think he wanted society to be like being alone.

NW: *One of the things that modern society gives us is ways in which people can learn about the past, and be educated by other people's mistakes and successes.*

ML: Education is a key issue for Rousseau: he tried to address that point by designing another form of education that could give us certain advantages of social life and culture, but without the fatal disadvantages that he thought education in the arts and sciences in his day would bring. He describes in *Emile*, published in 1762, the imaginary education of a boy by a single tutor. The boy is educated very carefully to only develop such intellectual capacities and such psychological desires that he will be able to fulfil. So, for example, if something goes wrong in his life, he should be taught to ascribe that to nature or fate so that he won't resent it—instead of thinking that he was being thwarted by some other individual, which might lead him to be sucked into a kind of psycho-drama with this other person that will then disrupt his own psychological peace. People said about Kant that when Rousseau's *Emile* arrived, it was the one time he didn't take his everyday walk that the villagers in Königsberg set their watches by. Kant was so overwhelmed and excited by this book.

NW: *And in this book nature plays a big role; it's not just the tutor who teaches the child, the countryside teaches him as well.*

ML: That's right, and that was another aspect of Rousseau's critique of modern society. The counterpart to advanced society is the ability to escape into nature; nature plays several roles for Rousseau. One is the role of fate which we have to come to accept. Another, especially in Rousseau's own later life in the *Reveries*, is the role of a refuge: we can lose our self, for example, in botanizing, we can find mental peace. This had a great impact on Rousseau's contemporaries. Rousseau's books were huge bestsellers across Europe, and many people tried to recreate his ideals in a natural and pastoral society: including, for example, Marie Antoinette who was famous for her deep immersion in the corrupt life of the court. She went to a little village outside Paris.

NW: *Quite a surprising aspect of Emile is that Rousseau is an early advocate of breast-feeding.*

ML: Yes, that's right. He thinks that breast-feeding is a natural way to nourish the child and to nourish the bond between mother and child. Rousseau's views on women and their role are significant. On the one hand, he idealizes women as mothers and thinks that they play a crucial role in educating children to have the sentiments of affection and of patriotism that a good society can spring from. At the same time, he thinks that for them to do that, they mustn't themselves be too rational, or play too much of a public role. So it's in one way quite an exulting role for women, but in another, a confining one. And Mary Wollstonecraft, one of the great feminist thinkers who lived just a little bit later than Rousseau, would excoriate him for this.

NW: *We've talked about Rousseau's prize essay. His* Discourse on Inequality *continues some of these themes.*

ML: Yes. 'The Second Discourse', as it's known, was published in 1755. It develops these themes even further into their political and economic significance and implications. In particular, what Rousseau comes to see as responsible for the worst turning points in that degeneration/development of human society is the institution of property. At the moment of the hut, there is property, but it's really just the use of land. For Rousseau, it's the ability to then start to monopolize property that leads to the division of society into the rich and the poor. In this picture, not everyone is equally treated in the development of society: we now have these two antagonistic groups, and Rousseau thinks that from that point on, it's not just psychological unhappiness that we have to contend with, but political oppression. He comes to see the origin of political power in society as a kind of bargain between the rich and the poor. He asks, why would the poor agree to uphold property, why should the poor not be storming the Bastille and storming the estates of the nobles? And he says, well, the rich persuade them that in order to hold on to the little that they have, they should accept the laws which then benefit the rich so much disproportionately more.

NW: *This is a pretty radical critique, isn't it?*

ML: It is radical and, indeed, I think that that aspect of the critique of bourgeoisie civilization and its effects on the poor profoundly anticipates Marx. We can get the real social criticism of the bourgeoisie as much from Rousseau as from Marx and expressed even more powerfully. Marx thought that bourgeois society was playing a crucial role, a historical role, a necessary role: it was providing the accumulation that would eventually lead us through to communism. For Rousseau, there's nothing good about it. My teacher Judith Shklar, a great Rousseau scholar, used to say that Rousseau is society seen from the bottom up; he shows us how society looks from the standpoint of the oppressed. This is again a turning point in western social and political thought.

NW: *Do you think there are things that we could learn now from Rousseau's thought?*

ML: Rousseau really challenges us to ask the fundamental question, Is commercial society making us happy? And in an age when commercial society and its externalization of costs has produced ecological crisis, these are very profound questions that Rousseau presses on us. How sustainable is the cycle of desires and wants that commercial society seems to require? Criticisms of the ad industry, for example, could have been written by Rousseau, in terms of the way that they continually awaken these desires for competition and status and self-advertisement in ways that can never be fully satisfied: we always need one more product, and Rousseau would have been able to prophesize that all too well.

NW: *Like some classical philosophers, Rousseau didn't just write about ideas, he actually tried to live them.*

ML: He did. And the *Confessions* is a profoundly significant document in the history of western thought for that reason. He makes his own life a kind of example of a uniquely pure and virtuous heart which has somehow been outraged and exploited and abandoned and betrayed by his contemporaries, by these Enlightenment philosophers, each one of whom he quarrels with and abandons. At a certain point in his life, he leaves Paris and goes to live in the countryside, turning his back on the fleshpots of Paris. This was a very significant thing to do, at a time when civilization was thought to have its world centre in Paris.

14

RICHARD BOURKE ON
Edmund Burke on Politics

Nigel Warburton: *When the fog of politics descends, it can be difficult to see clearly. Now regarded as one of the founders of modern conservatism, the eighteenth-century thinker Edmund Burke combined political experience with philosophical insight. Burke believed in the need to balance two aspects of our humanity: our competitiveness and our capacity for deference. For him, the French Revolution of 1789, enacted in the name of liberty, equality, and fraternity, was not only a failure in its own terms, but a terrible warning of what happens when political institutions are violently uprooted. Richard Bourke, a historian at Queen Mary, University of London, is writing a book on Edmund Burke.*

David Edmonds: *The topic we're talking about today is Edmund Burke. Can you explain something about who Edmund Burke was?*

Richard Bourke: Edmund Burke was born in Dublin in 1730 to a Protestant father and a Catholic mother. He spent his youth between Dublin and the Blackwater Valley in Cork, went to a Quaker school, proceeded to Trinity College Dublin where he took his undergraduate degree, and then to London where he studied law. His early career was spent as a man of letters in London, but he then moved into a career in parliamentary politics beginning in 1765–66, and that set the pattern for his life from then on.

DE: *His career was defined by a set of contentious political issues...*

RB: Yes; when Burke entered Parliament in 1766, the major issues of the day included the British government's attempt to tax the American colonies, which proved highly controversial and led to the Declaration of Independence and, in due course, to the war between Britain and America. There was also the hotly debated topic of the East India Company's presence in south Asia and how the Company should administer its affairs. Equally, events in Ireland were proving controversial. So, virtually everything that was to dominate his career was already on the table, so to speak, in 1766—with the exception of the crisis in France, which was not to emerge as an issue until much later in his career.

DE: *We'll get to the French Revolution later, but he was a supporter of the breakaway colonies in America?*

RB: He was a supporter of opinion in America against the British crown in the person of George III. I would not say that he was a supporter of all aspects of the American revolutionary position On the one hand, he was worried about the extent of religious radicalism in America and the extent to which it could be pacified. However, he did think that efforts should be made to win over American opinion; here, he stood apart from many of his colleagues in the House of Commons who thought that American opinion should be disregarded and that a policy of coercing the colonies should be pursued. His main worry at that period was the ambitions of George III. As part of his critical attitude towards what he saw as the overweening ambitions of the British monarchy, he took the side of the American colonists. However, he did not do so unquestioningly. For instance, he didn't credit the argument that there could be—in the phrase used at the time—'no taxation without representation', as a sensible view of politics, because it seemed to him structurally impossible for colonists thousands of miles away to have representation in Parliament.

DE: *So his support for them was an anti-George III stance essentially.*

RB: That's definitely the case. He was a Rockinghamite Whig who vehemently believed George III had disregarded the privileged status hitherto accorded to Whig connections under the Hanoverians. George III was taken to be subverting that privileged status by seeking to abolish party connections whilst accepting Tory aspirants into government. This, to Burke and his friends, seemed to be a violation of principle, a dangerous threat to the British constitution. It made them highly suspicious of the intentions of the new monarch and the extent to which he might have unconstitutional designs.

DE: *What did he think might happen if concessions weren't made to the colonies?*

RB: Well, his view was that if you couldn't conciliate America you would have to conquer America. To conquer America you would need an army. And you would end up with George III mobilizing troops in North America for a conquest that would not in any case succeed. You would have a military state abroad being supported ironically by a parliamentary government at home, and this seemed to Burke to be paradoxical, not to say disgraceful and bound to end in failure.

DE: *He's remembered as the quintessential conservative, and yet supporting the colonies doesn't sound like a conservative position.*

RB: Well, Burke was not regarded as a conservative as such until the nineteenth century, and that was basically on account of his reaction to the Revolution in France. In the eighteenth century, throughout his career from 1765 through to the French Revolution, he was regarded as a supporter of the cause of reform, and the cause of toleration of religious dissent.

DE: *Was he also concerned that, if no political compromise with the colonies could be struck, there was the possibility of a far greater rupture... America falling into chaos and anarchy?*

RB: Yes. For Burke, we live in the fog of politics. Success in that arena must be based on compromise. One is always dealing with human beings whose capacity for achievement is matched by their capacity for destruction. Burke's view of human nature was such that one always had to tread a careful line in political reform and also in one's preparedness to concede to dissent.

DE: *Does that make him a Hobbesian? Does Burke believe that, if you take away the power of the state, man will fall into war and conflict?*

RB: Burke had much in common with Hobbes, but wasn't exactly a Hobbesian. Burke's view was that there were two component parts to human nature; on the one hand, there was this driving force of competitiveness in the breast of human beings. But at the same time there was a tendency towards deference. That is to say, on the one hand, we compete with one another and that competitiveness, verging on envy and resentment, can bring us to the brink of conflict and, *in extremis*, destruction. But at the same time, Burke thought human beings are given to deference. They have a capacity for respect; they are in awe of greatness. This is a modifying disposition which can impose control on this other more unruly, frenetic, and factious tendency in human nature.

DE: *So these two tendencies, an inclination towards deference, an inclination towards competition, hold each other in some form of equilibrium?*

RB: In a well-regulated commonwealth, these two passions in human beings will be held in equilibrium.

DE: *Let's get on to the French Revolution of 1789. Does Burke witness events at first hand?*

RB: No. Burke had been to France 16 years earlier, as he himself records in his great book on the Revolution published a year after its outbreak, *Reflections on the Revolution in France*. He didn't visit France after the Revolution, and all his information about developments depended on reports, correspondence, and the newspapers.

DE: *What was his interpretation of the French Revolution? It proclaimed liberty, equality, fraternity: is that how Burke saw it?*

RB: Well, events moved very quickly in France. In the summer of 1789, Burke responded with uncertainty to what was occurring; it was an extraordinary event, and he would wait to see how it panned out. By the autumn, he was becoming alarmed and developed the following view: that although the French Revolution decked itself out in the colours of liberty, equality, and fraternity, it was in truth a sham performance. The French revolutionaries were proclaiming themselves defenders of equality, but in truth this was an insurrectionary oligarchy seeking to redistribute property in the name of equality. In fact, it was instituting an oligarchy of capitalist speculators.

DE: *But it also unleashed a wave of violence which terrified him.*

RB: That's precisely right. He saw a wave of popular passion as having been unleashed through the country which would be almost impossible to pacify. That was the emboldened, envious energy of resentment, such as an appeal to equality was bound to provoke.

DE: *Is that because in that equilibrium between conflict and deference, deference had been swept aside?*

RB: That's exactly right. Burke thought the appeal to equality gave added licence to competitiveness to verge over into violent conflict rather than controlled competition. The restraining influence of due deference, regard for authority, and acceptance of unequal relations as had previously existed had been cast into the wind.

DE: *His anti-revolutionary sentiments are the reason we know him to this day as a conservative; is it possible to put him on our political spectrum, from left to right, from Democrat to Republican?*

RB: Well, that's a difficult question. If I had to encapsulate my view in a nutshell, I'd say, 'no'. Many of the ideological slogans and labels that we employ today are a legacy of the nineteenth century, and Burke died at the end of the eighteenth. 'Left' versus 'Right' as a description of political positions derives from the period of the French Revolution, specifically from the question of whether the French monarch should retain certain powers or not. As regards local issues of the eighteenth century, it's clearly possible to align Burke; but it becomes much more complicated after the rise of modern democratic politics, modern socialism, and modern totalitarianism.

DE: *So, Richard Bourke, in one sense you're clearly a Bourkean, but are you an Edmund Burkean?*

RB: No, I'm not a Burkean. Burke held views about the organization of politics which have proved to be falsifiable. He believed, on the one hand, that property would only be secure if it was concentrated in the hands of the great. He believed an aristocratic order was necessary for stability in society. Subsequent history has proved this to be inaccurate. He also believed that any attempt at redistribution was a recipe for social chaos. But, of course, all the redistributive programmes in the United States and in post-war Europe have proved that not to be case. Social revolution didn't take place under Franklin D. Roosevelt, and social revolution didn't take place in Germany and Britain after 1945.

DE: *Give me an example of Burke's relevance today. Does he have anything to say to us about contemporary politics?*

RB: Well, I think Burke would have been opposed to the much-touted contemporary programme or policy of nation-building abroad. Given that Burke was a reformer and not a revolutionary, he would have seen a policy of nation-building in far-away places as precisely a revolutionary programme. Taking the example of Iraq, Burke might have thought that if you want to build nations abroad you ought to approach the task as if you were reforming your own. All reform is liable to encounter reaction. Radical revolutionary attempts at change are likely to provoke violent reaction. This will only be quelled by the intervention of military force, and you will then be in the paradoxical, not to say ironic, position of trying to deliver a reform programme by means of a military dictatorship.

DE: *He thought it wasn't possible to recreate a political structure from scratch—you had to work with the grain of a political system.*

RB: You had to work with the grain of existing political powers. The only alternative was and is to abolish them. But, of course, one of the great lessons of politics is, you can't abolish your enemies, you have to come to terms with them.

DE: *Do you think he was a great thinker?*

RB: Burke is unusual in combining great political insight with philosophical wisdom. He's not a great philosopher of the order of Thomas Hobbes, but he had great, great political experience compared, say, to Jean-Jacques Rousseau. Karl Marx had comparatively little, too. What Burke has to offer are the insights of a politician who's educated in the traditions of political thought.

15

A.W. MOORE ON
Immanuel Kant's Metaphysics

David Edmonds: *As the citizens of Königsberg in the late eighteenth century watched the professor of logic and metaphysics go for his regular daily walk at precisely the same time each day, they must have wondered what he was thinking about. Well, one of Immanuel Kant's preoccupations was whether we could work out things about the world without experience—without, as it were, leaving the armchair—and substantial truths, not just what Kant called analytic truths, in other words, not just truths of definition like 'all bachelors are unmarried men'. This apparently arcane issue is at the heart of Kant's investigation of the limits of human knowledge in his* Critique of Pure Reason. *Professor A. W. Moore dispenses a wealth of knowledge from his armchair in St Hugh's College, Oxford.*

Nigel Warburton: *We're going to try to explain Kant's metaphysics today! Could you start by addressing the question, 'What is metaphysics?'*

A.W. Moore: Metaphysics can be usefully characterized as the most general attempt to make sense of things, the attempt to understand what the basic structure of reality is like.

NW: *So, it's at the heart of philosophy—a drive to understand our relationship to our experience and to the world.*

AWM: Absolutely, it's the core part of philosophy. Other branches of philosophy all depend on metaphysics in various ways. You could say that it's the part of philosophy that holds the rest of the discipline together.

NW: *Immanuel Kant is most famous for his* Critique of Pure Reason, *and that's the work we're focusing on today. It's an incredibly complex, difficult book, but it has a central theme: could you summarize that theme?*

AWM: Yes, it's an extraordinarily complicated book, and it's difficult to summarize. Kant is fundamentally concerned with metaphysics in two senses. First of all, he's trying to do metaphysics in this book. He's trying to tell us something about the broad structure of reality, trying to make sense of things at the highest level of generality. But also, he's very interested in stepping up a level and raising questions *about* metaphysics, about its nature, its scope, and its limits— because one of the things that he was struck by when he looked at the work of his predecessors, stretching back over centuries, was that there hadn't been much in the way of consensus, not only about metaphysical issues themselves, but about how much was even possible within metaphysics.

His *immediate* predecessors had notably disagreed about what was possible within metaphysics. If we accept the standard cartoon sketch whereby his immediate predecessors divided into Rationalists and Empiricists, then we can say that, according to the Rationalists, it was possible by a pure exercise of reason to arrive at substantive conclusions about the nature of reality, whereas the Empiricists were altogether more sceptical. The Empiricists thought that reason was much more limited than the Rationalists took it to be and that the only way that we could arrive at substantive conclusions about the nature of reality was to do the sort of thing that we do in the natural sciences, which is to appeal to experience. So Kant was very interested in this fundamental disagreement between the Rationalists and the Empiricists, and, in a way, tried to act as referee.

NW: *One of the things he did in his role as referee was to come up with the notion of the synthetic a priori, which is fundamental to understanding the* Critique of Pure Reason.

AWM: Absolutely. Let's think of this in terms of that dispute between the Rationalists and the Empiricists. Kant was inclined to agree with the Rationalists that it was possible to use pure reason to arrive at substantive conclusions about the nature of reality. He was inclined to agree with the Empiricists that it was impossible to arrive at substantive conclusions about what was completely independent of us, without using experience. And part of what he wanted to do with this notion of the *synthetic a priori* was to reconcile these.

NW: *So, the first part of the synthetic a priori is the word 'synthetic',and that's contrasted with 'analytic'.*

AWM: Yes. Kant draws a distinction between what he calls synthetic knowledge and analytic knowledge. Analytic knowledge is knowledge that's available to us just by pure exercise of our concepts. By reflecting on the nature of our concepts, we can arrive at certain basic trivial truths about what things are like. We know, for example, that all sisters are female, not because we have gone out and investigated sisters to find out whether they fit the bill or not, but simply because it's part of our concept of a sister, that a sister should be female. So the truth, which it is, that all sisters are female would count as an analytic truth for Kant. That contrasts with, for example, the truth that some sisters are younger than their own siblings' children, which again is a truth, but which depends on the way things actually are. It's not written into the concepts involved, and to ascertain that that's true you do need to go out and investigate.

NW: *So analytic truths are true by definition, and synthetic truths are the kind which you require some kind of research to find out whether or not they actually are true?*

AWM: That's right, yes.

NW: *Now, how does another distinction, between the a priori and the a posteriori, differ from that?*

AWM: On the face of it, they look just the same. The standard way of characterizing a priori knowledge is as knowledge which is available without appeal to experience. A posteriori knowledge, or empirical knowledge, as it's also sometimes called, is knowledge which is grounded in experience. And it can easily look as if these are just two ways of drawing the same distinction. The two very examples that we considered earlier of analytic knowledge and synthetic knowledge would also serve as examples of a priori knowledge and empirical knowledge.

It's a priori that all sisters are female. You can tell that all sisters are female without appeal to experience. By contrast, although it's true that some sisters are younger than their own siblings' children, it's not something that can be ascertained without consulting experience. We actually have to investigate sisters to find out whether any sister satisfies that condition. It turns out that there are indeed some sisters who are younger than their own siblings' children.

Nevertheless, although, on the face of it, it looks as if we've got two ways of drawing one and the same distinction, Kant is adamant that these two contrasts come apart from each other. In particular, he believes that there is some knowledge which, on the one hand, is a priori and yet, on the other hand, is synthetic.

NW: *So, could you give an example of a synthetic* a priori *truth?*

AWM: Many of Kant's own examples are mathematical. Probably the most famous of all is that 7 + 5 = 12. This for Kant counts as a priori. It is something that you can tell just by an exercise of reason. You can do mathematics in your armchair. You don't need to go out and get your hands dirty and investigate what the world is like. So your knowledge that 7 + 5 = 12 is an example of a priori knowledge rather than empirical knowledge. But, Kant says, mathematical methodology doesn't consist in simply reflecting on the nature of your concepts either. No matter how carefully you analyse your concepts, that's never going to be enough to give you the insight that 7 + 5 = 12. You have to appeal to something else.

The arithmetical example is not necessarily the most convincing as far as that's concerned, but he did also often cite geometrical examples where it seems a bit more plausible. One of his favourite examples was that between two points you can only have one straight line. Again, he would have insisted that this was a priori, but not analytic. (Subsequent developments in physics have shown that this example is problematical in ways that Kant couldn't possibly have known, but let's ignore that.) However closely you investigate your concept of straightness and your concept of a point, and the various other concepts involved, that is never going to give you insight into this truth, Kant says. You have to consider the nature of space itself.

NW: *So we've got this puzzle. There are things which I can know sitting in my armchair without observing anything. I can think about things and discover truths about the nature of reality, not just about things which are true by definition. So, if Kant's right, he's got a real puzzle on his hands. How is it that we can discover things about the world without leaving the armchair? How does he solve that puzzle?*

AWM: He solves it in the following way. He says that what we're really uncomfortable with is the idea that there should be knowledge about what's out there independent of us, which we can nevertheless arrive at by pure reflection. And Kant agrees that such a thing is impossible. So his solution to the puzzle is to deny that the synthetic a priori knowledge that he's talking about is knowledge of what is out there independent of us. Although this knowledge doesn't consist in pure reflection on our own concepts, it does nevertheless consist in pure reflection on our own intellectual apparatus.

The metaphor that's often used in this connection, a very helpful metaphor, is that of a pair of spectacles. It's as if we have innate spectacles through which we look at reality. When we arrive at synthetic a priori knowledge of things, we're reflecting on the nature of our own spectacles. It's synthetic, because those spectacles themselves involve more than just concepts. We're not reflecting on the nature of our own concepts, but we are reflecting on the nature of our own spectacles. In particular, as the geometrical example might have led us to expect, Kant believes that these spectacles include space and time themselves. Even space and time are an aspect of how we view reality, rather than an aspect of reality itself.

NW: *So, for Kant, reality is not really accessible to us. What is accessible is the perceptual apparatus that we are endowed with, which is like a pair of spectacles. If these spectacles have a rose tint, everything we perceive necessarily has a rose tint. Space and time are like the colours that we take to be out there because of our perceptual apparatus rather than something independent of us.*

AWM: Exactly, you've just expressed it very well, Nigel. Kant believed that we can know that between any two points there's only one straight line because that's part of the intellectual apparatus that we carry around with us and that we impose onto reality when we're trying to make sense of it, when we're trying to come to know what reality is like. This is something that we can not only know but can know a priori; we don't need to go out and investigate whether space is like that, because it's part of our own intellectual equipment.

NW: *So does that mean that we can't really know how the world is, that all we can know is how we perceive it?*

AWM: That's exactly what it means. And here we come back to the issue that we began with, the issue of where Kant stands in relation to metaphysics. What he does in the *Critique of Pure Reason* is to follow through two separate projects: a positive project and a negative project.

In the positive project, he does as much within metaphysics as he feels can be done, spelling out how things must appear to us through our spectacles. He believes that there is a whole range of interesting and substantive conclusions that can be drawn about that, about how things must appear to us through our spectacles. But, as you just emphasised, 'appear' is the operative word. He's drawing a fundamental distinction between how things appear to us and how they are in themselves.

The fact that we carry these native spectacles around with us means that there must be such a distinction. We can never take these spectacles off. We only have access to how things appear to us. How things are in themselves is something that we can't know, and that is the thing that Kant wants to emphasise in the negative project, which also occupies a substantial part of the *Critique*.

It does mean, unfortunately, that a lot of the traditional questions of metaphysics have to be put to one side as just unanswerable. That includes questions about, for example, the Deity: whether there's a God or not; and, if there is, what the nature of God is. It also includes questions about our own freedom, whether we have free will or not, because Kant thinks that, in so far as such a question arises, it's a question about how we are in ourselves rather than about how we appear to ourselves.

NW: *So, what Kant's doing is setting the limits of what we can know in the process of telling us what we can know.*

AWM: That's exactly right, and he's concerned with both. He's concerned with what lies within the limits, and he's concerned with what lies beyond the limits—and he's concerned with making sure that we draw the limits in the right place.

NW: *It might seem to follow that, because we can't know about it, any discussion of reality, including whether there's a God or free will, is completely meaningless. Is that how Kant sees it?*

AWM: That's an excellent question, Nigel, and it's very important to emphasise that that's *not* how Kant sees it. That is how other metaphysicians have seen it. Arguably, that's how his great predecessor, David Hume, saw it, at least to an extent. But that's not Kant's way of regarding the matter. Kant is adamant that these questions are perfectly meaningful: there is a reality out there. The fact that we have spectacles through which we view things doesn't detract from the fact that there are things being viewed.

There is a reality out there. There is a way it is, irrespective of whether we can know what it's like or not. The point is simply that we can't know what that reality is like in itself. But we're at liberty to speculate and, as far as the great religious questions are concerned, we're at liberty to have faith that things are a certain way. So, it is an article of faith that some people have that there is a God. Kant is far from wanting to deny people that article of faith. He thinks that what they believe, when they believe that there's a God, makes perfectly good sense. They may be right, they may be wrong, but certainly it makes perfectly good sense. All he's doing is telling them that they can't have knowledge of whether what they believe is true or not.

NW: *Now, the* First Critique *is a massive tome, incredibly complex in its arguments, and you've done a brilliant job of pulling out the main threads of the book, but it's such a complex work that it must have been an intense labour to put it together. What do you think was motivating Kant in writing that book?*

AWM: I think the answer to that question relates directly to the thing that we were most recently talking about. There's one very revealing sentence in the preface that he wrote to the second edition of the *Critique of Pure Reason* where he said: 'I had to deny knowledge in order to make room for faith.' It seems to me that one of the things that was really motivating Kant was this desire to safeguard articles of faith.

But perhaps of even more fundamental concern to him was something that I touched on very briefly: the idea that our own freedom is also a matter of how things are in themselves rather than how they appear to us through the spectacles— because one thing that Kant was really concerned to do was to safeguard our belief in our own freedom and all that goes hand in hand with that belief, in particular the importance to us of morality (traditional Christian morality, as Kant saw it), which doesn't make sense unless we're free agents.

Kant was keen to safeguard all of that against the threatening pretensions of the natural sciences, which at the time that he was writing really *were* threatening. Science had made astonishing progress in the preceding century. In particular, Newton's work had seemed to show that almost everything, if not everything, could be accounted for in purely scientific terms. It looked as if the world was a place where everything was governed by inexorable mechanical laws. That in turn looked as if it posed a very serious threat to our belief in our own freedom and everything that goes hand in hand with that.

What Kant was able to do with this elaborate system that he had constructed was to show that we could both accept science in all its glory and cling fast to our belief in our own freedom by going back to this distinction that he drew between how things appear to us through the spectacles and how they are in themselves. Science is concerned with how things appear to us through the spectacles; science is concerned with the world of space and time, the world of nature. We can accept that, when viewed through the spectacles, everything is subject to inexorable causal laws, while at the same time accepting that we, as we are in ourselves, are free agents subject to the demands of morality.

NW: *So, for Kant, the unknowable is genuinely unknowable, but it's still protected. He's protecting things like the possibility of free will and the possibility of God's existence, even though we can't be absolutely sure about either of those things.*

AWM: That's absolutely right, Nigel, yes.

NW: *Given the way you've discussed Kant's work, it's clear you've got a great appreciation of him as a philosopher. How would you rank him amongst philosophers?*

AWM: My own view is that he's probably the greatest of all.

16

ROBERT STERN ON
G. W. F. Hegel on Dialectic

David Edmonds: *The late eighteenth-, early nineteenth-century German philosopher, Georg Wilhelm Friedrich Hegel, has had an enormous influence on western thought. Karl Marx, for example, was heavily indebted to him. But his prose is notoriously complex, and he's not someone to open with in Philosophy 101: that would be like learning to read with* Ulysses, *or starting the piano by attempting Rachmaninov. It takes a lucid mind to decode him, and so* Philosophy Bites *turned to Professor Robert Stern, who's based at the University of Sheffield. We asked Professor Stern to explain the one idea in Hegel that even most non-Hegelians have heard of: thesis–antithesis–synthesis, the idea that's usually known as Hegel's* Dialectic.

Nigel Warburton: *The topic we're going to focus on is Hegel's* Dialectic. *I don't know much about Hegel, but I know the caricature of the dialectic is that somebody puts forward a thesis, then there's an antithesis, a contradiction of it. And somehow, miraculously, from the clash of these two things, a synthesis emerges. Is that about right?*

Robert Stern: Yes, you are right that the idea is often associated with Hegel, and it is a bit of a clichéd caricature, as you say. In fact, Hegel very rarely used those terms, 'thesis', 'antithesis', and 'synthesis'. But, on the other hand, there is certainly a large element of truth to the basic story.

NW: *So is this just a way of describing what characteristically happens in a debate or does it refer to episodes in history? What is it?*

RS: The best place to start is to think of it in the way that Hegel presents it, that is, by going back to Plato and to dialogue and discussion, but adding to that the particular concern that Hegel had, which was that, especially in philosophy, one should avoid dogmatic presentation of your views, just insisting that you're right, and that the other person's wrong. If you do that, you don't really establish that what you're thinking is right, as against the other person. You can't legitimately just insist that you're correct, and they're not, as they will have reasons for their view, just as you do for yours. So, one way of handling that situation, and making progress in enquiry in a non-dogmatic way, is to try and find problems within your opponent's view, that they themselves can be brought to recognize—what's sometimes called 'internal critique'.

For example, if you think you're a great defender of freedom, and think of yourself as a great liberal, and I can show you, 'Well, yes, but if you followed through your views, you'd end up with a very repressive society'—that should show you that, in your own terms, you've gone wrong. And you might then feel that you had to change your views entirely and go to the opposite extreme—by abandoning liberalism, for example, in favour of an authoritarian position. So, you might give up one view, and move over to the opposite, equally one-sided view, in Hegel's terms, which has its own internal problems. Then you have to show that the only real progress is somehow finding a balance between these competing positions.

So, to take an example, which isn't directly Hegel's, we can obviously have debates in philosophy between people who believe in free will, and those people who believe in hard determinism—roughly the view that because every event has a prior cause or is governed by a natural law, we lack freedom. If you can show in various ways that both sides are one-sided, or are inadequate, that they leave out important accounts of the issues at stake, then you're working towards a position that might involve, or incorporate elements of, both views. That's the sense in which you're looking for some kind of *synthesis*. But then, again, that synthesis can often turn out to be premature, to involve problems of its own. So you move on to another view that competes with that one. And so on. So, this process gives a structure to a discussion, a structure that is found in a lot of Hegel's works, not unlike a series of pyramids.

NW: *So, are you saying dialectic is really a method for discovering truth?*

RS: Yes, I think that's broadly speaking right. You're using certain sorts of principles of reasoning to move from one position to another, better one—and you can also again see how Hegel's works have this sort of structure, as a method of enquiry. Obviously, if you're going to use that method for reaching the truth, and if you're going to claim to get to truth at the end, you're first of all going to have to make sure that you move through the positions in a pretty systematic way so you haven't left anything out, because that would then be a view that you haven't considered, and therefore whose truth you hadn't assessed, as a possible rival to the final position you end up with. So you need a structure that's going to take you systematically through various positions. Also you need to start from the right place. So you have to start from the simplest position on the issue, because if you start too far down the line, again you'll have missed out various options that you should have considered earlier on. Often the structure of Hegel's work begins from very simple positions. So, Hegel's *Logic*, which is the first part of his system of philosophy and basically concerns metaphysics, famously begins from a view that just thinks there is Being. That's its theory of reality: all there is, is being, not individuals, properties, events, and so on—just being. That is as simple a view as you're going to get. Similarly, the *Phenomenology of Spirit* begins with a very simple view of knowledge: that knowledge is just taking things in immediately through perception, and no more. So that gives a beginning point to the way the enquiry's going to work, and from which it can unfold. And then, of course, you are also hoping that you're going to reach a stable end point, because, of course, there might be a worry that you just have one position and it ends up collapsing into another, and then into another, and into another, and you never end up with anything that's stable.

NW: *Just to get a grasp on this notion of dialectic though, is it the equivalent of saying, 'The truth is always in the middle'? It sounds a bit like that: here's one side, here's another side, synthesize them: there's a bit of truth in both of them.*

RS: There's something in that. The phrase, 'Hegelian middle' is often used: the third way. I used to describe this as 'the third way' in lectures before the term was hijacked by

politicians. But that's often how Hegel likes to present
things, and again some background to this is useful. One
important figure in the background for Hegel is Kant. An
important element in Kant's story about metaphysics is that
metaphysics ends in antinomies which are literally
unresolvable contradictions. For Kant, these partly show the
inability of the human mind to settle these questions, and
partly that they're somehow bad or flawed questions that we,
as human beings, get ourselves into. One way of thinking of
Hegel is as someone who thinks these debates are genuine,
but where he is more optimistic than Kant—he thinks the
antinomies can, on the whole, be resolved.

Some terminology he uses to discuss this is the distinction
between what he calls 'the understanding', 'dialectic', and
'reason'. The understanding is characterized as a form of
thinking that thinks in a relatively limited, though important,
way. It just thinks 'freedom is freedom', say: to be free is to be
able to just do what you like, that's what freedom is. And
taking it in that way, it seems an obvious contrast with there
being any moral obligations or having to respect the claims of
other people, as these limit what you can do. And you might
think, 'Well, freedom is one thing, moral demands on us are
obviously something different, and these cannot be reconciled,
so to be free I must reject morality.' That's the view of the
'understanding', which just sees a clear contrast here. The
dialectical moment is when that position leads into a kind of
contradiction. So, for example, to the person who just thinks
that 'freedom is doing whatever you like', you might say, 'Well,
what happens if what you like is taking drugs?' Or, 'Why is
doing what you like free, because after all what you like comes
from your desires and your tastes or your upbringing. And

things that aren't within your control, so why is that freedom?'
And that might make the person then see, 'Well, hang on,
freedom is obviously more complicated than that.' The
dialectical moment, which Hegel associates with a kind of
scepticism, is a sort of despair. You might think now, 'Well, yes,
freedom is this great mysterious thing, I really can't
understand it at all.' And that's a point again where Hegel
associates it back to a Platonic moment. Again in Plato's
dialogues, the confident interlocutor of Socrates starts by
thinking he knows what he's talking about, and then realizes,
'Oh my goodness, you know, it's all falling apart, I don't
understand this at all.' But then the moment of resolution is
when you say, 'Well, wait, maybe it's all falling apart because
I'm thinking about freedom in this one-sided and inadequate
way. And when I become more sophisticated about what
freedom is, then I can perhaps see it is more reconcilable with
moral obligations than I thought it was.' That's the sense in
which you then end up with a kind of middle position, because
you see that the one-sided view isn't really opposed to its
opposite. Understanding always thinks in terms of either/or,
Hegel says. *Either* free will, *or* determinism. Or, *either* freedom, *or*
moral obligations. Or, *either* no state, *or* tyranny. And the
dialectical moment is when you begin to see that basically things
are much more complicated than that, and that both sides need to
be brought together somehow. Hegel thought, 'This is why
philosophy's so hard: because it requires us to think through both
sides of the problem.' And that's why the perspective of reason,
which is this resolving moment, is very difficult from the
standpoint of normal human understanding, which wants to keep
both sides apart and distinct from one another—so it can't see
how freedom is compatible with determinism, and so on.

NW: *I don't understand why that's not begging the question, because you can't assume that the truth lies in the synthesis. I might dogmatically assert that 'torture is morally wrong, in every circumstance'. Somebody might contradict me, and from that kind of clash of statement and its antithesis I might still emerge quite rationally justified in believing torture is always morally wrong. Hegel seems to be assuming that the truth will lie in the synthesis, not in the initial position.*

RS: Well, of course, the wrongness of torture may be just the stable end point you are after! In that case, there may be no further synthesis to be achieved. But I assume you are imagining people who question this claim of yours, who contradict you. But why should you be moved by that, why shouldn't you just stick to your view, rather than feel pushed towards some sort of synthesis? Obviously, this will depend on them having reasons for their view: they aren't just claiming this for fun; for example, they may think torture is justified to get vital information from the enemy, and so on. I think Hegel's point is that you can only emerge rationally justified in your own position if you can find some way to show your opponent that something goes wrong with their position, in terms they would accept—otherwise, you are dogmatically insisting that you alone know right from wrong here. Of course, this may be very hard to do, and so it may be hard to get anywhere, and the dialectic may break down. I think, first of all, Hegel would say that he's not assuming anything here, this is just his pattern of how he hopes things might turn out. And if they do turn out like that, we can make progress. But there's no guarantee, there's no a priori guarantee at the beginning of this exercise that that is how they will turn out. On the other hand, there's no a priori reason for scepticism, either. So, all you can do is try and conduct this dialogue.

NW: *I can see how that could work as a tentative method for philosophical debate, and it could be very productive in certain areas such as the free will debate that you've discussed. Now, if I've got it right, Hegel doesn't stop there, though. He's talking about the dialectic applied to historical change. How does Hegel employ the dialectic in relation to history?*

RS: Well, again, we have to be slightly wary of a caricature here. But in a broad sense, Hegel's view of history is a kind of idealism in the sense that it relates to ideas and thinking, and the way cultures and civilizations have thought about the world. Ideas make a big difference to history, as far as Hegel's concerned. And he will then say, I think, that these ideas then played out in this broadly dialectical manner. So, again, coming back to the case of freedom, Hegel thinks that one important movement in history is the movement from thinking that just one of us is entitled to freedom (a king, say), to some (the patricians of ancient Athens, say), to all of us, where obviously this development relates to changing views of what freedom is, what we are, how we relate to one another, and so on. Hegel thinks that, again, that's been played out in this broadly dialectical way, as different views have come along, that have conceived of freedom in an inadequate manner.

So, one example of that, in Hegel's own time, would be the French Revolution. For Hegel, the French Revolution was the main historical event of his lifetime, and, like a lot of intellectuals of the period, he initially viewed it with great enthusiasm, but then was horrified by the results: the Terror, and so on. Hegel has an interesting discussion of where the notion of freedom involved in the French Revolution is one-sided. You've got a contrast between thinking of freedom as doing what you want—roughly, following your own particular interests—and thinking of freedom as transcending all your interests, which are seen as limiting you in some way: instead, freedom consists in acting to further the general good, or the universal, rather than the particular. So, I'm not free unless I'm working for the good of society as a whole. If I'm just working on my own particular projects, then I'm merely particular, I'm merely confined to acting for myself. The danger of no longer seeing yourself as a particular individual in this way, is that you basically set yourself up as speaking for everyone, for the general will. But then the problem is: who represents the general will? Who can be that one person who speaks for all? This problem provides Hegel with his dialectical diagnosis of the French Revolution. Anyone who stood up and said, 'I am the Revolution, I represent the general will', met with the response, 'Well, you're not, you're just some particular person, you know, you're not really representing the universal in this sense. So you have to be cut down', and so the French Revolution, by the nature of its inner logic, could have no leader, and could only degenerate into the kind of senseless killing, which Hegel diagnosed in this way.

Now, that's a case where Hegel's saying that an idea—here, a certain conception of what it is to be free, a certain conception of how we might represent society as a whole, by somehow giving up all our different interests, concerns, and roles—has had an historically real and disastrous effect. Now, he's not claiming to offer a full historical explanation of the French Revolution and the Terror here, it's not that he is claiming that all there is to history is ideas. But he does think that those ideas are nonetheless important to how history goes, how societies change, and so on—and, again, such developments still have this dialectical relation to one another, on Hegel's account, as different one-sided viewpoints are played out over time.

NW: *What strikes me as different about Hegel, from many thinkers, was that he saw things as progressing to a better state. I don't know if everybody feels that way today—certainly lots of philosophers are more pessimistic about the idea of progress. I wonder if you could say something about Hegel's views on progress.*

RS: Yes, I think that's interesting. Broadly speaking, I hold the view that he is, as you put it, optimistic. There are darker sides to Hegel and, as we've mentioned, when he talks about the dialectic itself, it goes through this rather dark moment. He calls the *Phenomenology*, which is one of the works where this is carried out, a 'highway of despair', because all the views you might start with turn out to be internally problematic and are taken away from you, as they are shown to collapse. And, as I said, there is always a risk that in being taken away from you, there will then be no further progress. But the works themselves, broadly speaking, point towards a kind of resolution. You're right that one contrast between Hegel and his successors is that they're much less optimistic. So, if you take Adorno's idea, say, of the negative dialectic, you can tell by the name, the idea is that, in a sense, it breaks down, that there won't be the moment of resolution. Or, Kierkegaard famously writes a book called *Either/Or*, which is precisely a deliberate echo of Hegel's distinction between the understanding and reason that we discussed earlier: where

Hegel thought that the 'either/or' of the understanding could be resolved by reason into some sort of more unified position, Kierkegaard thought that these different views must remain at odds with one another—so that you are ultimately faced with a choice between them. So, for example, Kierkegaard holds that no reconciliation is possible between the religious outlook and more secular views—you are faced with a choice. On the whole, analytic philosophers are more on Hegel's side than some of these 'continental' thinkers, in making more optimistic assumptions about enquiry. The business of finding philosophical problems, and then trying to find ways of doing justice to both sides of the debate, and making careful distinctions, and finding different conceptual options that might do justice somehow to both sides—I think that's not uncommon in analytic philosophy. A lot of contemporary analytic philosophers spend their time trying to do this.

NW: *I was thinking of parallels with John Stuart Mill. In his discussion of freedom of speech, he talks about the importance of having your view challenged by somebody who actually believes the opposite of you. The process of the collision of truth with error is a really important way of discovering and energizing the truth that you eventually end up with.*

RS: Yes, I think that's right. And there are connections to do with other ideas in Mill, such as fallibilism. Because, again, to engage in this discussion you're going to have to, in a sense, be open to the thought that what you think can be challenged. It doesn't mean that you have to think you're actually wrong, but you have to be able to think, 'Well, it's worth at least listening to the other person, because I might be mistaken.' For Hegel, that's an important part of modernity, that we don't claim infallibility for our views. We do take justification and being able to defend our views seriously. And that's why in the end you'll have to be drawn into this dialogue and discussion.

NW: *I can see how Hegel's approach, with something like freedom, could be very illuminating. But if you take another example, say, homeopathy, where there's this internal explanation that the more dilute a substance, the more effective it is as a drug. Now, that is considered absurd by many doctors, but within the homeopathic community it's internally consistent.*

RS: Yes. I think it's right that one of the threats to the approach is that you potentially run across a position that has this kind of internal coherence. What you would want to find is presumably that there are links between these claims about homeopathic medicine and some commitment to evidence concerning cures, and how it successfully deals with illnesses, and so on. That's going to be part of the story, presumably—and then, of course, homeopathy is open to challenge if you can produce evidence of this kind that it does or doesn't work, and so on. So again, in theory, one can see the worry here: that two equally coherent positions might face each other, with no obvious internal problems forcing the one to take account of the other. But, in practice, in the positions Hegel discusses, he claims that this is not how things work out.

NW: *Obviously, you've immersed yourself in the works of Hegel. What's so rewarding about reading his work?*

RS: Well, this may be a matter of temperament, but I find the project of working through these really quite formidable difficulties, and looking for positions that will resolve them while somehow doing justice to both sides, to be a very exciting project. Hegel worked across a whole range of different problems. We've talked mainly about freedom, but there are issues he dealt with in political philosophy, issues in art, in religion, and so on, as well as many in metaphysics and epistemology. So, there is a wide-ranging and complex programme here. And the notorious difficulty of Hegel's writing, though often off-putting to some, is not, I think, gratuitous if you see it in these terms: because he is trying to think through both sides, or more than one side, and show you how each passes over into the other. It is inevitably hard for him to articulate this in a straightforward way, as you could if you were just defending one position and refuting the other. So, I am prepared to forgive him here. And, again, going back to Kant, I think the difference between a Kantian and a Hegelian sensibility, is that Kant leaves you with these antinomies and a number of dualisms. For Kant, both sides are equally plausible; really, there's nothing much we can do about it. I think wanting to go further, and look for some sort of resolution, is a natural enough stance. Most philosophers I've met have that desire in them, to do this kind of thing, because that's often why we're in the business of philosophy at all. We have an interest in thinking through these difficult issues, and not being satisfied with one-sided solutions, and so on. So, I think it comes naturally to us—or at least it does to me.

17

RICHARD REEVES ON
John Stuart Mill's *On Liberty*

David Edmonds: *John Stuart Mill was given an upbringing by his father so demanding, so arduous, so rigid, that many blame it for his subsequent mental breakdown. By age three, he was learning Latin and Greek. Economics, geometry, and logic soon followed. His father, James Mill, was a friend and disciple of the utilitarian Jeremy Bentham and a notable philosopher and economist in his own right. John Stuart Mill was a sort of laboratory test; an experiment in raising a utilitarian child. To a degree, it worked. John Stuart went on to become a Member of Parliament and a brilliant philosopher and economist. He was an early advocate of women's rights and was the architect of modern liberalism. He eventually found personal happiness through his long friendship and subsequent marriage to Harriet Taylor. Richard Reeves has written a biography of Mill and so is well placed to link Mill's ideas to his highly unusual life.*

Nigel Warburton: *The topic we're focusing on is John Stuart Mill's great book,* On Liberty. *That book was described by him as a 'philosophic textbook of a single truth'. What was that truth?*

Richard Reeves: *On Liberty* is fascinating both because it's the best short version of his philosophy but it's also revealing about his life. People generally know about the Harm Principle—that you should be free to do what you wish as long as you don't harm others; they tend to think that that's the single truth he was referring to. But actually the single truth at the heart of *On Liberty* is that each individual should be free to develop to the fullest of their own potential. That's what *On Liberty* is about: it's about individual flourishing. The Harm Principle is a part of his liberalism, but it's not the essence of his liberalism.

NW: *I don't know if this is too crude a reading, but he had a very constrained childhood: could you see* On Liberty *as a reaction to that?*

RR: Mill's intellectual journey, which culminates in *On Liberty*, results from the fact that he felt the need to prove that he was self-made. He was described as a 'made man', as 'manufactured' by his father James Mill and Jeremy Bentham who set out to create a utilitarian disciple, somebody who was going to take forward the philosophy of utilitarianism—the doctrine of the greatest happiness of the greatest number. So it's important for Mill to believe that he's made himself: he wants to show, 'I wasn't made by my father and Jeremy Bentham. *I made me.*' But this then becomes the beating heart of his liberalism and his philosophy: that this should be true for every single man and woman.

NW: *In* On Liberty *he sets out the broad conditions under which people could flourish in that way?*

RR: That's right; it's a description of a good liberal life, but also of a liberal culture and the society within which you'll be able to live out your life to the full. So, there are rules, the most famous being the Harm Principle, that is, other things being equal, as long as you're not harming me, you should be free to do what you want to, even if it's a stupid and self-destructive thing to do. The freedom to fail, the freedom to engage in activities which others would consider to be immoral or reprehensible or just silly is very important to liberalism. In addition, there needs to be a set of liberal institutions, assumptions about tolerance, and so on, and a belief in the possibility that each individual can become a better version of him or herself. That's the optimism at the heart of his liberalism: that we can become better versions of ourselves.

NW: *But it's not just about the legal institutions: he was very strongly opposed to what he called 'the tyranny of the majority'.*

RR: Mill famously said: 'Protection against the tyranny of the magistrate is not enough: you also need protection against the tyranny of public opinion.' He called it 'the despotism of custom': we do things because other people are doing it. He said that someone who chooses to do something merely because it's the custom makes no choice at all. It is very important to him that we are actually following our own path and that we aren't being driven by what we now might call 'the done thing'.

Much of the force of his argument is to do with intellectual freedom. He was explicit that *On Liberty* is not about political freedom (we tend today to still treat it in that way). There will be arguments about 'should the government ban gambling?', 'should the government make us eat better food?', etc. But what animates Mill is intellectual and moral liberty, whether or not we are living in an environment and have the capabilities to construct a life of our own choosing.

NW: *But in the area of free speech, is he not using a political argument? Provided nobody is harmed, people should be free to express opinions, because that's the best way to arrive at the truth.*

RR: What he's arguing for in *On Liberty* is not merely the absence of restraint on free speech: he's advocating dissent, and argument and disagreement. Indeed, he says that if there isn't an opposing view, we should conjure one up. He says that even the Catholic Church appoints a devil's advocate to argue against someone being canonized as a saint, and we should do the same thing. Because there is nothing more dangerous than 'the deep slumber of a decided opinion', in Mill's words. He would be very unhappy with a society in which we had the formal legal freedom of free speech, but everybody just went around agreeing with each other. He positively wants argument, positively wants dissent, and he believes that's necessary because it's in the collision of the half-truths which constitute most of our opinions, that the real truth will emerge.

He said, very famously in Parliament, 'Each of us knows that some of our opinions are wrong, and none of us know which they are. For if we did, they would not be our *opinions*.' He hated politicians who said, 'I will never change my mind', 'I'm right', and so on. Of course, he was passionate in his own convictions. But if we ever give up the possibility that what we believe is right is actually wrong, then we're in real trouble. The formal structures of liberalism are only a very small part of his liberalism. He's actually arguing for something much more demanding.

NW: *It's demanding of individuals, but not so much of society.*

RR: It's demanding of both. Mill is not only asking us to criticize ourselves but to hold each other to account, and for there to be a constant scrutiny. That was quite difficult for a lot of his readers. There is a lovely moment in Thomas Hardy who was a big fan of Mill's. In his novel, *Jude the Obscure*, one of the characters, Sue Bridehead, reads Mill and she says to her husband, 'We must constantly be choosing our own opinions; these are John Stuart Mill's words. Why can't you act upon them? I always wish to.' And her husband, Richard Phillotson, says, 'What do I care about J. S. Mill? I only want to lead a quiet life.'

What's lovely about that is you can imagine Hardy's reader going, 'That's right. Does John really want us to be questioning everything? I too only want a quiet life.' Of course, for Mill, that sort of quiet life, the deep slumber of decided opinion where we stop questioning ourselves and each other, that's when things get dangerous. That's exactly the point at which liberalism is under threat.

NW: *There's a slight irony, as well, in that she's citing Mill as if he were an authority, whereas presumably he doesn't want to set himself up as the absolute authority: he might be fallible on liberalism as much as anything else.*

RR: One of the tensions in his work is how one handles authority. Actually, he wanted the more learned and cleverer people to be more influential than the uneducated mass, and he was famously worried about universal suffrage, until levels of education had risen. But, on the other hand, he did actually explicitly accept on various occasions that he was wrong about some things; he changed his mind, for example, on one of the tenets of his economics. He was immediately converted to proportional representation by what he considered to be a killer set of arguments by Thomas Hare.

So, he has the authority of someone who's thought very hard about a subject, and is willing to state 'here's what I think is the truth'. But when a counterargument is made and he thinks it's sufficiently strong, he himself was willing to change his mind. In a sense, the danger of Mill—and you can see it happening already in Hardy—is that he's becoming a national treasure: everybody wants to quote him; he's a fairly safe establishment figure from our liberal past. So he's lost some of the dangerousness that is essential to his liberalism.

NW: *It's true that some people carry around copies of* On Liberty *and read it as if it were a religious book.*

RR: It was actually described by a lot of his contemporaries as having a feel of a gospel. And it certainly retains some sense of being a New Testament of liberalism, because it's short and well written, and polemical, and because it can be reread by each generation in a different way. As a work of political theory and of philosophy, it retains much more authority than most. In fact, the former leader of the liberal party, Joe Grimond, was asked, 'How do you keep your liberalism alive?' He said, 'Every New Year's day I reread *On Liberty*.'

NW: On Liberty *was first published in 1859. Can you give us a sense of the climate of that time?*

RR: One of the paradoxes of *On Liberty* is that its strongest arguments are against the tyranny of public opinion: Mill was worried that mass communication, mass media, mass travel, universal suffrage, would create the way things are thought about and done. He was afraid that individualism, eccentricity, being heretical, would become more difficult. But he defended *On Liberty* as being less about his own era than about the future. His book was published in the same year as Darwin's *Origin of Species*; the Liberal Party was born that year too, and this was a period of great intellectual openness and flowering. So, in a sense, *On Liberty* sits uneasily in its own historical context.

One of the reasons why *On Liberty* has survived so well is that, whereas some of the legal arguments and the institutional arguments resonated well with his own era, his arguments about what it means to live a free life and to make and remake your own opinions and to construct your own life are more relevant at the beginning of the twenty-first century than they were when he actually wrote *On Liberty*.

NW: *In the book, Mill gives a great deal of credit to Harriet Taylor. If you believe Mill, she was the co-author of his book. Is that a substantiated claim or was it an act of generosity on his part?*

RR: Mill made exaggerated claims for the intellectual influence of Harriet Taylor because he was deeply in love with her. She was his controversial companion for many years, and then later his wife. It's clear that they worked together intellectually and that she had some influence on him. But the essence of his liberalism was born before she became a serious intellectual collaborator. *On Liberty* was sent to the publisher a matter of weeks after Harriet Taylor's death; it had been written before her death. There's a physical memorial to her in the cemetery just outside Avignon, but this was the literary memorial, this was his way of thanking Harriet.

NW: *You've devoted quite a lot of time to reading and rereading Mill and putting his work in the context of his life. What have you taken away from that?*

RR: What Mill gives us is a way to think about many contemporary social problems, which in many cases were social problems then, as well. But, in *On Liberty*, Mill explicitly addresses such questions as: 'How does one regulate alcohol consumption?'; 'What about gambling?'; 'What about prostitution?' He didn't tackle obesity because it wasn't an issue then: but I'm sure he would if he were writing about it now. He also gives us a framework for free speech laws, and so on. So he gives us a way to think about the rules, the institutions that surround a liberal society. The Harm Principle, and the free speech rules that he set out, remain as good a place as any to begin discussions about the regulation or otherwise of personal behaviour.

Mill gives us something else too. He gives us a picture of how to live and what constitutes a good life. This resonates even more strongly now than it did then. He argues that the only good worthy of the name is that of a life which is led by the individual themself, a scrutinized, autonomous life. To the extent that my life is a good one, it's one that I have chosen: I am deciding what constitutes a flourishing life and I am pursuing my definition of the good life. What makes Mill's liberalism so muscular is his view that I am the expert on what constitutes a good life for me, and that's the basis upon which both good lives and good societies are built. It is not for the state or for the church, or for any other set of institutions, or for the majority in their public opinion to dictate to me what constitutes a good life. A good life is an autonomous life, and that is a message which resonates across the world today as strongly as it did then. This message should be informing not only our politics but also our personal reflection to this day.

18

CLARE CARLISLE ON
Søren Kierkegaard's
Fear and Trembling

David Edmonds: *God tells you to kill your son. Should you obey His will? Søren Kierkegaard was a nineteenth-century Danish philosopher and Christian theologian. He had a prolific but short life: he died in 1855 aged 42. In his book,* Fear and Trembling, *written, like several of his works, under a pseudonym and in different voices, Kierkegaard focuses on the biblical story of God's call on Abraham to sacrifice Isaac—and on the anguished choice Abraham then faces.* Fear and Trembling *is one reason why Kierkegaard is credited with being, among other things, a father of existentialism. Clare Carlisle is a Kierkegaard scholar at King's College, London.*

Nigel Warburton: *The topic we're considering is Søren Kierkegaard's book* Fear and Trembling. *It's a book that focuses on a particular biblical story.*

Clare Carlisle: It focuses on the story of Abraham and Isaac from the Hebrew Bible. God commands Abraham to take his only son Isaac up to Mount Moriah and to sacrifice him there. Abraham embarks on a three-day journey, takes Isaac to the summit, prepares the altar. Isaac is lying there on the altar and Abraham raises his knife and then as he does so, an angel says, 'You don't need to sacrifice Isaac, you can sacrifice a ram instead.'

NW: *Kierkegaard turns this story into philosophy, by exploring some of its implications.*

CC: Yes, that's right. Kierkegaard uses the story to make several points about Christian faith. Abraham is often described as the father of faith. So, Kierkegaard offers an interpretation of the story that raises questions about the nature of religious faith and, specifically, Christian faith because that's the tradition that Kierkegaard himself is thinking and writing within.

NW: *But he does it not in his own voice but through the voice of a pseudonym.*

CC: The book is written under a pseudonym who's called Johannes de Silentio, or, in translation, John of Silence. When the book was first published in 1843, Kierkegaard's name didn't appear anywhere. So, on the face of it, the book is written by this character called Johannes de Silentio. He's not just a pseudonym, he's not just a name that Kierkegaard adopts: he's a character in his own right. He has his own perspective, and this is all part of Kierkegaard's literary strategy, because he wants to get the reader to reflect and to ask questions.

NW: *Encouraging the reader to think things through from the perspective of a pseudonymous author is something that he does in much of his work.*

CC: Kierkegaard's authorship splits into what's called the aesthetic, or pseudonymous, literature and those texts that Kierkegaard signed with his own name: the latter are usually explicitly religious in tone. But there are many pseudonymous works, and many different pseudonyms, and they often reflect, indirectly, on religious questions.

NW: *In* Fear and Trembling, *Johannes de Silentio explores the story; he takes us through some possible scenarios.*

CC: The book has several different sections, but one of the earliest sections is called 'Atunement', and there several different versions of the story are told. In one of these interpretations, Abraham despairs; in another interpretation, he refuses to sacrifice Isaac; and so on. This offering of different interpretations serves a few purposes. One is to emphasise that there are various ways in which Abraham might have responded to God's command. This helps the reader to focus on Abraham's response itself: in particular, on the existential situation that Abraham was being put in, and the fact that, when he was faced with this command, there were several possible ways of responding to it. His response was his choice; he chose one possibility, which was to respond with faith—but of course there were different options open to him.

It also gets the reader to focus on the journey that Abraham makes. Kierkegaard thinks that people often go straight to the conclusion and say, 'It was alright in the end, he didn't have to sacrifice Isaac.' But Kierkegaard wants to remind the reader of Abraham's journey, the fact that he had to walk for three days. He wants to emphasise the anguish that Abraham must have felt. He also wants to emphasise that each physical step that Abraham takes expresses and symbolizes his repeated commitment to the decision that he'd made; and this is a model of existence in general: the fact that we're always in the process of becoming, we're temporal. So, at each moment, we are renewing our actions, choosing again in whatever situation we find ourselves.

NW: *From a rationalist perspective, just because you hear or receive a message that you ought to sacrifice your son, it doesn't follow that you should sacrifice your son. Most of us, put in that position, would question very hard the source of the message.*

CC: That's right. This is something that Kierkegaard wants to accentuate in *Fear and Trembling*. It's emphasised very strongly that Abraham's actions and decisions can't be understood through reason; they're not rational. They can't be justified on any ethical basis: they're immoral. Kierkegaard wants to highlight the fact that Abraham's faith appears to be paradoxical—it appears to be morally abhorrent.

NW: *So it's morally abhorrent but yet conventionally approved of because the obvious reading of the Bible is that Abraham was a good guy: he did the right thing.*

CC: That's right, and that's precisely what Kierkegaard wants his readers to question—because Kierkegaard perceived among his fellow Christians a kind of complacency, an assumption that faith was something easy. It was something that one is simply born into by virtue of growing up in a nominally Christian society, and involves going to church, going through the motions of being a Christian. Kierkegaard wants to challenge that kind of complacency, the assumption that people have that they are already Christians. Kierkegaard thinks that this assumption is something that blocks the project of becoming a Christian.

If you think you're a Christian already you don't think it's any kind of existential task. So Kierkegaard is trying to unsettle people who might have had a fairly uncritical, unquestioning acceptance of the story of Abraham, that Abraham is the father of faith. Kierkegaard is saying, 'If Abraham is the father of faith, then what is faith? What does it require of us?' It seems to be a terrible thing that cannot be rationalized, that can't be based on any ethical grounds. So what is it?' Other questions that Kierkegaard wants to accentuate are: 'What if Abraham was wrong, what if he was mistaken?', 'What if it wasn't God's voice that he heard?', 'What if it was some kind of hallucination?' Kierkegaard relates this possibility of doubt to the situation of Jesus' disciples. His disciples could've been mistaken; they could've doubted who Jesus was. They didn't have the outcome to fall back on, the outcome of the success of Christianity. Historically, in that situation, they didn't know what the future held, just as Abraham didn't know that Isaac was going to be given back to him.

NW: *So it's a bit like the Socratic method. Socrates would take something which people took for granted and actually reveal to people that they didn't know what they thought they knew. Here, faith seems to be central to Christian teaching. But God's putting a very strange demand upon believers—to have faith in the absence of evidence.*

CC: Kierkegaard saw himself as a kind of Socrates of Christendom; he was interested in Socrates and inspired by Socrates. He wrote his doctoral dissertation on Socrates, and there are very clear parallels. Just as Socrates thinks that people assume that they possess knowledge and that assumption means that they don't bother seeking it again, Kierkegaard thinks that people assume that they're Christians, and this assumption prevents them from seeking to *become* Christians. So there's a clear parallel with Socratic philosophy that Kierkegaard himself was very conscious of.

NW: *It's still hard to see how Abraham's actions are admirable at all.*

CC: For Kierkegaard, Abraham is a solitary figure who can't be understood, and can't be admired, on the basis of any socially acceptable notion of morality. Abraham's willingness to sacrifice Isaac doesn't benefit any other human being: it doesn't benefit Isaac, of course, but there's no benefit to anybody else either. It's not that he's sacrificing Isaac for the sake of some greater social good. Moreover, Isaac symbolizes society because he's Abraham's only son and Isaac is the future tribe of Israel. Abraham is going to be the father of a nation, and so that nation is symbolically, as Johannes de Silentio puts it, contained in Isaac's loins. So in sacrificing Isaac, he is in fact sacrificing society as well.

NW: *One of the difficult aspects of reading Kierkegaard is knowing what Kierkegaard actually thought. What do you think Kierkegaard's message is here?*

CC: He wants the reader of the text to think for him- or herself, to raise questions. Somewhere he writes that his texts are a mirror that offers an aid to self-reflection, self-understanding, self-examination. Just as the story of Abraham is open to endless interpretations, so *Fear and Trembling* is also open to interpretation. My own understanding of the book has changed over the years. Now I think that Kierkegaard's message is in the form of a question, and it's the question of whether the Christian ideal, the ideal of faith, is in fact even attainable, whether it's even possible. Could any of us really have acted as Abraham acted? I think that's the question he wants readers to ask themselves. Then another question would follow from this: if Abraham is the father of faith and if I could not have acted as Abraham acted, then do I have faith, can I have faith, is it even possible to have the kind of faith that Abraham demonstrates?

NW: Fear and Trembling *appealed particularly to a number of existential thinkers, notably Jean-Paul Sartre. What is it about the book that they found so relevant to their interests?*

CC: There are several aspects of the book. One is the way in which it raises the question of the relationship between faith and reason, and more broadly, the question of the relationship between human existence, human subjectivity itself, and reason. A message that can be taken from the book is that the truth of human existence can't be adequately grasped or expressed in terms of rational thought.

Another aspect is the theme of choice, of responding to a particular situation, of being in an ethical dilemma—which several of Kierkegaard's heroes find themselves in—and not having any grounds on which to make a choice between two alternatives. Precisely because what Abraham does is irrational—in a sense he's left the sphere of reason—he's faced with his own freedom, and that, of course, is an experience of anguish which Kierkegaard emphasises. Of course, the anguish of freedom is one of the central themes of Sartre's own existentialism.

NW: *Why should anybody read* Fear and Trembling *today?*

CC: If the reader is a Christian, then they'll probably find some kind of inspiration from reading the book. If the reader is a philosopher, then they'll find a challenge to their own faith perhaps in philosophy. In this book, as in several of his other books, he's critical of academic philosophers who don't necessarily reflect on their own existence. They might ask abstract questions in order to avoid reflecting on more pressing questions, as Kierkegaard would see it, about what we are to do, what we are to commit to, and so on.

But *Fear and Trembling* is one of those books that doesn't just appeal to academic and religious readers. One of the reasons for this is that it addresses themes that are universal human themes, such as love, and suffering, and loss. At the centre of the book are a father and a son: a father who's faced with the prospect of losing his son and generally of losing, or having to give up, what is most precious to him. This is a human situation that we're all likely to find ourselves in at some point. So, the book has an emotional resonance that is one of the reasons why it continues to be read and talked about by a very wide range of readers.

19

Friedrich Nietzsche on Art and Truth

David Edmonds: *Does art teach us truths, and is that its purpose? Friedrich Nietzsche was, by critical consensus, a tin-eared composer— and by universal consensus, a virtuoso writer. Nietzsche took art seriously. Until they had a massive falling out, he was a close friend of Richard Wagner. For Nietzsche, the function of art—of music and theatre—was to give us a hint of a truth—the truth that the world was chaotic and meaningless; but equally, art had to shield us from this dreadful reality. Aaron Ridley is a Nietzschean scholar at the University of Southampton.*

Nigel Warburton: *We're going to focus on Nietzsche's ideas about art and truth. Could you say a little bit about Nietzsche's relationship to art?*

Aaron Ridley: Nietzsche was arguably the most art-obsessed philosopher there's been. Throughout his life he regarded himself as a serious poet; he also regarded himself as a serious composer, though the evidence of his own compositions was to the contrary. He assigned a very significant place to art.

NW: *In his first book,* The Birth of Tragedy, *he focused on the art of tragedy, but it illuminated other things about art and truth.*

AR: Nietzsche wrote *The Birth of Tragedy* under the spell of Schopenhauer who had thought that the world was an utterly vile and ghastly place, and if one really grasped the nature of it, one would see that the whole thing, that existence itself, was a terrible mistake. Nietzsche took that thought over from Schopenhauer in a way. But where Schopenhauer thought that that was a good reason for renouncing everything and saying no to the world, no to existence, Nietzsche thought that the ancient Greeks had found a way of using the truth that the basic nature of existence is awful to make their culture more energetic—and that they had done so through tragic art. He held that the flourishing of Athenian culture was a function of this. Through their tragedy, the Athenians allowed themselves to get just enough of a hint of the dark irrational forces that the world really consisted in, while saving themselves from the full impact that the recognition of that would have, by laying over it a veil of illusion. So you got a glimpse of the truth, but the truth was made palatable, the pill sweetened by a structure of illusions. That was what was characteristic about their tragedy. You need the truth to energize itself, the well-springs of the life-force are irrational through and through—but then you need the illusion that art also provides to prevent the energy from blowing you apart.

NW: *He expressed that through the notion of the Apollonian and the Dionysian.*

AR: Yes, he uses these two god figures to personify various metaphysical levels. The reality, which he associates with the god Dionysus, is that the world is ultimately chaos and destruction and meaningless striving. Illusion, surface appearance, the stuff we lay over the Dionysian reality to protect ourselves from it, he associates with the god Apollo. He thought that in classical Greek tragedy some absolutely ingenious balance between letting in the Dionysian truth and making it palatable via the Apollonian illusion had been achieved, and that this was the unique achievement of classical Greek tragedy.

NW: *Then in came Socrates and upset that.*

AR: Then in came Socrates and brought about the death of tragedy. Nietzsche's *The Birth of Tragedy* is in fact largely devoted to the death of tragedy and to explaining how, in his view, a very different world view gets put into place—a world view that he associates with the figure of Socrates—where the irrational is ultimately regarded as unreal. So, what Nietzsche had taken the Greeks' insight to be, that the fundamental nature of the world is chaotic and irrational, and so on, was, from the Socratic perspective, impossible. There could be no such world as that because in the Socratic world view there was an equation between reason and reality—and, indeed, goodness.

So, from Nietzsche's point of view, what happens is that a certain version of the Apollonian which had previously just been regarded as an illusion which hid reality from you, *becomes* reality. And if you start to think of the world like that, in Nietzsche's view, tragedy can no longer do the work that it did—since, on this picture, there is no longer any Dionysian reality to get a glimpse of or indeed to protect yourself from.

NW: *But, surely, Nietzsche himself believed the Dionysian was an important force in the world. He didn't accept the Socratic picture.*

AR: That's exactly right. Nietzsche thought that Schopenhauer and the Greeks had been on to something, that in its

innermost nature the world was chaotic and dreadful, and that
the pre-Socratic Greeks had found a way of drawing strength
from that, through their tragedies. Whereas post-Socrates,
that sort of reality got denied and, in Nietzsche's view,
everything got thinner, robbed of a fundamental primal
energy that was stolen along with Dionysus.

The end of *The Birth of Tragedy* was actually about the
rebirth of tragedy or the possibility of the rebirth of tragedy.
He thinks that now—he was obviously writing in the late
nineteenth century, but 'now' means modernity in general—
it might be possible to have this kind of culture-sustaining art
again. The reason for that is that the Socratic world view,
which led in one way or the other to the Christian world view,
is beginning to lose its grip on us. So if the Socratic/Christian
picture starts to be chipped away, then the Dionysian is on
offer again, and we ought in principle to be able to bring off
that incredible balance between glimpsing the Dionysian
truth, while at the same time making life livable through the
illusions of Apollo.

NW: *So in that phase of his writing, Nietzsche was certainly treating
art as something which made life livable: if we saw the world as it really
is we wouldn't be able to carry on.*

AR: In Nietzsche's view, that's certainly the case. The world
is just a meaningless procession of becoming and destruction:
there's no sense to it, there's no pattern to it, there's no reason
to it. Moreover, and this is something he also took over from
Schopenhauer, if that's the correct understanding of reality,
then individuality itself—the individuality of particular people,
particular things, particular objects—that's a kind of illusion,
too, part of the Apollonian world. What are we? We're just

the froth on a maelstrom of waves breaking for no reason on to nothing. Getting that picture, Nietzsche thinks, is energizing, but too much of it and it's psychologically utterly destructive. 'There is no me: all I am is a random confluence of currents and splashes and thunderings, here for a few moments and that's that: there's no point to any of it!'

So, he thinks that, from the point of view of our individual existence, if we were to come into being aware of ourselves as the illusory individuals that we really are, then the very best thing for us would be never to have been born at all, and the second best thing would be to die soon. If you really were to get a clear take on the illusoriness of your own individuality, then you could only think of your life as being a mistake. So you need some illusions to protect yourself from that. Again, the Apollonian steps in to save the day, to reinforce or rescue our sense of ourselves as properly individual beings.

NW: *What you're saying is that for Nietzsche, in this early phase, the arts served to give us the illusion that gives shape and coherence to something which is ultimately just flux.*

AR: Exactly that. What the Apollonian is doing is peddling a kind of untruth in order to protect us from *the* truth, and it can do that in a number of different ways. Some of the Apollonian devices here are things like having recognizable characters with coherent motives, who act in a way that we can recognize people as doing. But this, of course, is Apollonian because the fact of the matter is that it's all just strife and chaos. Then, by giving us a plot which is intelligible and characters who interact with each other in intelligible ways and a story that unfolds with that famous inevitability that tragedy is meant to have, again, all that this is doing is reinforcing a certain set of illusions to the effect that life makes sense.

NW: *How did Nietzsche's views about art change as he grew older?*

AR: There was a very seismic change shortly after he wrote *The Birth of Tragedy*. I said that the last sections of *The Birth of Tragedy* held out the promise that there might be a rebirth of tragedy. At the time that he was writing the book, he thought this was going on in the music dramas of Richard Wagner for whom Nietzsche was a very willing propagandist—indeed, possibly the most able propagandist any artist has ever had. *The Birth of Tragedy* is in part a song of praise to Wagner: here it is! For the first time since Aeschylus, we've actually got proper art, doing the sort of thing that art ought to be doing.

But very shortly after writing *The Birth of Tragedy*, he fell out with Wagner. He became utterly disenchanted and decided that what he had thought was a great reborn tragic art form, was in fact everything that he hated most about Christianity—only in disguise. I think he was absolutely wrong about Wagner, but that's neither here nor there. Nietzsche became very committed to that view. And it's no coincidence that the minute that he decided that Wagner was a charlatan and not the saviour of modern culture after all, art is massively downgraded for a few years in his pantheon of important things.

NW: *How had his views about truth changed?*

AR: Well, at much the same time that he became convinced that Wagner was a charlatan, he also became convinced that Schopenhauer was also an enemy of everything that was good, too. This was Nietzsche having his oedipal moment, growing up and wanting space—and doing it in the classic way, by rebelling against his intellectual mentors. But once he had decided that Schopenhauer was also really bad news, that made him very sceptical about the Schopenhauerian metaphysics which had underpinned what he was doing in *The Birth of Tragedy*. It's curious what survived. He comes away from him, even once he's repudiated him, thinking that the world is chaotic, that the world lacks meaning, but no longer thinking that this was a deep metaphysical point—a point to the effect that, if we see behind the appearances, then we'll see that everything is just turmoil and nonsense.

He now thinks, for a short period in the late 1870s, that the best route we've got to the truth is science, and that what science shows is that our ordinary take on the empirical world is hopelessly inadequate: compared to *that* take, he says the world is indeed a veritable mish-mash. But, because science allows us a better apprehension of what the empirical facts actually are, it also holds out the prospect that we might, through that knowledge, attempt to make the world a straightforwardly better place. However, he thought that a lot of the things we'd uncover during the process of becoming more knowledgeable about the truth would be very disturbing. So from that point of view, he thought that, although ultimately we ought to be able to do without art—art as the provision of illusions—and, indeed, although we *will* come to do without art, once we've got used to the truth and have steeled ourselves in the appropriate ways against it, nevertheless, for the time being, during the period of transition, we'd still hang on to art: art still has a protective role to play as we gradually uncover the truth about things through science.

NW: *You said that this was a short-lived phase. What happened next?*

AR: Well, he realized it had nothing to do with him, that he'd spent a couple of years being somebody else! A very good symptom of this is that one of the things that that we'd be able to do as we became more knowledgeable would be progressively to abolish suffering, and moreover that that would be a thoroughly good thing. This is possibly the most un-Nietzschean thought that Nietzsche ever had. In *The Birth of Tragedy,* he thinks that glimpsing the horrible reality of things and suffering from the illusoriness of one's own individual existence can make one stronger and more vibrant—so, suffering is good for you.

And he reverts to this view: he returns again and again and ever more vehemently to the thought that there's something actually valuable about at least some suffering. So, the attempt to abolish suffering altogether as a way of making life better, Nietzsche went back to thinking, is in fact a classic expression of a life that no longer has the energy for itself, of a life that is declining into complacent uninterestingness.

NW: *The way in which art shapes an apparently formless reality was also mirrored in what he said about how we might approach our own lives.*

AR: That's right, yes. Once he's come out of the positivist period, he still thinks that the world is inherently chaotic, indifferent to human purposes and human needs. It's a meaningless world, and this presents us with some challenges particularly if we don't want to avail ourselves of some of the more obvious ways we might have of dealing with apparent senselessness. One way would be the Socratic/Christian way, according to Nietzsche, which would be to say that this meaninglessness is only apparent; and that if one looks hard enough and thinks hard enough one will see that actually it's all for the good, it's all for the best in the best of all possible worlds (where the best is a world that in fact transcends this one). Nietzsche thinks that that's a fantasy—a dangerous fantasy, that we should have learned to do without.

In effect, what we're left with, for Nietzsche, is a chaotic, meaningless world but not one in a deep Schopenhauerian sense, just in a straightforward, immediate, and direct sense, which we ought to know better than to try to make palatable to ourselves by telling wholesale, big lies about it in the way that he thinks that Socrates told just big lies and Christianity tells big lies. What we have to do, instead, he thinks, is to tell little lies, lies that don't falsify the entire character of existence but which locally have the effect of making portions of existence bearable. He thought we can do that by the way in which we think about the world that we live in. But also, as you say, we can do it by making something of an illusion of ourselves—by, as he famously puts it, giving style to our character. The idea is that we might become works of art, that we might improve ourselves through a certain self-directed artistry.

NW: *You've given a description of an interpretation of Nietzsche's different views about art and truth. But where do you think he was right about the relationship, or are his views just of historical interest?*

AR: It's more than of just historical interest. What's unusual about Nietzsche's position about art is the consistent thought that art is something which trades in illusions, in deceptions, in partial visions—and, indeed, that that's a lot of its point.

This is a very unorthodox position in the history of thinking about art and particularly in the history of thinking about the relationship between art and truth. What almost all philosophers have wanted to do is say that art is a good thing, and that it's a good thing partly because it has some connection to knowledge, which is valuable for us. That's been the dominant trend—the attempt which can often seem pompous and unconvincing, to defend our investment in art by equipping it with high-minded epistemic purposes. But this is a defence which, although very, very common, is something we might want to look at with a certain amount of suspicion. So I don't think that the study of Nietzsche is of merely historical interest. He offers us a richer and more challenging conception of the relation between art and truth than any other philosopher has done, and it is a conception that we have yet to come properly to grips with. How much do we *want* to know about ourselves and our world? How much would it be *good* for us to know? These are the unfamiliar questions that Nietzsche's philosophy of art forces us to ask.

20

PETER SINGER ON
Henry Sidgwick's Ethics

David Edmonds: *The most important philosopher in the utilitarian tradition . . . ? Who would you go for? Jeremy Bentham? John Stuart Mill? Peter Singer of Princeton University puts the case for a less familiar nineteenth-century thinker, a man little known outside academia: Henry Sidgwick.*

Nigel Warburton: *The topic we're focusing on is Henry Sidgwick's ethics. Who was Henry Sidgwick?*

Peter Singer: Henry Sidgwick was a late nineteenth-century Victorian philosopher, professor of philosophy at Cambridge University. He produced what many people—and I'm one of them—think is among the greatest works of ethics ever written, the *Methods of Ethics*, published first in 1874. Throughout his lifetime he kept reworking it, so the final edition is the seventh, published posthumously in 1907.

NW: *What kind of a philosopher was he? What was his central theme?*

PS: Sidgwick was a utilitarian. When people talk about the classical utilitarians, they tend to talk about Jeremy Bentham,

John Stuart Mill, and Henry Sidgwick. I regard Sidgwick as the greatest of them as a philosopher. Obviously, Bentham was a pioneer and did an enormous amount of work about political reform, law, and jurisprudence on a huge range of topics—an incredible polymath. John Stuart Mill was a wonderful popular writer, and his *On Liberty* was a classic; his *Utilitarianism* was also very popular and sold well, and helped spread his ideas; and, of course, *The Subjection of Women* was far ahead of its time. But Sidgwick, without a doubt, is the most careful and thorough philosopher of the three, very fair-minded, always thinking of objections, and always clear and precise in his concepts.

NW: *Within utilitarianism there are many different forms. What kind of utilitarian was he?*

PS: Sidgwick was a *hedonistic* utilitarian. That means that he thinks that the good to be maximized is pleasure or happiness: the greatest possible balance of that over the amount of pain or suffering. He was also what today we would call an act consequentialist, judging each individual action in terms of whether it leads to better consequences. (In contrast, rule consequentialists first decide what rules would have the best consequences, if generally followed, and then judge each act in terms of whether it conforms to those rules.) These terms were not part of Sidgwick's vocabulary. But, I think, he's really saying that every act we do ought to be judged in terms of whether it produces the best consequences, even though, in judging the individual act, we ought to take into account whether it is likely to weaken support for a useful rule.

NW: *So, if I were to lie to you now and tell you the interview will be over in a few seconds, judging that ethically would be just a question of looking at the consequences or likely consequences of my saying that?*

PS: Yes, that's right. Now, Sidgwick might say that, for ordinary, everyday life we know that telling the truth is generally a better thing to do, so you should not really even think about telling a lie unless you have reason to believe that there are some rather exceptional circumstances. Still, what you said is correct. It's not the fact that there's a general rule against lying that would make your lie wrong, but rather what the particular consequences are going to be.

NW: *That makes him sound like Jeremy Bentham whose utilitarianism is hedonistic, and also based on individual acts. So what's the difference?*

PS: Bentham is not really a very systematic philosopher in terms of developing a view, stating it precisely, and looking at difficulties with it. The other difference is that Bentham is a *psychological* hedonist as well, a psychological *egoistic* hedonist: that is, he thinks that everything we do, we do for the sake of our own pleasure and the avoidance of pain. Sidgwick thought that was a mistake, and I agree with Sidgwick there.

But in any case, in the *Methods of Ethics*, Sidgwick is trying to do something different from Bentham. He's trying to investigate in a fair-minded way what possible ways there are of thinking about ethics or, to put it in other words, of answering the question, 'What ought I to do?' He discusses what he calls the 'method of egoism', that is, that the right answer to that question is: 'I ought to do what's in *my* interest.' He also discusses at great length—it's a wonderful part of the book—common-sense morality, or intuitionism: the idea that we *intuit* a range of common-sense principles, including, say, the principle 'Do not lie' or 'Tell the truth', which you were imagining violating a moment ago. He tries to put that principle in its best form, and then argues that common-sense morality doesn't really stand up by itself once you examine it and try to clarify the principles. He shows that common-sense morality needs to be supplemented by an underlying principle which turns out to be identical with the underlying principle of utilitarianism.

NW: *How does common-sense morality end up being justified on utilitarian grounds?*

PS: Well, let's take the example that you used a moment ago about lying. There's a common-sense rule that says, 'You should tell the truth' or 'You should not lie'. But then, when you think about that rule a little bit more, it's clearly not absolute. Common-sense morality doesn't believe that you should *never* lie. It has a whole range of situations in which you can lie. There are rather trivial ones in which your wife comes to you just before you go out and says, 'Do you like my new dress?' Common-sense morality doesn't really condemn you if you say, 'Oh, you look lovely, dear', when you don't quite think so. And, then, at the other extreme, there are the cases where the only way to prevent some disaster is by telling a lie: suppose that only by lying can you prevent an evil dictator from killing many people. Common-sense morality says you may lie in those circumstances too. So there are several situations where this rule—like many others—is not clear and precise. And if you ask, 'How do we decide which are the justifiable exceptions to the rule against lying?',

Sidgwick's argument is that the answer always is to look at the consequences of what you're doing. So, to Sidgwick, this suggests that the rule, 'Do not lie', is not really a self-evident intuition: it's a subordinate principle, and underlying that, there has to be a more basic intuition which is in fact the intuition of doing what will have the best consequences.

NW: *Well, lying is quite subtle, but with some possible actions, like torture, many people believe there is an absolute prohibition on torture. There are no exceptions. Could Sidgwick have coped with that sort of case?*

PS: I think Sidgwick would cope with that case in a way that has been rather controversial. Probably the rule, 'Do not torture', has good consequences because if you don't have a rule that says 'Do not torture', then you'll get a lot of abuses. But there may be some cases where even though it's good to uphold, in public, an exceptionless moral rule, it could be justifiable to do a particular act in breach of the rule. This is what Sidgwick calls *esoteric* morality: it may be right to do something *only if the fact that you do it can be kept secret*. So, if you take what is sometimes called a 'ticking bomb' scenario— imagine that a terrorist has planted a nuclear bomb some- where in London and the only way to get him to reveal where it is in time to stop it going off is to torture him, or maybe even to torture his young daughter in front of him—Sidgwick might say, 'Well, it would be justified to torture in those extraordinary circumstances, but it would not be justified to have a rule that says you may torture, because if you do, people will abuse it.'

NW: *One of the great virtues of Bentham's and Mill's utilitarianism, is that they take each individual sentient being seriously and seem to treat*

them equally in the calculation that they make about pleasure and pain.
With Sidgwick, it's almost as if there's an elite who are clever enough to
foresee the consequences and they can transgress rules but the general
population are too stupid to see the consequences of their actions.

PS: Sidgwick might not have wanted to characterize it quite
that way, but he does think that sometimes some people
might be in a special position of knowledge where they are
justified in doing things that other people not in that position
of knowledge would not be justified in doing. I don't think
this is contrary to any principle of equality that Bentham
accepts—Mill, I'm less sure about—but Bentham is really
talking about 'each to count for one and no one to count for
more than one', and Sidgwick would be completely on board
with that. He would say, 'Yes, we count the interests of those
people equally, but we must recognize the reality of the fact
that some people *do* have particular knowledge or particular
abilities that makes it justifiable for them to do things that are
contrary to a rule that we should uphold publicly, because
other people, without that special knowledge or ability, are
likely to go astray.' You might think this is an elitist view.
Certainly, Bernard Williams thought that: he called it 'Government
House Utilitarianism', which conjures up the image of
colonial administrators who know what best to do, but believe
that they cannot trust the 'natives' with the truth. I think that's
a somewhat unfair characterization, but there is an element of
this elitism in it, I wouldn't deny that.

NW: *Isn't there a risk that if some politicians read Sidgwick's*
Methods of Ethics, *they would come to believe that they are in this*
privileged esoteric group and justify and rationalize to themselves actions
which aren't genuinely justifiable by utilitarianism?

PS: There is that risk, and this is the paradox of even talking about esoteric morality. Maybe we should have kept it in a little seminar room somewhere for a hand-picked audience because as soon as you start talking about it, you have exactly the possibility that you mention, that people may think that I'm one of the group that is justified in torturing. So yes, there's a danger in the doctrine, but I also think there's something true in the doctrine. I think, for example, the situation with regard to torture is very hard to get around. I certainly think it's better that we have a rule that says you should never torture. On the other hand, I can't really say to myself that torture would be wrong if we were facing the obliteration of London, and torture were the only way to stop that.

NW: *Sidgwick is a philosopher's philosopher: he's not known in the way Mill and Bentham are. You hinted at why that might be: because he's writing in a much more complex style. Is that the only reason do you think?*

PS: Well, the *Methods of Ethics* is some 500 pages long, and Sidgwick's prose doesn't leap off the page and really excite you to go on with it in quite the same way as Mill's often does. It's one of Sidgwick's virtues that he's so careful: he considers all the objections, he qualifies all the claims he makes. It makes him so much better as a philosopher than Mill. You read Mill and you think, 'What does he mean here? Does he really mean that? Isn't that inconsistent with what he said back there?' You don't get that with Sidgwick. But, on the other hand, you do get something that requires more concentration and more effort to read.

NW: *If we lived in a world run by Henry Sidgwick, what would it be like?*

PS: Henry Sidgwick would have rejected that possibility; he never saw himself as a leader or a ruler. But I suppose he hoped that the people he was educating would be rulers. So, for one thing, I think that they would have an overriding concern for the general happiness, that counts everyone equally. I think that they, interestingly, would also have a concern for the welfare of animals, because Sidgwick does mention animal welfare, as do all the utilitarians: they're much more aware of the fact that animals count than any other ethicists of that era were. He is also very concerned about looking at the long-term future, emphasising that we should be concerned for all the moments of our existence and for all the others who may come after us. He was one of the first to raise the question: 'If we can affect the size of the population that exists in the future, what kind of principles should we look at?' In fact, I think he was *the* first explicitly to raise that question, which Derek Parfit and others have discussed at greater length more recently. I think that in today's world he would have been a strong environmentalist. He would have been appalled at the failure to act on climate change. I think he also would have wanted us to be more aware about global poverty. So, I think the world would be a better place if his influence were more prevalent.

21

ROBERT B. TALISSE ON
The Pragmatists and Truth

David Edmonds: *Baseball may be popular in America, but the sport hasn't really taken hold in many other countries in the world. Its philosophical equivalent is Pragmatism: it's sometimes called 'American Pragmatism' because its three major figures, Charles Peirce, William James, and John Dewey were all Americans, writing in the late nineteenth and early twentieth centuries. Pragmatism is described as a movement, which masks the fact that its leading figures had major philosophical differences. Opponents of Pragmatism say it's dangerous in all its forms. It's a type, they say, of pernicious relativism. For some objective truth about Pragmatism we turned to a leading authority on the subject: Robert Talisse of Vanderbilt University.*

Nigel Warburton: *Pragmatism in philosophy is different from the way the word 'pragmatism' is used in everyday life. Could you outline what it is? What is this movement known as Pragmatism?*

Robert Talisse: Pragmatism begins at the turn of the twentieth century, primarily with the writings of Charles Sanders Peirce, William James, and then John Dewey. It began with Peirce as a conception of the meanings of terms and statements. The claim is that the meaning of a sentence such as 'this knife is sharp' is to be understood in terms of the kinds of actions one would perform with the object. So, 'this knife is sharp' means, for the Pragmatist, 'if you rub it up against many other substances, it will cut'. The idea is that the meaning of sentences is to be brought down to a description of a kind of experiment—if you perform *a certain* kind of action you will get *this* sort of effect.

NW: *Just to get that straight, most people would say that what it is for a knife to be sharp is that it cuts things. But Pragmatism isn't just common-sensical, is it? It's actually a philosophical reaction against a different way of conceiving what a word like 'sharp' could mean.*

RT: That's right. It's an attempt to functionalize all of our philosophical concepts rather than an attempt to make them more lofty or abstract or, for example, to talk about the property of sharpness. So you can imagine a Platonist, a follower of Plato, saying '"x is sharp" means that it manifests or partakes in the form of "the sharp"'. The Pragmatist wants to say in response, 'That's not the right kind of analysis. It's not that the Platonist gives the wrong theory of properties, it's instead that the Platonist is barking up the wrong tree.' To say that something is sharp is to say that if you perform certain actions with it, you will get certain types of results. So, the idea is to bring everything down to what's practical and to avoid abstract theorizing and appeals to transcendental properties.

NW: *But Pragmatists don't just focus on whether or not knives are sharp. What sort of topics interest Pragmatists?*

RT: The effort is to bring philosophical analysis more in line with scientific practice. Pragmatists offer this conception of

meaning as a way of dismissing, or removing from the
philosophical agenda, certain kinds of philosophical problems
which had been puzzling philosophers for thousands of years:
questions about properties, and essences, and substances and
these highfalutin abstract concepts. The Pragmatists' objective
is not to give answers to the question of what substance is, or
what essence is, but to dismiss such questions entirely, to say
that these are the wrong questions to ask. So, there's an
agenda that has as much to do with answering the question of
what philosophy can do as it has to do with trying to give
philosophical theories. The Pragmatists' thought is, 'once you
start talking about things that aren't verifiable, or that couldn't
be brought down to some real difference in human experience, you're philosophically off on the wrong track'.

NW: *It sounds as if Pragmatism is close to what's called Logical
Positivism—the idea that a statement is meaningless if it's not empirically
verifiable (if it can't be tested) or if it's not true by definition.*

RT: That's right. The earliest Pragmatist, Charles Peirce,
sometimes writes in a way that brings him very close to the
verificationism of Logical Positivism that prevailed in the first
half of the twentieth century. But Pragmatism is different
from Logical Positivism. The difference between the Pragmatists and the Logical Positivists comes up most starkly in the
work of William James who sees a problem in Peirce's
statement of Pragmatism. James thinks that, for example,
Peirce's Pragmatism is insufficiently sensitive to matters of
value. It seems from some of Peirce's writings that value
drops out of the Pragmatist picture because you couldn't do a
test in a laboratory to find out whether something is good or
beautiful. Peirce was angered by James to some considerable

extent—in fact, Peirce eventually declares that he's no longer a Pragmatist, and renames his view 'Pragmaticism'. Peirce says he wants to distinguish his view by giving it a name that is 'ugly enough to be safe from kidnappers'; he sees William James as one of the kidnappers.

James sees this positivistic element in Peirce's Pragmatism, and so offers an alternative version of Pragmatism. In response to the verificationist element of Peirce's Pragmatism, James says, 'Well, we mean by "experience" something much broader than philosophers typically mean.' So, James thinks that the meaning of a sentence is the implications in experience for somebody who believes that sentence to be true. To put the contrast starkly, Peirce thought that the meaning of a statement consists in the empirical consequences of its *being true*; while James held that the meaning of a statement consists in the empirical consequences of its being *believed to be true*. In this way, James would say questions about religion, about God, about value, about beauty are all very deeply meaningful. They're not dismissible because you can't do a laboratory experiment to verify their truth. Instead, you have to ask yourself, 'What would it be to believe that?'; and James thinks that if believing in God gives you the right kind of psychological comportment towards the world so that you can get on with your life and not be depressed, that's all the justification one needs to adopt the belief. And, more importantly, those enabling psychological effects are part of the meaning of the belief.

NW: *I can see how that then makes sense of James' famous book* The Varieties of Religious Experience *as part of a Pragmatist project, but it also raises a problem for Pragmatism, which is that a lot of people believe that either God exists or doesn't exist as a metaphysical entity. The truth is outside of the human in some sense: the truth is the way the world is.*

RT: That's right. This is a particularly difficult problem for William James. James says famously, 'Truth is what works.' He holds that the truth of a proposition is equivalent to how successfully it guides action. So, it looks as if James is saying that if you believe that the bus leaves at 8 a.m., and that belief guides your actions in such a way that you actually get on the bus, that's what it is for the belief to be true. But, as you say, what gets left out is the conception that the truth of the sentence has something to do with how it maps onto, or corresponds to, or hooks up with the world.

Having said that, James has some pretty interesting arguments to suggest that the conception of correspondence or 'hooking up' with the world is philosophically muddled. James is very keen to say, 'Look, it's unclear what the metaphors of "correspondence" or "hooking up with", or "latching on to reality" mean; how can we cash those out philosophically?' He thinks that standard correspondence views of truth trade largely in metaphors that never get fleshed out. So, he asks how could a sentence—a string of sounds, or scratches on paper— bear that kind of relation—'correspondence'—to tables and chairs, dogs and cats, and things?

NW: *But religious people believe that God exists. They don't think that God is just a convenient idea that makes their lives go better.*

RT: That's right. I think that you're right to point out that there might be a bait and switch in James' defence of religious belief. He's saying to religious believers, 'Religious belief is philosophically above board and you shouldn't be brow-beaten out of it by clever philosophers.' But then, when you look at what he gives as the analysis of the content of religious belief, it's a *psychologized* version of religion. For James, belief in God means hope for the improvement of the universe. Belief in God means, having what James calls 'the strenuous mood', the psychological comportment to the world that will enable you to fight for its improvement, and fight for what you see as good; religious belief for James has nothing to do with the afterlife, or angels and folks with long beards and white hair up in the sky.

Let's bring this down to a particular example. James gives an analysis of transubstantiation, the part in the Catholic mass where the wine and bread are transformed by the priest, so the doctrine goes, into the actual blood and body of Jesus. Charles Peirce thought that transubstantiation was 'meaningless gibberish'; for him, it was just a metaphysical doctrine that should be dismissed as nonsense. James, however, says, 'No, the idea that we could actually feed on the body and blood of God is psychologically potent. It is truly the pragmatic application of the idea of substance.' He says that the doctrine of transubstantiation is psychologically useful in helping us to sustain our motivation for improving the world. Now, whether that's going to move any religious believer or not is of course a different question.

NW: *It seems to me that Pragmatism ought to have quite a lot to say about science. Is that historically true?*

RT: Yes, that is true, and in fact we get the explicit focus on science and philosophy of science most heavily in the work of John Dewey. For Dewey, the theory of inquiry—the theory of actual experimentation, hypothesis-testing, and production, and all the rest—was a central occupation. One thing to say about Dewey's view of science is that it shares some of the motivations of the Logical Positivist but tries to work with a broader conception of science. The idea is that *experimentation* is the heart of science. The activity of manipulating, checking for results in light of that manipulation, going back and revising hypotheses—this ongoing process of a sophisticated version of trial and error—is what Dewey means by science.

Dewey thinks that scientific experimentation as it's practised in the laboratory is just a refined or more systematic version of ordinary human thinking generally when it's done properly. So, the thought is not the Positivist one that science is a special kind of practice, and we now need to model philosophy on it. The Deweyan Pragmatist thought is that all thinking manifests in some very general way the pattern of inquiry that gets practised in a more systematic way in the laboratory. We need to take note of this fact and revise our philosophical concepts in light of the experimental methods of science.

NW: *It seems to me that the Pragmatists could almost dispense with the notion of truth once they've started cashing it out in terms of behaviour and belief and so on.*

RT: That's right, at least for many versions of Pragmatism. Dewey is pretty explicit about this. He argues that we could replace the concept of truth with the concept of warranted assertability or warranted assertion; he thinks that scientific inquiry is really after warrant or justification for hypothesis, rather than truth. For Dewey, truth talk is going to fall out, warrant talk is going to come in, and warrant is always going to be contextual, historical, or sociological.

NW: *Pragmatism didn't stop at the turn of the century: it's had an afterlife. In my lifetime, the one philosopher who stands out as having been heavily influenced by Pragmatism is Richard Rorty. How is he a Pragmatist? What did he do with the tradition?*

RT: Well, Rorty, I think, is the inheritor of Deweyan Pragmatism. And, just to pick up on what we were just saying about replacing the concept of truth with warrant—which on Dewey's view is always contextualized and historical—Rorty takes that view a step further and says things like this: 'Truth is just a pat on the back that we give to sentences which seem to be paying their way.' Or elsewhere he says: 'Truth is simply what the people you're speaking with will let you get away with saying; Truth is just what your conversation partners will all nod "Yes" to when you say it.' And, further, Rorty claims that there's nothing more to say about truth. So he has an eliminativist view of truth. It's not that truth is too hard, or that there's no good theory of truth. Even looking for a theory of truth is a mistake for Rorty. Truth is the kind of thing we should not take to be a philosophical matter at all.

NW: *Now, I know Rorty had this thrown at him, but what about the Nazis? What the Nazis did was backed by many millions of people in Germany, Austria, and parts of Poland. And yet now we look at it as the most horrific thing ever done. Is it all relative? That can't be right, can it?*

RT: Well, I agree with you. I'm not a Rortyan Pragmatist; in fact, I'm an anti-Rortyan Pragmatist. And you're right this is the standard line against Rorty, and I think it's a powerful line. Rorty's response, though, is very interesting, and disturbing. His response is to say that there's nothing that you can really do to show that the Nazis or anti-liberals like Nietzsche are wrong. All you can do is say they're not part of the community of conversationalists that I like to get on with. Like all Pragmatists, he's got this second-order view about what philosophy can achieve. Rorty wants to say that the whole point of philosophy, the whole point of Pragmatist philosophy as Rorty understands it, is to encourage us, as he says, to stand unflinchingly for our commitments even once we've realized that there's no philosophical justification that can be given for them. He says that all philosophical justifications of liberal democracy are circular: they're all just restatements of what people like us liberal democrats say about freedom or about violence. When we criticize the Nazis, we're really just addressing the audience of people who are just like us—fellow liberal democrats. He says it's an error, encouraged by traditional philosophy, to say that if we can't give an argument that even Hitler would have to be moved by, well, then, liberal democracy is somehow enfeebled or jeopardized. Ultimately, Rorty would have to say that Nazism and western liberal democracy are the same: neither enjoys any greater philosophical justification than the other. And, yes, that's relativism. But Rorty says that there's no alternative to relativism, so there's nothing to the charge that a view is relativist; one can criticize a view for being relativist only if one accepts that it's possible for a view to be non-relativist, which is something that Rorty denies. He claims that all views are relativist; the only difference between them is that some are self-aware of their relativism, and others are deluded about it.

NW: *That seems to be a theme in twentieth-century philosophy. We had the Logical Positivists such as A. J. Ayer saying that moral judgements are just expressions of emotion, they're purely subjective. Then there are the existentialists embracing something not dissimilar to what you've described in Rorty: this idea that there's a contingency about human values, but you have to stand up for the values that you yourself endorse. And we have the later Pragmatists as well. Three sorts of philosophical movements pushing in that direction. Interesting, but disturbing, too...*

RT: Very much so. Rorty, as you have described him, is even taking A. J. Ayer one step further. Rorty's not saying that moral judgements are *only* expressions of emotion or *merely* the expression of emotion. He'd object to the 'only' and 'merely' in those statements, because, according to him, there's no alternative. Remember that the Logical Positivists think science gives us the model of objectivity. They hold that, since moral statements can't fit into that model, moral statements are non-objective. Rorty wants to say that what Ayer thought was the case with respect to moral statements is also the case with respect to scientific statements. There's no objectivity to be had; there's just, as he says, *solidarity*: making community with the people who are like you, and saying things to each other that you all endorse as a way of feeling community with others. And that's all there is. And that's all philosophy can do, on the Rortyan view.

NW: *We've travelled quite a long distance here talking about the key Pragmatist thinkers running right through into the late twentieth century. Yet, despite it being a practical philosophy, there does seem to be some-thing missing. Pragmatism misses that sense of awe and wonder that is the start of philosophy, the idea that we are trying to explore a reality that's beyond us.*

RT: I think you're right that there is a sense of something missing to the philosophical enterprise in all the Pragmatists' views. I think that's deliberate. Pragmatists adopt something like the view of the later Wittgenstein that traditional philosophy is a kind of dysfunctional urge or a symptom of something wrong. Wittgenstein held that we need therapy to get over certain kinds of philosophical longings, and philosophy traditionally had been a way of trying to pursue those sickly aspirations. Pragmatism often sees itself as a way of trying to cure us of those aspirations.

Now we can ask: Who is right? Is traditional philosophy right to hold that there's something essential to the human condition that requires us to ask these deep questions; or is Pragmatism right that the deepest traditional philosophical questions—the questions that bothered Plato, Aristotle, St Thomas Aquinas, Descartes, and all the way up through Kant—are somehow misguided or have set us off on the wrong path? That is itself a deep philosophical question, of course. But you're right; that's what's being offered by the Pragmatists: a rejection of the traditional philosophical concerns. Pragmatism is not simply a philosophy that doesn't get at these deeper things; it is an explicit rejection of the thought that we should pursue traditional philosophical aspirations.

22

BARRY C. SMITH ON
Ludwig Wittgenstein

David Edmonds: *Gardener, primary school teacher, architect, engineer, war hero, millionaire who gave away most of his money, hospital porter—and arguably the most significant philosopher of the twentieth century, Ludwig Wittgenstein was born in Vienna in 1889, the youngest child of a wealthy steel magnate. He moved to Cambridge in 1911 to study under Bertrand Russell and to pursue his interest in logic. Russell would write the forward to the* Tractatus Logico-Philosophicus, *the only philosophy book Wittgenstein published in his lifetime, completed in the trenches of World War I. The* Tractatus, *Wittgenstein initially believed, solved all the fundamental problems of philosophy. But by the time he returned to Cambridge in 1929 he was having second thoughts. His legendary charisma, his frenetic mental energy, his beguiling prose, his deep originality—all helped ensure that a new generation of disciples would absorb, adopt, and transmit his ideas. Barry Smith is a Wittgenstein expert and the director of the Institute of Philosophy.*

Nigel Warburton: *We're talking today about Ludwig Wittgenstein's view about what philosophy is. He's often described as a philosopher's philosopher.*

Barry C. Smith: I think he is a philosopher's philosopher because, as well as giving us philosophical ideas, theses, and positions for us to explore, he's actually interested in the *activity* of philosophy. What is philosophy about? What's its subject matter? Unlike science, there is no automatically demarcated domain of enquiry or set of facts that we're studying. So, he's self-conscious, all the time when he's doing philosophy, and he's wondering what he is up to.

NW: *In order to make sense of how he got to his later philosophical views about what philosophy is, we need to fill in some details about his philosophical background. He began as a student of engineering, came to England before World War I to study with Bertrand Russell. What was his view of philosophy at that point?*

BCS: As an engineer, he was interested in rather abstract problems: he was into aeronautical engineering. But to do that, you had to have a concern with mathematics and this was where he really began to have his first philosophical thoughts. What was mathematics about? What made mathematical statements true? We don't doubt that $2 + 2 = 4$, but when we arrive at these undoubted truths, what is the subject matter? We don't trip over numbers in the world, we don't spill our coffee on them, and yet we seem to be talking about something that's absolutely sure and certain. The subject matter of both mathematics and logic became a central preoccupation, and he found out that in Cambridge there was a philosopher, Bertrand Russell, who was interested in the nature of logic, and who had got these questions going.

NW: *But his interest was not just in the philosophy of mathematics; he was interested in how our thoughts relate to the world.*

BCS: All our thinking, if it is in good order, is logically correct thinking. But what are the truths of logic truths *of*? What actually gives us some grip on the idea that there are some things that are logically right and logically wrong? And again, rather like mathematics, logic doesn't seem to describe the world. And yet, if logic describes something beyond the world, something more mysterious and transcendental, how does it apply to us in our thinking and in our lives? So, really, his quest is to find a way in which logic *is* in the world and is actually the structure and the boundary of our thinking.

NW: *But how can logic, which is essentially the structure of arguments, relate to the world at all?*

BCS: Well, we come to hold many beliefs about the world, and we hope our beliefs are true, and we can't necessarily tell, we have to go around and find out and check, and look for evidence, and so on. But if we know to begin with the fact that our beliefs are contradictory, that we both believe something and believe its opposite, then we know these beliefs can't both be true at the same time. So, unless our thinking is at least consistent, there's no chance of it fitting the world, there's no chance of us getting things right.

NW: *So, I can't believe that I'm in London and in Cambridge simultaneously.*

BCS: Exactly. If you tried to believe *that*, we would doubt that you had one or other of these beliefs.

NW: *Logic, then, structures the limits of what I can think. And that presumably was what interested Wittgenstein. He wasn't just interested in mathematics per se, he wanted to know about our relationship to reality.*

> BCS: We want to describe reality. We want to figure all the ways reality can be, not just as it is, but as it could be. Logic seems to provide us with some limits to the way things could be. It *could* have been raining today; you *could* have been in Oxford instead of in London; but it's not the case that you *could* have been both in Oxford and not in Oxford at the same time. So, what is it that provides this logical boundary or logical constraint on the way reality could be?

NW: *One aspect of his answer was what's come to be known as the picture theory of language.*

> BCS: Yes. If you think that language can describe states of affairs, it can describe situations. We're sitting in a room just now recording this podcast, but if we think of all the ways we can describe the world, and if we could do that exhaustively, then we could use that very language through rearrangement of parts of the sentences into new sentences to describe not just the way it is, but the ways it could be, alternative versions of the world. If you have sentences which work to describe reality correctly, Wittgenstein thought they were in some sense pictures of reality—just as a picture of reality, like a painting, needn't be of an actual scene, it's of a *possible* scene.

NW: *At that stage, what did he think the activity of philosophy should be?*

> BCS: He wanted to see how philosophy should describe the limits of language as the limits of how things could be in

reality. The job of the philosopher is not to describe reality; perhaps that's the job of scientists. But, instead, what we should say is, 'Here is how language can actively be used to describe how things might be, and here are the limits on what we can think or describe as the way reality could be.' The limits of language for Wittgenstein were the limits of reality.

NW: *So, if I've got this straight, part of what Wittgenstein was trying to do was distinguish what we can talk about and make sense of from mere nonsense.*

BCS: Yes. But there are two types of nonsense, for Wittgenstein. If you put words in any order, 'the man of of the on', for example, that doesn't make any sense. But Wittgenstein was also interested in statements which purport to describe reality but (he thought) didn't do so. They might nevertheless show us something important about reality. When you say that a proposition cannot be both true and false at the same time, you're not describing a fact purporting to picture some part of reality, but it's nevertheless showing you some of the limits and boundaries on how we can describe reality, or on how reality could be. So, for Wittgenstein, some of these nonsensical statements were actually quite illuminating. The laws of logic, the limits of intelligibility are the ways of showing what those limits are without stating them.

NW: *Wittgenstein thought he'd solved the problems of philosophy. He left Cambridge; during World War I, he was in the trenches with the Austrian army; but he gradually came to realize that there were some things that he needed to get straight still, and came back to Cambridge in 1929. Then he developed a new conception of language. Instead of thinking of language in terms of a picture of the world, he put forward this notion of meaning as use.*

BCS: Yes, I think he comes back to philosophy because, although he thinks he has solved the problems of philosophy in the *Tractatus*, stating what the limits of intelligible thought and language are, he realizes that philosophers still hanker after some form of explanation and he wonders what we want when we want explanations. What are we trying to explain? He comes to diagnose our problem in philosophy as the search for explanations where none can be given. He recommends instead a way of avoiding explaining and returning just to describing how things actually are. So, now his view of language is, 'Don't try to explain how language would work if it were in perfect order. Try to describe how it really works; just see how we use language.' So, philosophers who thought of revising language to make it fit for the job of describing science or mathematics, wanted a revision to our ordinary practice. But, as Wittgenstein pointed out, we don't have any problems with our ordinary practice: we use language as second nature, we're comfortable with it. If we're going to understand how it actually works, as opposed to how philosophers think it should work, we ought to just describe it. But to do that you have to attend to it very carefully and get it right.

NW: *That makes him sound more like a sociologist describing how we happen to use language. That's not a traditional picture of what a philosopher does.*

BCS: The philosophy is in trying to persuade you that you don't need explanations: you just need description and you need a lot of philosophy to persuade other philosophers to accept that. But in terms of describing language, he wants to describe language as it is actually used, look at how it is put to work by ordinary folk, and yet he knows there is such a thing as using language correctly or incorrectly. If a word is to have any meaning, it has to have a definite application; we can't use a word to name just anything we like and suppose the word still has some significance. We use the word 'red' for red things, and if we didn't use it selectively, that way it wouldn't have that meaning. So, now, he's interested in what it is that makes the difference between the correct and the incorrect use of a word. He thinks that, when we use a word correctly, we seem to be following a rule for its correct use. But now he's left with the terrible philosophical problem of explaining what it is to follow rules, and to follow them correctly.

NW: *On that question, we're in danger of going down a completely different track. I want to pull this back to the role of philosophy. He said philosophy begins when language goes on holiday. I wonder if you might give us a gloss on what this means.*

BCS: He thought philosophy was in trouble when language went on holiday: in other words, when we start using language in a philosophically prescribed way, instead of using it in its normal way. People are not puzzled by their use of language; they use these words and they listen to these sounds, and they hear them as immediately meaningful. And yet philosophers make this seem a puzzling activity. How could these mere sounds, these mere noises, manage to convey something about the inner contents of my mind? How could they make it available to you, another mind, who doesn't have the ability to scrutinize my thinking. Now, Wittgenstein saw those philosophical puzzles as only arising because people had misconceived the relationship between language and thought, and the relationship between language and other people. In the *Tractatus*, he's worried about the relationship between language and reality.

How does language capture reality? What are the limits of language that show us the limits of reality? By the second period of his philosophical life he's interested in the relationship between language and us. We seem only to become creatures capable of wondering, thinking, discussing, philosophizing when we're already in the midst of a language, when we already speak language and use it to communicate our thoughts to one another. And he wanted to show that language not only involves a relation to other people, without which you couldn't have meaningful significance for your own words, but that language also ties you to the world. There is no predicament of the sort the Cartesian philosopher envisaged, of us sitting by ourselves in our own library, wondering if anybody else existed and if we were the only thinkers. That picture was deeply flawed, because even to have the materials to start thinking and asking those questions you're already immersed in a practice of using words in exchange with others in a way in which you all jointly maintain the significance of that language.

NW: *So that's what he means by 'meaning as use'. Part of that is a reaction against a view of philosophy which comes down through Plato where we have Socrates—the character in Plato's dialogues—challenging people to define key concepts such as 'justice': and the people he asks prove incapable of actually explaining it. What Socrates is trying to do is get someone to give necessary and sufficient conditions for something being justice. But Wittgenstein challenges the notion that a definition in use is anything like that.*

BCS: Yes, he does and he uses a rather good and a rather famous example. We all know what it is for something to be a game. We play games with one another in teams, sometimes by ourselves, and the question is, what are the conditions for something to be called a game? How do we use the word 'game', how do we define it? And Wittgenstein points out that any set of conditions that you come up with which are supposed to define the meaning of the word 'game' will fail to cover some cases that we happily recognize as cases of games. So, what is it that all of these cases have in common that makes them all equally covered by that term? And his answer is not going to be a single set of necessary and sufficient conditions; rather, there is going to be a family resemblance between the activities of one game and another, as in the way that members of a family might resemble each other and have more or less distant resemblance to other members of the family. We don't all have our father's nose, but there is some way in which we become grouped together by resemblances between members of that family. Similarly, in the activities we call games, they are enough alike, they are enough overlapping, for us to think of this as a family resemblance.

NW: *So, football is a game with winners and losers, teams, and a ball. So is baseball. Lots of similarities there. But a game may be just one person throwing a ball against a wall and catching it: with no winning or losing. So there are lots of different features in things we call games. There is no single essence, no essence of gameness that makes all these things games.*

BCS: Yes, that's right. Ring-a-ring-a-roses played by children is a kind of game but it doesn't have winning or losing. It's not even about getting better at doing it. It seems to be just about the repetition of a certain activity over and over again. Now, the idea that there's no essence to a game, there's no single thing it has, is, as usual with Wittgenstein's philosophy, going to illustrate a much bigger moral.

Because the moral he's interested in is the fact that there's no essence to language. In the *Tractatus*, he had seen language as a logically, perfectly ordered, functioning system doing a very precise job. Here we see a number of different uses that language is put to, but there's no single thing they have in common, there's no underlying essence to language. He also has a very nice metaphor of how language is an organic entity. He talks about being in a city and starting in a square and moving into different districts and coming to know some of them and re-encountering them from different directions. And realizing that the city doesn't have buildings of all the same period but that it's been laid upon again and again with new architectural styles and finding one's way into these different periods of time and space is one way in which we see the organic growth and outgrowth of language.

NW: *There's also the image of different levers that look the same but you find they're pulling different strings, different mechanisms. These images are characteristic of the unusual way in which Wittgenstein did philosophy.*

BCS: It's very unusual. He tends to work by example more than anything else. But the real philosophical work is trying to understand what the example is doing. He thinks that we have to be reminded of how language works instead of how we believe it works. Bertrand Russell and perhaps his earlier self thought that the real essence of a language was that words stood for objects, the naming relation, the relation between the name and the thing—this was the foundation of all language. But when we get the *Philosophical Investigations*, which is published posthumously in 1953, we realize that a word has more uses than just standing for an object, it could also describe an activity. He imagines at the very beginning of the *Investigations*, a builder and an assistant, and the builder is asking the assistant to bring more materials and he says 'slab'. Now 'slab' can either be the name of the piece of concrete he wants, it can be a request to bring the slab towards him, it can be a gesture suggesting there are no more slabs left and the assistant will have to get them. The very same word can perform different functions. That's one side of the story. The other side of the story is not to think time and time again that because, on its surface, language looks the same that it's actually performing the same function. Sometimes we have sentences that describe the way reality is—it might describe the number of books in this room or the arrangement of the furniture. But we have sentences which look equally fact-stating but are not actually descriptions of a state of affairs.

NW: *Can you give me an example?*

BCS: Yes. When we use psychological predicates to describe our mental states—I have a headache, I'm in pain, I'm wondering whether Nicolas Sarkozy will be elected in the next French election—these look like fact-stating sentences, like the way we might describe the railway timetable, the weather, the arrangement of furniture. But for Wittgenstein, they're not doing any such thing. These sentences are not describing a state of affairs as though it was an object I could scrutinize and then comment on. They actually express my state of mind. He thinks that by uttering this sentence I literally speak my mind and I put it into public view for others rather than report on it by observing it myself.

NW: *This was all in the* Philosophical Investigations. *And in that book, Wittgenstein delivers a completely novel view of philosophy, where the point of philosophy is to dissolve problems that people get into by misusing language, by pushing language too far. So philosophy has become a kind of therapy, he talks about showing the fly the way out of the fly-bottle.*

BCS: I think the idea of therapy is supposed to be to help those who need help, and who are already in trouble. And Wittgenstein's idea of philosophy as therapy is first of all to coax people into the problems to see why it's tempting to think in the way we do as philosophers, and then to try to explain to them why these ways of thinking are actually setting up spurious problems. And if they understand the situation properly and what they're doing and the activities they're engaged in, they'll no longer find them puzzling. But you've got to be first tempted to fall into the mistakes, and to make those mistakes. And he invites us, by his writing, and by his style—usually by engaging with an imaginary interlocutor who's putting problems and puzzles and questions to him—to fall into those mistakes, to feel ourselves in the grip of those problems. Because only then, when you see that they're tempting, can you exorcize them, can you do real philosophy to get yourself out of there.

NW: *So have you got an example of how philosophers get bewitched by words?*

BCS: There's a nice example Wittgenstein gives when he's dealing with a question from his philosophy student and literary executor Elizabeth Anscombe. Anscombe says to Wittgenstein, 'You can see why people thought the sun went round the earth.' 'Really? Why?', he says. And Anscombe replies, 'well it looks that way'. And Wittgenstein remarks,

'And how would it look if the earth went round the sun?'
There we can see very nicely the way our thinking can
mislead us if we don't see the whole picture. And by effecting
a change in the way of seeing, not a change in the facts, the
problem goes away.

NW: *We're in the twenty-first century. Wittgenstein was very much a*
philosopher of the twentieth century. What was his impact on philoso-
phers who've come since?

BCS: Many philosophers have regarded Wittgenstein as
creating some really rather good problems, some very
haunting problems that we are still exercised by. And even
though it may have been the official Wittgenstein moral to see
these problems as things we should resist or that needed to be
dissolved, philosophers have continued to find them important
and troubling, and gone on working on them. I think one of
his lasting legacies, though, perhaps beyond philosophy, is the
idea of trying to give up the need to explain everything. Now,
we're convinced that science will find explanations of so many
things, states of the brain, our emotions, and so on. And
Wittgenstein very poetically and very aptly reminds us that
sometimes explanations are not needed or won't help. In his
remarks on J. G. Frazer's book, *The Golden Bough*, he says 'to
the man who has lost in love, what will help him, an
explanation?' It's a question clearly inviting an answer 'no, not
an explanation. That's not needed and it won't help.'

23

HUGH MELLOR ON
Frank Ramsey on Truth

David Edmonds: *Who was the greatest Cambridge philosopher of the twentieth century? Wittgenstein? Bertrand Russell? G. E. Moore? Hugh Mellor, emeritus professor at Cambridge, wants to nominate a figure virtually unknown outside academia: Frank Ramsey. Ramsey, the son of a mathematician, himself became a mathematician, though his awesome intellectual talents were applied to many areas: he learnt German in next to no time, and translated Wittgenstein's famous book, the* Tractatus Logico-Philosophicus, *when he was just 19. He died seven years later, at the peak of his powers. His brother, Michael, who became the 100th Archbishop of Canterbury, said Frank 'was interested in almost everything'.*

Nigel Warburton: *We're going to focus on Frank Ramsey on truth. Could you say something about who Frank Ramsey was?*

Hugh Mellor: Frank Ramsey was born in 1903, the son of a mathematics don at Cambridge. He got to know quite a lot of mathematicians, philosophers, and economists in Cambridge—contemporaries of his. Then he studied Maths at Trinity College, Cambridge, and graduated in 1923 with the top First in the subject—he was a brilliant mathematician. He won a research fellowship at King's College a year later, and became a University lecturer in mathematics in 1926. That was the post he held until he died, just before his 27th birthday in 1930, which makes it all the more remarkable how many other things he did in that very short life.

NW: *What else did he do?*

HM: He founded a branch of mathematics which is now called 'Ramsey Theory'—don't ask me to explain it, I don't understand it. He founded two branches of economics—Keynes asked him to write articles in the *Economics Journal*. One is a theory of savings, the study of how much of its income a nation should save, and the other is a theory of optimal taxation, that is, if you need to raise a given amount of revenue in tax, how should you do that while minimizing the loss of utility to the people who are paying the taxes? Then he wrote an article which is the foundation of modern subjective decision theory. To do this all before he was 27 just shows what a waste it is he died then.

NW: *Why did he die so young?*

HM: He developed the symptoms of jaundice, but it was misdiagnosed as gallstones. In fact, he had hepatitis, and the combination of hepatitis and being operated on for gallstones killed him.

NW: *We're going to focus on his work on truth. In general terms, what did he say about truth?*

HM: His work on truth is an important part of what he did most of—even though he was a lecturer in mathematics—

which was work on all sorts of aspects of philosophy. On truth he developed a theory which has become famous—or notorious, depending whether you like it or not—which is often now called the Redundancy Theory. Most people who wrote about truth thought you needed a theory of what truth is, just as you might need a theory of what stars are, for example, so that you know what you're talking about. But Ramsey's view was that you don't need a theory of truth: the concept, he said, is really redundant. He gave as an example: 'If you say "it's true that Caesar was murdered" that just means "Caesar was murdered".' The concept of truth here is redundant.

NW: *Does that mean he didn't have any time for people who ask 'what is truth?'*

HM: It's true that he wouldn't have been very impressed by Pilate's question. He thought what was more important was to answer the question of what it is to believe one truth rather than another—what's the difference between different truths? What's the difference between *kinds* of truth: for example, between mathematical truths on the one hand, and scientific ones on the other?

NW: *So, he's a kind of zoologist of truth in the sense that he's looking to identify all the different species of truth.*

HM: That's right, and he's also interested in why truth matters. Why, in other words, if you're going to have a belief about something it's a good idea to have a true one.

NW: *One area in which people talk a lot about truth is mathematics. Truths of mathematics seem to be necessarily true. What did he say about mathematical truth?*

HM: He was in Cambridge at the same time as Bertrand Russell, after Russell and A. N. Whitehead had written *Principia Mathematica*, their famous work on the foundations of mathematics, in the 1910s. Their view of mathematics was that it consisted of propositions which were completely general, not about any one thing or kind of thing in particular, but all kinds of things. Ramsey thought that wasn't enough. Take a proposition like 'any two things differ in at least 30 ways', which is completely general and, he said, might well be true. But, even if it is true, it isn't mathematics because it *could* be false. So he tried to plug this gap by taking over from Ludwig Wittgenstein's *Tractatus Logico-Philosophicus* the idea that a necessary truth, or a logical truth, is one which can't be false: a proposition such as, for example, 'it's raining or it's not', which is going to be true whatever the weather. 'Either it's raining or it's not' isn't a *mathematical* truth, though, because it's not general, it's too specific.

So, Ramsey's view was that you put the two together, so that mathematical truths are truths which are completely general but also logical, i.e., tautological: they can't be false. That was the way in which Ramsey fixed a defect in *Principia Mathematica*.

NW: *So what you're saying is that for Ramsey '2 + 3 = 5' isn't about adding two apples to three apples and getting five apples. It operates at a very general level. But it's also tautological: so it's the equivalent of saying that A = A.*

HM: Yes, that's right, it can't possibly be false. And it's the combination of those two features—of being completely general and of being necessarily true—that makes it mathematical.

NW: *Obviously, not all truths are mathematical truths. What did Ramsey say about contingent truths, the truths that could have been otherwise?*

HM: He said that what matters about beliefs that *could* have been false is that you want the ones you have to be true; and his question was, 'Why?' Answering that question, he said, will tell you what it is that distinguishes one truth from another.

NW: *Could you give an example of that?*

HM: Suppose I want to go and buy some milk from a local shop. Of course, I'm not going to go until and unless I believe the shop is open. That's the function of belief: a belief that a shop is open and sells milk, combined with my desire to get some milk, will get me to go to the shop. But unless those beliefs—that the shop is open, and sells milk—are true, then I won't get what I went to get, namely milk. So, for Ramsey, what's good about having true beliefs is that if you act on your beliefs when they're true you'll get what you want to get, and if you act on them when they're false, you won't.

NW: *That's surely not true, though, is it, because you can act on false beliefs and by a bit of luck get what you want?*

HM: You never act on just one belief: you act on a combination of beliefs, and if they're all true you *will* get what you want. If two of them are false then they may, as it were, cancel out. But truth is the property of beliefs, says Ramsey, which *ensures* that if you act on beliefs all of which have that property you will get what you want.

NW: *So you can only be sure of getting what you want if you believe true things.*

HM: That's right.

NW: *Now how does that amount to an improvement on what went before?*

HM: Ramsey builds this idea up into a theory which has since been called Success Semantics, which says that the conditions under which your actions succeed—your shop is open, it has milk, etc.—are the conditions in which the beliefs you acted on are true. If you ask what a contingent belief—the sort we're talking about—is *about*, i.e., what its *content* is, then a standard answer is that its content is its truth conditions, i.e., the conditions under which it will be true.

This makes Ramsey's theory the basis of a semantics which says that a belief's truth conditions—what it's about, what has to be the case for it to be true—are given by the conditions under which any actions it would make you perform will succeed. That's what's meant by saying that the *success* conditions of the actions that beliefs cause are the conditions under which those beliefs are true. It tells you what beliefs are about in terms of how they make you behave and when that behaviour will succeed in getting you what you want.

NW: *The example you gave about getting milk from the shop seems fairly straightforward. If I want milk, I'll go to the shop to get it— believing that the shop is open, that it sells milk, etc. But with many of our actions it is not absolutely clear to us what our beliefs are. Does it follow from what Ramsey is saying that somebody else might know better than we do what our beliefs are?*

HM: They might well. There's nothing in this theory that says that you have to be conscious of the beliefs you act on; in fact, very often you're not. For example, when I'm about to cross the road I habitually look to the right where traffic might be coming from. I do that without thinking about it; but what makes me do it is my belief that traffic here keeps to the left, so you need to look to the right to avoid being run over. And if that belief were false because I hadn't realized that I was in France, for example, my looking right instead of left might well be fatal.

NW: *But usually when we use the word 'content'— the 'content' of a belief—we're thinking of something linguistic: we obviously use sentences to communicate. But it sounds as if, for Ramsey, a belief doesn't have to be conscious and perhaps doesn't even have to be the kind of thing you could put into a sentence yourself.*

HM: No, it certainly doesn't. One of the virtues of Ramsey's view for me is that it explains how animals have beliefs; when cats learn how to recognize the approach of a dog, they will believe it's a dog, and take appropriate action; if they believed, falsely, that it wasn't a dog, they could be in bad trouble. So there's no presumption that, in order to believe something, you have to be able to put it into language. And even if, like us, you *can* use English sentences to say what you believe, the content of those beliefs isn't given by what those sentences mean: it's the other way round. The theory of meaning that goes with Ramsey's view is that we use sentences to *communicate* beliefs whose content is given by how they enable us to act in ways that will get us what we want. In other words, it's a 'belief first' theory of the meanings of sentences.

The rival theory which—oddly enough, in my view—is more popular, is the 'language first' theory. This says that unless you've got a language you can't have beliefs, which seems to me absurd, and that what a belief is about—its content—is given by the independently established meaning of sentences that express it. For some reason, which is not clear to me, that view, which goes back to Frege, is the dominant view in the philosophy of language and the philosophy of mind.

NW: *Ramsey was an atheist; his brother ended up Archbishop of Canterbury. They both had beliefs about God, different beliefs, how would that cash out in terms of what we've just been talking about?*

HM: One of the things that as a fellow atheist I rather regret is that if the people who believe in an afterlife, for example, are wrong, they will never know. If I'm wrong, I probably will know. This is mildly irritating. But the theory of Success Semantics, as I'm calling it, doesn't say that you have to *know* whether your actions are successful, and sometimes you don't. Suppose you make a will, for example, because you want to leave particular things to particular people, and you believe that they will get these things after you die if you make this will. And they will, if this belief of yours is true. If your belief is false, they won't get them; your will-making action will fail. But either way you won't know. So in this case the truth of your belief, about the efficacy of your will, will make your action succeed even though you won't be there to see its success. And the same goes for beliefs about the afterlife.

NW: *From the enthusiasm of your exposition of Ramsey's ideas it's obvious that you think that he was right on many topics. How would you rank him as a philosopher?*

HM: I think Ramsey is one of the philosophical geniuses. If you wanted a musical analogue, it would be Mozart—except that Mozart lived on to the ripe old age of 36. Ramsey was ten years younger than that when he died, having founded a branch of mathematics, two branches of economics, subjective decision theory (also widely used by economists), a new theory of truth, a theory of semantics, and several other things that I haven't even mentioned. Most philosophers at their best do less than half of that in a life three times that long.

24

MARY WARNOCK ON
Jean-Paul Sartre's Existentialism

David Edmonds: *Jean-Paul Sartre, the twentieth-century French novelist and philosopher, was one of the founders of existentialism. He rejected God and the Nobel Prize for literature; he opposed the Vietnam war and French involvement in Algeria; he embraced Marxist ideas, but later changed his mind. Perhaps his longest commitment was to his life-long companion, Simone de Beauvoir—his relationship to her is usually described as 'unconventional'. Mary Warnock is a philosopher who now sits in the House of Lords; she's also the author of a book on Sartre.*

Nigel Warburton: *The topic we're focusing on is Jean-Paul Sartre's existentialism. Obviously, Sartre is one of the best known philosophers of the twentieth century, not least because of his novels and plays, but he's also the quintessential 'existentialist'. What do you understand by the term existentialism?*

Mary Warnock: I think of existentialism, of which, as you say, Sartre was one of the founding fathers, as a minor offshoot of mainly German phenomenology, which Sartre had gone to Germany to study in 1939. Sartre was not an original thinker, but like our Samuel Taylor Coleridge, a picker-up of other people's ideas, sometimes misunderstanding them, but with a genius for using them at the right time, just when they will catch and enhance the spirit of the age. So, existentialism now seems to me as much a sociological as a philosophical movement; indeed, philosophically it is all but forgotten.

After the unique mixture of humiliation and courage that marked France during the war, Paris needed a philosophy that would give to individuals a belief in themselves and their own powers to see through humbug and make their own decisions. And this is a large part of what Sartre gave them, in the kind of flamboyant, essentially Germanic, metaphysical wrappings so dear to the French.

NW: *Sartre described existentialism as the idea that for human beings existence precedes essence.*

MW: Whatever that means! You need to unpack what he meant by that. I think he meant that there was no given human nature: we all make our own lives by the choices that we make. That was a very important thought for him because he argued that everything is a matter of choice, and if you say that you are bound to do this, or have to do that, whether you mean you are morally bound to do it or whether you mean your childhood influences determine you to do that, whatever you mean, you're wrong—because actually you *could* do otherwise.

NW: *And he used this famous example of a student who came to see him in wartime with a dilemma: should he stay at home with his mother, or should he join the free French and fight the Nazis?*

MW: Yes, that was a wonderfully vivid example of there being a genuine choice for the student and nobody could make it for him. The great thing that Sartre brought, certainly to British philosophy, when he eventually crossed the channel, was his brilliant real examples. Sartre was a storyteller and dramatist through and through, and his stories, embedded in the philosophical text, served as proof of the theories. This was something English moral philosophers were very bad at doing, and Germans, for that matter. In England there was an obscure but influential philosopher, H. A. Prichard (1871–1947) who, in writing on moral theory used absurd, trivial, and highly unrealistic examples, and that was the tradition. Sartre was like a breath of fresh air. In his big book *Being and Nothingness* he had a story to show what he meant by 'bad faith' where a waiter pretended that he *had* to get up at 5 o'clock in the morning, he *had* to attend to his customers; he'd created a situation in which these duties had to be fulfilled if he were to fill the role of the waiter properly. But it was a role, a part he was playing and even overplaying. And once he had created these duties and obligations, as Sartre said, they sprang up like partridges all round his feet. He had duties all over the place. Reading this story, you suddenly recognized that there were lots of people who were in bad faith in that way: people who wouldn't think beyond the fact that they had to get up in the morning and catch the 8.30 train or whatever it was, and their life was dominated by these false necessities and the part they had decided to play.

NW: *This notion of bad faith is obviously central for Sartre in* Being and Nothingness. *Can you say a little bit more about what it is?*

MW: Bad faith is pretending to yourself something which if you thought about it for 5 minutes you would realize was not true. It's acting or overacting a part. The waiter, who pretended that he was really bound by duty, was acting the part—and overacting the part—of a conscientious waiter. When I read this, I suddenly recognized all kinds of people I knew who seemed to me to be playing the part of an Oxford philosopher, or playing the part of a committed mother of five—and you took on this persona and you pursued it, and actually you were an actress. And I found this fascinating.

NW: *So what is actually wrong with being in bad faith? We're pretending to ourselves—but maybe that's just a condition of interacting socially—we have to tell ourselves stories like this.*

MW: It is true that we have to tell ourselves stories and we do have to have a narrative of our own life. But bad faith is probably objectionable only if it is carried too far—to the extent that you may suspect yourself or even other people— more often other people—of being insincere, of having no real self, of just being hollow, playing one part after another. So it was wonderful to have all that blown away and to be told that you could do anything you like.

NW: *But surely Sartre was wrong when he said that we're completely free—we're free to choose whatever we want. There are influences upon us that are overwhelming.*

MW: Well, I think he was wrong in two ways. First of all, he was wrong to discount all the influences from one's childhood or past and equally from one's genetic make-up. But he was more importantly wrong in saying there was no such thing as actual moral right and wrong, and that only thinking makes it so. This relativism in moral philosophy was a very pernicious influence and is actually itself morally wrong.

NW: *That's interesting because in 'Existentialism and Humanism', a 1945 public lecture, subsequently published as a short book, he did say that when you choose for yourself you choose for everyone, his philosophy had that universalizable aspect. Sartre was saying that when I make a choice, say, I choose to marry, that's not just an idiosyncratic personal thing: I'm saying that human beings in my epoch should marry, and maybe have certain kinds of family relationship. I must be choosing the best choice, otherwise I'm being insincere in some way. And so I act as if everybody's acting in the same way.*

MW: Of course, one has to distinguish between choices. If you choose to have a boiled egg rather than a scrambled egg for lunch—that has no general implications for humanity as a whole. But if you make a moral choice that you're going to keep a promise on this occasion though it's to your own hindrance, then you are choosing for humanity as a whole. Now that is what he said in that essay, in that lecture, but he never said it either before or later. He was presumably trying to defend his moral theory against the widespread criticism that it was destructive of morality and essentially self-indulgent; he was quite capable of stealing an idea from Kant and using it for his own purposes, and then discarding it. So, it was probably produced out of some kind of pressure not to be so relativist, egocentric, in his view of morality as he was at that time inclined to be. But, of course, later, in the second phase of his life when he was struggling to reconcile Marxism with existentialism, then he had to be making choices for the whole of humanity, and he changed gear completely in the middle of his career. So his second enormous book (*Critique of Dialectical*

Reason, 1960) really had little relationship to his original existentialism days.

NW: *I find Sartre's later work incomprehensible. A lot of his later work was written when he was taking speed and it seemed to have quite a bad effect on his writing. And perhaps he'd reached the stage when he wasn't edited in the way that he might have been as a younger philosopher. Do you have any thoughts about the style in which he came to write?*

MW: It was appalling—absolutely ghastly. I didn't like the style in *Being and Nothingness*, though I enjoyed the anecdotal part of it, and I enjoyed the huge metaphysical structure that it was all built around. But it appalled me when I first read it. However, it was nothing compared to the incomprehensible and really shoddy way that the *Critique of Dialectical Reason* was written. But I don't think it was caused by a failure of proper editing. I think Sartre himself was in bad faith. He was playing the part of a French intellectual, specifically a great philosopher with a vast theory of history that would change the world, and he hardly knew, in his befuddled state, the difference between reality and pretence. However, we must remember that, when the *Critique* came out in 1960, we hadn't yet had the benefit of yet more incomprehensible—deliberately incomprehensible—French philosophers such as Jacques Derrida, who really are unreadable, and meant to be so.

NW: *Meant to be so? Why would they want to be incomprehensible?*

MW: Because they wanted to be profound. They were unduly influenced by the German philosopher Martin Heidegger, who thought philosophy had to have a whole special vocabulary and a way of going about things that nobody could possibly understand. From Hegel onwards, one branch of philosophy did delight in obscurity and I think that's a totally mistaken view of what philosophy should be about.

NW: *Going back to Sartre, what would you say is his enduring legacy? You began by saying he's more or less been forgotten.*

MW: He has been forgotten and probably rightly so. But what he did, historically, was to open our eyes to the fact that moral philosophy could be an exciting and totally relevant subject, involved not only in intellectual questions but in emotional questions as well. I admire him most for his having embraced the philosophy of Edmund Husserl and the German phenomenologists who thought you couldn't separate the intellect from the emotions and who preceded Wittgenstein in breaking down the distinction between the inner and the outer. What's going on in your head is not completely separate from what is going on in the outside world. When he was very young Sartre went to Germany to discover what was going on with the phenomenologists and he introduced Husserl to France, and wrote a wonderful, terribly overexcited article saying, now at last we are free from Descartes and Descartes' dualism, and he saw that, he understood that, and he emotionally adopted this huge step which was taken by the phenomenologists and was later explored by Wittgenstein.

25

CHANDRAN KUKATHAS ON
Friedrich Hayek and Liberalism

David Edmonds: *'This', said Margaret Thatcher after becoming leader of Britain's Conservative Party, 'is what we believe'. And she banged a book down on the table. It was called* The Constitution of Liberty, *and it was written by Friedrich Hayek. Hayek, the Nobel Prize-winning economist and political theorist, was born into an aristocratic family in Vienna, but left Austria after his doctorate and went on to teach in London, Chicago, and Freiburg—he's probably best known for his book,* The Road to Serfdom, *written during World War II, a passionate defence of liberalism, as it faced possible extinction. For a while, Hayek was based at the London School of Economics—now the academic home of Professor Chandran Kukathas.*

Nigel Warburton: *The topic we're going to focus on is Friedrich Hayek and liberalism. Many people don't think of Hayek as a liberal at all: he's regarded as the quintessential conservative thinker. Could you explain what he has to do with liberalism?*

Chandran Kukathas: Hayek started his intellectual life as an economist, but turned his attention to political philosophy late in his career. When he did so he set out to defend a philosophy of liberalism—this is how he put it himself. He thought that what was most urgently needed at that time was to counter what he saw as the malign development of totalitarianism in the regimes of Nazi Germany and Stalinist Russia, and he thought that these ideas were going to take hold in western democracies. The antidote was to offer a restatement, a rearticulation of the philosophy of liberalism. That was basically his research agenda for the next 40 years or so.

NW: *So, why do people see him as a conservative?*

CK: That's complicated because the term 'liberal' has a different resonance on the two sides of the Atlantic. In the United States, from the European point of view, liberalism really means something a bit closer to socialism. On the European and English side of the divide, liberalism is something that you would contrast with socialism. So when Hayek writes about liberalism, his target is really socialism; whereas in the United States, when people write about liberalism, their enemy is conservatism. But Hayek himself recognized the difficulty of the term, and apart from offering a defence of liberalism, also tried to be quite explicit about the fact that he repudiated conservatism. The famous postscript of *The Constitution of Liberty*, is titled 'Why I'm Not a Conservative'.

NW: *Central to his liberalism is a suspicion of the power of government.*

CK: That's a little bit of the story, but it's not the whole story, because Hayek is not quite as hostile to government as people think, especially if you look at some of his earliest philosophical and political writings. What he's concerned to do is not so much criticize government as to explain what its proper role is. Indeed, he has quite an extensive role for government, which is one of the reasons why he drew criticism from libertarians.

But in an early essay, he argues that one of the problems with twentieth-century liberals was that they took too uncritically the phrase 'laissez-faire', as if laissez-faire would simply solve all problems. So, he saw his task as to try to articulate what were the things that were best done by the government, and what should government stay clear of.

NW: *Let's start there, then. What are the areas within which government should operate?*

CK: Firstly, I would draw a distinction between the earlier and later Hayek. The Hayek of the 1930s and 40s right up to the Hayek of 1960, when he wrote *The Constitution of Liberty*, had a much more extensive role for government than later. But as time went on, he became more and more sceptical about some of the things that he'd assigned to government. So, for example, at the early stage he would have seen the role of government as trying to provide stable institutions of law, to provide stable institutions of money, to attend to the provision of various public goods, to be concerned about the environment. He thought that the government had a role to play in some sort of provision of education. But later on he became more sceptical about allowing too much scope for government legislation. For example, he became concerned that the legislative process itself was overly infected by particular interests, and so did not really reflect the government's concern to act in the interest of all.

He also became concerned about whether government was capable of providing a sound and stable currency. So, in his later years, he put forth some quite radical proposals for the denationalization of money, for example. On the whole, his thought developed in a more libertarian, almost anarchistic direction. But he always retained a certain view that there were some things that you needed government for.

NW: *But, in the area of the market, he certainly believed that there were respects in which spontaneous order could emerge and actually produce better results than a government overseeing the market.*

CK: Yes, he thought that markets would address a great many of the problems that human beings face. He saw markets as coordinating mechanisms. The virtue of markets was that they allowed individuals through the use of their own independent knowledge to coordinate their different purposes, to achieve ends, and to produce goods that no planner could satisfactorily do. But he also thought that to work, markets required certain sorts of institutional structures. Although some of these institutions would appear spontaneously, it was still necessary to think hard about how these institutions would work, what sorts of institutions you need. So, what he was against was the idea that you could somehow plan outcomes.

At that time, the claims that were made on behalf of socialism were really quite extensive. So Hayek's concern then was to try to say, 'Well, I don't think you can achieve this, I don't think it is practically possible. But also, if you tried, the human cost would be enormous.'

NW: *Could you outline what his main criticisms of large-scale social planning were?*

CK: Well, here Hayek was building on some important insights of the Austrian economist, Ludwig von Mises, who wrote a very important book that came out in 1920 called *Socialism*. Mises tried to try to show that, in a socialist economy, economic planning was impossible because in the absence of market pricing there would not be signals to tell producers precisely how much they needed to produce: there were no feedback mechanisms informing people of what was needed or demanded.

Hayek took this further; what he tried to show is that the nature of the knowledge problem was even more substantial. The problem was that you could not even get the faintest idea of what sort of knowledge was out there. Many socialists had tried to argue that technology would resolve the planning problem; more and more powerful computers would allow us to plug in information that we had about people's preferences, demands, production resources, and so on, and somehow come up with conclusions about what is the best way to allocate resources in society.

What Hayek tried to show was that knowledge was not only so thoroughly dispersed that it would be difficult to gather and put into a computer, but also that knowledge was not something that simply existed independently of institutions. Knowledge was something that was being generated and disappearing all the time. A lot of knowledge was of a kind that was transient or fleeting: you may be the owner of the truck and suddenly you find that someone whose goods you were planning to deliver doesn't have these goods, you've got an empty truck. Nowadays, you'd probably put up a notice on Craigslist saying, 'going to Birmingham with an empty truck, all offers taken'. This knowledge is going to disappear in about two hours. You couldn't gather it; it would be impossible. Well, this is how the market operates, Hayek thinks. It's a matter of people constantly and spontaneously trying to coordinate their activities, and Hayek thought this was where the market was at its most dynamic. Planning was something that would stifle this element of it to the disadvantage of everyone. What he thought you could do is plan to have good institutions, but what you couldn't control was the outcome of human interaction.

NW: *So what does a good institution deliver? Does it deliver freedom—liberty—as you'd expect from a liberal thinker? Does it deliver equality, justice? What is the good result we're seeking to achieve?*

CK: The short answer is that it's not any one thing. If you have good government, then what you will have is a society in which there is freedom, in which there is the administration of justice, and in which there is also a coordination of human purposes such that you have a measure of prosperity as well as equality. Equality is extremely important for Hayek, although in his case, not so much equality of economic outcomes but equality before the law, which he thinks of as the most important achievement of liberalism.

One of the things Hayek and most liberals are wary of is the idea that there is some single ideal, or even some cluster of ideals, that a liberal society or a market society for that matter is supposed to deliver. The problem is how to coordinate our actions given that we have so many different purposes, given that we have different values.

NW: *What role does he assign to the law?*

CK: The law is there to smooth relations among people. It's there because in our relations with one another we can come into conflict—since we have different ends, different purposes, and different desires. Given that, the problem is how do we figure out a way of getting along? The law is one mechanism to enable this to happen, just as the market is a mechanism for enabling us to coordinate our economic purposes.

NW: *What would Hayek say about the fact that markets can actually deliver severe inequalities of outcome?*

CK: On the whole, he's not really concerned about distributive outcomes. In fact, he thinks that it's dangerous to try to engineer particular sorts of outcomes. But he was concerned that the outcomes of markets could mean destitution for some people. In spite of his critique of socialism and the welfare state, he did on the whole defend institutions such as a welfare minimum to ensure that people couldn't fall below a certain point, to ensure that if the market didn't provide for some people they would not fall on hard times.

NW: *Would it be fair to say, then, that the usual summary of Hayek as a conservative thinker, the ally of Margaret Thatcher and Ronald Reagan, is slightly misleading?*

CK: That's correct. Those two leaders themselves were quite interested and sympathetic to Hayek's thinking. But how much he actually influenced them as opposed to the fact that they came to him because they were already sympathetic to those ideas, is another matter. Of course, politicians always pick and choose the ideas that are going to be suitable for their own purposes. Both those figures had things on their agenda, and they would draw on Hayek when it suited their purposes.

Hayek was quite happy to accept that. But there were also issues on which they simply disagreed: Thatcher, for example, was much more conservative than Hayek.

NW: *The way you've been talking, it would be hard for me to believe that you're not sympathetic to Hayek. Are you a Hayekian?*

CK: I'm very sympathetic to Hayek's ideas, but I always think back to the first time I heard Hayek in person. I was a student at Oxford, a dinner had been organized at which Hayek was the guest of honour—it was at a small Chinese restaurant. Towards the end of the evening, someone stood up and proposed a toast to Professor Hayek and he of course had to respond. He got up rather wearily—I think he had had enough of these sorts of occasions by now—he was in his eighties. He only said one simple thing: he said thank you very much, and that he appreciated the gesture. The only thing he wanted to say was that he hoped that there would never be Hayekians in the world, because he thought that followers were always a bad idea, and followers were always worse than the people they followed. Marxists were much worse than Marx; Keynesians were much worse than Keynes; and so he really hoped there wouldn't be any Hayekians. So with that in mind, I hesitate to call myself a Hayekian, but I have been very significantly influenced by his thinking.

26

JONATHAN WOLFF ON
John Rawls on Justice

David Edmonds: *Many contemporary political philosophers are proud to call themselves 'Rawlsian'—disciples of John Rawls. Among academics there's an extraordinary degree of consensus that the most important work of political philosophy from the second half of the last century was Rawls'* A Theory of Justice, *published in 1971. The book's influence has been felt well beyond the university campus. Its radical claim that what matters most in society is the position of the worst-off has filtered through to politicians and policy makers. Jonathan Wolff is a professor of philosophy at University College London.*

Nigel Warburton: *We are going to focus on John Rawls'* A Theory of Justice, *probably the most famous work of political philosophy of the twentieth century. Could you tell me a bit about John Rawls and who he was?*

Jonathan Wolff: John Rawls was an American philosopher who worked from the 1950s until the end of the century—so he had a long working life. He concentrated on political philosophy for most of his life. He began writing important papers in political philosophy in the late 1950s and never stopped—and, in a sense, still hasn't stopped, because there is still more of his work being discovered even 10 years or so after his death.

He was based for most of his life in Harvard and, as you say, his major work was *A Theory of Justice*, published in 1971. That was a continuation of work he had started in the 1950s, and after he finished work on the theory of justice he carried on developing his theory, seeing new problems, seeking solutions, new applications, and so on. It was his life's work.

NW: *What was the key idea in this book?*

JW: Rawls put forward what looks at first like a very simple theory of justice: what he called his 'Two Principles of Justice'—in fact there are three of them, so it's quite a mystery why he called them the 'two principles'. The first of Rawls' principles is known as the 'Liberty Principle', which says that each person is entitled to an equal and extensive set of basic liberties. Everyone is entitled to the sort of civil rights and liberties that one tends to have in liberal, highly developed societies. The second principle gets a bit more interesting, it splits into two: one of them is known as the 'Difference Principle'; and the other is known as the 'Fair Opportunity Principle'.

The 'Fair Opportunity Principle' again seems rather bland; it says that everyone is entitled to fair equality of opportunity, although Rawls interprets this in a more radical way than those on the political right would do. But the 'Difference Principle' is where things get really interesting. The 'Difference Principle' concerns the distribution of income and wealth in society. Now Rawls' view is that there is a sense in which fairness requires an equal distribution of income and wealth, but he says, it may be that inequalities in society could be to everyone's benefit. For example, a competitive economy with higher wages going to very productive people could create incentives, and that could make everyone better off. So, his view is that although fairness in a sense requires equality, if everyone, literally everyone, would be better off by inequality, then inequality is justified. And that's the 'Difference Principle'. The 'Difference Principle' says that inequality is justified *only* if it makes the worst-off as well-off as possible. This is Rawls' highly distinctive contribution to political philosophy.

NW: *But he didn't just pluck these ideas out of the air, did he? He had a particular way of arriving at these conclusions.*

JW: That's right. When you say he didn't pluck them out of the air, one way of understanding that is that someone must have had those ideas before he did, and another is that he must have had arguments for them. Now, Rawls was very respectful to the traditions in political philosophy, and if he could possibly attribute any of his ideas to anyone else, he would do. He was, in a way, the opposite of many of us: he didn't seem to crave originality, he craved the reverse. So he tried to stick his ideas on other people, and he could do that with the 'Liberty Principle' to some degree, and the 'Opportunity Principle', but one of the remarkable things is that not even Rawls could find anyone who held the 'Difference Principle' before him. True, it has been argued that inequalities were justified if they were to the advantage of the worst-off. This was a common thing to say in the 1940s, for example, by British Labour politicians, who suggested that inequalities are justified if they make all of us better off. But Rawls added a further twist: it's not enough that they should make us all better off, they have to make the *worst-off* as well-off as possible. Rawls seems to have been the first person to suggest such an idea.

NW: *But how did he get to that position? What reasoning led him to that conclusion?*

JW: Well, what is so interesting about Rawls is that he didn't just have a radical theory, a new theory: he had a radical new argument. Rawls realizes how difficult it is to argue for any principle in political philosophy, but in Rawls' case, he used the method of a hypothetical contract, also known as the 'Original Position'. Rawls' idea is that, quite often, people disagree about justice because they're biased by their own interests. If I knew that I was rich, I might be very much against taxation; if I knew I was poor, I might be very much in favour. Who's right, the rich person or the poor person? Rawls' response to this is to say, 'Well, let's take these two people and let us imagine that they don't know if they are rich or poor, could they then come to an agreement of some sort?' What type of taxation would you like in your society if you didn't know whether you were rich or poor? Would you agree to racial discrimination in your society if you didn't know what race you were? Would you agree to sexual discrimination if you didn't know what sex you were? Rawls' basic idea is to say: let us strip things that could bias people—in imagination, of course. You have to imagine yourself stripped of anything that might lead you to be prejudiced in your own favour. Accordingly, Rawls proposes that we should imagine people getting together, not knowing how wealthy they are, what race they are, what sex they are, not even what their conception of the good is, in other words, what they like in life. Then he asks: how would these people design society, what principles of justice would people in this hypothetical contract situation agree to, behind what he calls the 'veil of ignorance'?

NW: *So, in this imaginary case, I'm behind the veil of ignorance, I don't know what position I'm going to occupy in society: that's what Rawls calls the Original Position. I have to think through what principles would create a fair society in that situation. Is that right?*

JW: It's half right. It was right up until the last point where you said that people behind the veil of ignorance have to ask themselves what would be a fair society. In fact, Rawls says that the veil of ignorance itself ensures fairness. What these people should be asking is what in their selfish interests they would want. If you didn't know what your role in society was going to be, how would you *selfishly* want society to be designed? If you didn't know whether you were going to be a manual worker or whether you were going to be a city banker, what wage differentials would you want to have in society between the city banker and the manual worker? Possibly not the ones we've got at the moment.

NW: *So Rawls reaches these radical conclusions about how we should structure society. But what does this mean in practice? If we always have to increase the income of those worst-off, does it mean there won't be opera, or people won't be able to go on holiday to the Bahamas?*

JW: Well, the principles he draws up are at a fairly abstract and high level. They're principles to regulate what he calls the basic structure of society: they're not meant to be principles that guide our day-by-day behaviour. Rawls himself doesn't say that you as an individual have a moral duty to make the worst-off as well-off as possible; he's not telling you to give your money away: that will be dealt with by the tax system.

So, for us, we will have all the freedoms under a Rawlsian society that we have now. There could be opera if people want it, and are prepared to pay for it, maybe even at public expense if people want to vote for that. But the main thing that Rawls wants to say is that, ultimately, the institutions of our society should be arranged to guarantee equal basic liberties and fair opportunity, and the economic system should be set up so that simply by living our normal lives—going to work, paying our taxes but otherwise spending our money how we wish—the worst-off will become as well-off as possible. He does not think he is asking for heroic self-sacrifice.

NW: *That's the theory. Now, there are objections that can be laid against this, surely? For instance, it's not obvious that I wouldn't want the opportunity of a big pay-off. I might want to gamble from my position behind the veil of ignorance because it would be quite nice to enter with a ticket for the lottery that might just win.*

JW: This is a criticism that Rawls faced probably from the first day he ever wrote his theory: that he's saying that behind the veil of ignorance you should really play very, very safe. You should try to arrange things so that the worst-off are as well-off as possible. And you're saying, in response to Rawls, well maybe it's worth a bit of a gamble. Maybe I could gamble a little bit for the sake of great wealth, and wouldn't it be rational for me to do this? And, in particular, utilitarian critics say, 'Well, why shouldn't we gamble quite considerably? Isn't it rational to gamble under some circumstances, even if you know you can lose?'

Now, what Rawls did later on in his work was to try to clarify the difference between his view and the utilitarian one. First of all, he asks, what are you prepared to gamble with? Of course, you talk about gambling with your money, but would you gamble with your liberties? Would you gamble with your opportunities? Rawls thinks it's not rational to gamble with your liberties or opportunities, and so, he says, the Liberty Principle and the Opportunity Principle are fairly resistant to the gambling argument. Rawls says the first victory against utilitarianism is to establish the Liberty Principle and the Opportunity Principle.

Having done that, he says, well, maybe someone will come back and suggest a mixed principle of justice with the Liberty Principle and the Opportunity Principle, and then a utilitarian principle for distributing money. Now Rawls' first answer to that is that this is just too risky: if you were in the Original Position and had to think about your total life prospects, it would be irrational to take a big risk. It would be ridiculous to risk your livelihood for the sake of a lottery game, because you could end up in the gutter. But there's an obvious reply to Rawls, which is to say, well, let's rule out the grave risks. Let's have a safety net. Instead of making the worst-off as well-off as possible, why not have the Liberty Principle, the Opportunity Principle, the safety net, and then a bit of utilitarianism for gambling. Even so, Rawls still thinks it would be more rational to go for the Difference Principle in the Original Position. Partly, this may be a view about money not being terribly important; a rather romantic socialist view: once people have got enough, why should they strive for more? And that may be fair enough, if you do have a high minimum, why would you want to gamble some of that for the sake of crazy gain? So, in the end, I think, your choice behind the veil of ignorance would come down to a matter of temperament. The argument for the Difference Principle is not in my view stone cold, but it's pretty good.

NW: *As I understand it, John Rawls gave precedence to liberty above all his other principles. Why was that?*

JW: That's correct. The Liberty Principle for Rawls has 'lexical priority' over the other principles, at least once we all have enough to eat. It's a hard thing to argue for, but the sorts of examples people use concern things like the justification of slavery or, more recently, apartheid in South Africa. Some defenders of apartheid argued that white rule in South Africa was actually better for the blacks because of economic prosperity, and therefore it was better for black people not to have the vote. This is an argument that has been made time and time again; that if poor people are given the vote they will mess things up. Now, you might argue against that on empirical grounds, arguing that black people in South Africa would use the vote very responsibly. But Rawls' answer would be, well, that's not the criterion. If people don't have the vote, if they're not given basic political liberties, if they are discriminated against, then that is enough reason to change the system, whatever the consequences for economic prosperity.

NW: *That seems to suggest another criticism of Rawls: who's doing the imagining in the Original Position? A bunch of liberal philosophers in a Harvard seminar? We're not talking about a bunch of fascists here. What would the fascists choose? The structure of this thought experiment allows you to smuggle in your prejudices.*

JW: Well, that's a very important point. The basic motivation for Rawls' theory, in my view, is the thought that ignorance is a way of modelling impartiality. If you make people ignorant of certain things, they have no choice to be partial. But there is a question, as you rightly say, about what you should be made ignorant of. You're made ignorant of your race, of your sex, of your earning power, but why *those* things? If you're made ignorant of what Rawls calls your conception of the good, the things you like in life, well, you don't know that you even like liberty or opportunity, and so how can you make a choice at all? What Rawls says is that we've got to assume that people value what he calls the primary goods. These primary goods are roughly speaking liberty, opportunity, what he calls the social basis of self-respect, and money: income and wealth. And Rawls' justification for this is that these are the things that you would value, whatever else you valued in life. Whatever your conception of the good, whatever you want out of life, liberty, opportunity, and money, and the social basis of self-respect, are all-purpose means for achieving it.

NW: *But, surely, there are people who've got completely different conceptions of the good: a monk for instance, who wants to spend a spiritual life meditating, and is not in the least concerned with money. Money wouldn't even enter into his world.*

JW: Money might even be an obstacle. It is true there are some people who choose to be monks. Rawls would say, they have chosen to be monks. They weren't forced to be monks, they have made that decision, therefore they value liberty, they value the liberty to be a monk, and they value the opportunity to be a monk. If they weren't given that opportunity, that would be a problem for them. It is true that they may not want to have wealth, but nevertheless they might still want to live in a society where the worst-off are as well-off as possible. Monks do good works: they want to try to improve the material conditions of other people, even if they opt out for themselves on the whole. So, Rawls could say that these are all-purpose means. But there is a residual worry here. The monk may value a type of community, because of social solidarity, or ideas of collective, or common good. It's less clear that opportunity, liberty, and money, are ways of achieving *common* goods. This was a criticism made by Michael Sandel and other communitarians: that the theory of John Rawls is biased towards liberal individualistic conceptions of the good.

NW: *Rawls' theories have been tremendously influential in academic circles, but did they actually change anything politically?*

JW: It's always hard to trace the connection between ideas and practice. In the early 1980s, at a Social Democratic Party conference, a proposal was made to adopt Rawls' theory as the official philosophy of the party. This was turned down on the grounds that no one could understand it. But Gordon Brown read Rawls, and many of the current crop of both Labour and Conservative politicians studied Rawls' theory and have taken in Rawls' ideas. If you look across public policy now, there is a special concern for the worst-off in society: that a failing society is one that fails the worst-off, and where there is an excluded group of people with no stake in society. Broadly across politics, at least in Europe, and maybe now in America, although things have been rather different there over the last decades, there's particular concern with how the worst-off are faring and with important social programmes to address disadvantage. Further-more, within the civil service, until fairly recently, a type of utilitarianism was dominant. Civil servants were very interested in cost–benefit analysis: they were interested in promoting programmes if the benefits outweighed the costs. This is still true, but there is now a concern for the worst-off, and the distribution of benefits. A few years ago, the Treasury made changes to the Green Book, its official guidance, introducing a weighting system, where the benefits to the poor were counted as more important than benefits to the rich, a change which is arguably influenced by Rawls.

NW: *So Rawls has probably had some impact on the real world of politics. But he has had a huge impact on academic political philosophy. I wonder if you could just summarize that impact.*

JW: We can date political philosophy, at least in the twenti-eth century, to pre-Rawls and post-Rawls. Between John Stuart Mill and Rawls, there's no one of the same stature. You can spend a lifetime, and people have, as a scholar of Rawls. There are very few political philosophers between Mill and Rawls for whom that would have been a sensible way of spending your time. What Rawls did was completely change the mood in political philosophy. His first substantive papers came out in the 1950s. To understand the impact, it's quite interesting to look at what else was going on at the same time. We were in the late legacy of Logical Positivism, and ordinary language philosophy. Most work in political philosophy was a matter of pretending to clarify terms. There would be books called 'The Vocabulary of Politics', and papers discussing 'the grammar of sovereignty'. Political philosophy was very inward-focused and cautious, and to the outsider looked moribund. Then along came Rawls, with a theory and an argument for it. At that time, even to present a theory and an argument was very unusual, and no one had set out such a systematic and plausible theory for perhaps a hundred years.

27

ROBERT ROWLAND SMITH ON
Jacques Derrida on Forgiveness

David Edmonds: *There's surely no figure from the twentieth century who so divides philosophers. Some Anglo-American philosophers insist he was a charlatan and claim his writings were intentionally obscure—there was a huge fuss when Cambridge University decided to award him an honorary doctorate. But Jacques Derrida also has numerous admirers and disciples. Born into an Algerian Jewish family, Derrida moved to France in 1949 when he was 19. Over the next two decades, he began to develop a new approach to philosophy— 'Deconstruction': his best-known book,* Of Grammatology *was published in 1967. But here Derrida specialist Robert Rowland Smith discusses a theme from another of his works,* On Cosmopolitanism and Forgiveness.

Nigel Warburton: *The topic we're going to focus on is Derrida on forgiveness. Could you say a little about who Jacques Derrida was?*

Robert Rowland Smith: Jacques Derrida was a French philosopher. He was born in Algeria in 1930 and he died in the early part of the twenty-first century. He came to Paris as a young man of 19 where he studied at the École Normale Supérieure and ended up taking a series of posts in Paris, ending with a position in the École des Hautes Études en Sciences Sociales.

NW: *He's most associated with 'deconstruction'.*

RRS: That's right. It's a word that he inherited partly from Heidegger. But I ought to clarify what Derrida meant by deconstruction. There is a myth about Derrida that deconstruction is a form of twentieth-century nihilism, that it suggests that there's no such thing as meaning, that everything is about text and language. That's a peculiar caricature of what Derrida's work is about. I would describe that version of his work—the version that was taken up in the United States into literary criticism—as deconstructivism. On the other side, I'd put something—which we'll call deconstruction—which encapsulates many more things, including work on language, and also work on forgiveness and other matters.

NW: *So what did Derrida say about forgiveness?*

RRS: His starting point was to observe that the rhetoric of forgiveness was becoming all the more prominent in the world as politicians queued up to ask for forgiveness for various crimes they'd committed: crimes committed either in their own name or by other people. So, his starting point is a political one. What he wants to get to, though, is a notion that forgiveness is not as straightforward as we might think it is—and that, in a certain sense, forgiveness is impossible. That is a peculiar thing to say because we forgive people every day. If you were to steal some money from me, Nigel, I would probably forgive you depending on how much it was and how quickly you returned it. But it's not something that feels to me an impossible thing to do; on the contrary, it's something that I could do on an everyday basis.

NW: *That's good to know. Forgiveness though doesn't seem to be at all paradoxical. It's one person acknowledging that they'd been wronged and saying, 'I'm going to wipe the slate clean.'*

RRS: That's right. At one level, it seems pretty straightforward. But what Derrida says is that if I can forgive you for stealing that tenner from me, in a sense it was pretty easy. You were forgivable, and Derrida then smells a rat. If it is possible to forgive you, it means you were forgivable. So why did it need me to forgive you for it? Why will I have to be involved in the forgiving?

NW: *But lots of things are edible though they haven't yet been eaten. So doesn't it make sense to say something is forgivable but hasn't yet been forgiven? I don't see why just because something's forgivable there's no sense in forgiving someone.*

RRS: Derrida is not necessarily talking about what happens over time; rather, he's interested in the conditions that apply when we forgive or don't forgive other people. He's saying that for us to forgive somebody, it must be possible for them to be forgiven. But if it is possible for them to be forgiven, why would we need to forgive them in the first place? What they're doing is *de facto* forgivable. So, there's no real value that attaches to the forgiveness that I might grant to you. And that leads him to pose the alternative side of the equation, which is to say that actually it's only the *unforgivable* which really calls for forgiveness. It's those things which are so criminal, so heinous, so atrocious that activate the need—the moral need, even the political need—to do something about them. But, of course, once that need is activated, we cannot do anything with it, because to forgive the unforgivable is by its very nature impossible. We're caught in a double bind between forgiveness and the impossibility of forgiveness.

NW: *It seems to me that there are degrees of difficulty in terms of forgiving things. If I steal fifty pence from you, you'll forgive me. If I steal £50,000 from you, you may find it harder to forgive. If I murder your family, that's harder to forgive still. If I wipe out a whole race, that's even harder to forgive. They're all forgivable in principle; they are not unforgivable.*

RRS: That's a good challenge. One of the philosophers that Derrida reads in turn in his book on *Forgiveness* is a man called Jankélévitch who says that forgiveness died in Auschwitz. It was impossible, essentially, to be in a position of forgivability after the crimes committed in the Holocaust. So, there is a degree of truth in what you say.

Derrida would counter as follows: actually two things come into play when you forgive either something trivial or something relatively serious. On the one hand, it's possible to forgive you and I do forgive you whether you've stolen that money from me or done something worse. But, at the same time, my act of forgiveness always has to refer to an unconditional unforgivability, otherwise it debases and devalues the forgiveness that I'm currently acting out in front of you. So, he says it's not so much a question of being on the spectrum between A and Z, as evoking or convoking those two conditions at the same time. So, I forgive you and it's possible to do that, but it's always with a view to another horizon which is the unforgivability of whatever you might do.

NW: *Within Christian ethics, if I've understood it correctly, almost everything is forgivable. So what is it that we could have a difficulty about forgiving here?*

RRS: Derrida talks about the relationship to Christian forgiveness. He says that in Christian forgiveness you are always forgiving the person as well as the act. Once you've forgiven the person, you are implicitly placing a condition upon them, and the condition is: 'I will forgive you so long as you repent or change or reform in some way.' So the tendency in Christian thinking is to attach conditions to forgiveness, implicitly, to be sure—but they're there. So, when you forgive, you will only ever forgive the person who will change. Whereas Derrida is saying that true forgiveness, if it's about forgiving the unforgivable, doesn't impose that condition. It says, 'I forgive you even though you have committed this terrible thing and you may continue to commit this terrible thing and will possibly commit it again and again in the future.'

NW: *I don't think that's true because lots of people say that they forgive the dead. I forgive my father for being horrible to me. But he's dead now; he's not going to change.*

RRS: He is not going to change, but what you will have done is internally transform your image of your father into somebody who is now forgivable. So, you have worked the transformation on him to render him forgivable in your own mind's eye, and therefore you have subtly managed a kind of christianization—I use that term with a small 'c'—upon your father to make it manageable for the two of you to come to this agreement across the line of death.

NW: *So let's try and get Derrida's paradox clear. Derrida is saying that if you forgive something which is intrinsically forgivable, that's not a great deed. The great deed is to forgive what is by definition unforgivable, but that's impossible. So, therefore, the only thing worth forgiving is the very thing which you can't forgive.*

RRS: Correct. Derrida has a philosophical point which he couples with that insight. The practical point is forgiveness and unforgivability go together. The philosophical point is that forgiveness requires two contradictory conditions to be met. On the one hand, that the act is unforgivable, but on the other that it has to be forgivable for it to take place at all.

NW: *Presumably then, ordinary acts of forgiveness become of lesser value than they have been previously. Once you read Derrida you're going to be saying, 'I was forgiven, but that was easy for the forgiver.'*

RRS: That's a good challenge again, and I think that there are two responses. The first is that there is a call on your conscience that Derrida wants to raise. When you forgive someone, be a bit more self-conscious about whether it's a difficult or an easy act for you. If it's easy, then you will be seeking to gain some kind of emotional or political capital out of it. So, that's the first rather practical point.

The second point is even in relatively trivial instances of forgiveness—you accidentally spill your glass of water on me and I forgive you—forgiveness always evokes in some subtle or minimal way that larger horizon of unforgivability at the same time too. So, forgiveness, by its very nature, has to occur as if there were the unforgivable on the scene at the same time.

NW: *Derrida was the bugbear of Anglo-American philosophers, particularly in the analytic tradition. They got very angry with him, tried to prevent him getting an honorary degree at Cambridge, wrote abusive things about him. Why does he stir up so much disgruntlement amongst philosophers?*

RRS: That's a good question. He's not been the most popular character among people in that tradition. Incidentally, he was awarded the Cambridge degree in the end after quite a lot of debate (in 1992, but an honorary degree in Literature, not in Philosophy).

Why the hostility? I don't think it's mischievousness on his part, but he does try and pull the rug from under the feet of the philosophical tradition by exposing what he sees as a number of prejudices in it. For example, there are prejudices towards reason as something that is intrinsically non-contradictory. Why should that be the case? Why should reason be something that isn't prone to its own particular tics and prejudices and so on? So, one of his main concerns is to think about the history of reason as such—and to show that, like the history of anything else, it is subject to infiltration, to personal preference, to politics, and so on. So, there's no neutral history of reason, there's no neutral rationality. And he talks about different rationalities, psychoanalytic rationalities, for example, as well as so-called logical rationalities. I think the project is more about putting things into perspective rather than disrupting things *per se*.

NW: *The way you describe Derrida, he sounds very much in the Socratic tradition. The tradition of Socrates playing the gadfly, irritating people by asking the questions they don't want to, or can't answer . . .*

RRS: Derrida would be delighted with the analogy. In one of his books—on Socrates and Freud—he talks about this movement from behind, coming to surprise people when they're least expecting it. So, you draw a pretty good analogy: he's Socratic in that sense. The main difference is that the values that he espouses are not necessarily Socratic values.

NW: *You knew Derrida personally. Was he in any way affected by the opposition that he encountered from Anglo-American philosophers?*

RRS: Yes. But there are equal and opposite forces in play. For every hostile analytic philosopher from the US west or east coast there was at least one *aficionado* from somewhere in *mittel-Europa*.

NW: *A lot of Derrida's writing is extremely difficult to understand and, to outsiders at least, it's quite dry. Is that what he was like as a man?*

RRS: First of all, there's a huge range of writings of Derrida, some of it pretty playful. I don't know how many volumes it will come to when the collected edition comes out, but I imagine it would be in the fifties or sixties, and within that there's a huge spectrum, from the more obscure to the more transparent. What was he like as a man? Extremely engaging, an affectionate, witty man. I remember picking him up from Heathrow airport, when he came over to deliver the Oxford Amnesty Lectures on human rights. Being a Frenchman, he tried to get into the driving position, I tried to shift him over to the other side and he said, 'typical, I'm obsessed with rights'—an off-the-cuff remark in English, and very witty.

NW: *So, do you think he forgave the Anglo-American philosophers?*

RRS: I think that would be impossible.

NOTES ON CONTRIBUTORS

Sarah Bakewell studied philosophy at the University of Essex and is a former curator of early printed books at the Wellcome Library in London. *How to Live: a life of Montaigne in one question and twenty attempts at an answer* (2010) is the most recent of her three biographies, and won the U.S. National Book Critics Circle Award and the Duff Cooper Prize. She teaches Creative Non-Fiction Writing at City University in London, and is working on a book about existentialism.

Richard Bourke is Reader in the History of Political Thought in the School of History at Queen Mary, University of London. He has published extensively on the intellectual history of the Enlightenment, with a particular focus on the political ideas of Edmund Burke. His *Empire and Revolution: The Political Life of Edmund Burke* is forthcoming from Princeton University Press.

John Campbell is Willis S. and Marion Slusser Professor of Philosophy at the University of California, Berkeley. He has published *Past, Space and Self* and *Reference and Consciousness*.

Clare Carlisle is Lecturer in Philosophy of Religion at King's College, London. Her books include *Kierkegaard's Philosophy of Becoming, Kierkegaard's Fear and Trembling*, and the first English translation of Félix Ravaisson's *Of Habit*.

John Dunn is a Fellow of King's College and Emeritus Professor of Political Theory at Cambridge University. His books include *The Political Thought of John Locke, Modern Revolutions, Western Political Theory in Face of the Future, The Cunning of Unreason: Making Sense of Politics*, and *Setting the People Free*.

David Edmonds is a BBC World Service radio documentary maker and a senior research associate at Oxford's Uehiro Centre for Practical

Ethics. His books include the international bestseller, *Wittgenstein's Poker* (co-written with John Eidinow).

A. C. Grayling is Professor of Philosophy and Master of the New College of the Humanities, London. His books include *Ideas that Matter*, *To Set Prometheus Free*, *Thinking of Answers*, and *The Good Book*.

Angie Hobbs is Professor of the Public Understanding of Philosophy at Sheffield University. She has published widely in the field of ancient philosophy, including *Plato and the Hero*, and is currently producing a new translation of and commentary on Plato's *Symposium* for Oxford University Press.

Terence Irwin, FBA, is Professor of Ancient Philosophy in the University of Oxford and a Fellow of Keble College. From 1975 to 2006 he taught at Cornell University. He is the author of: *Aristotle's Nicomachean Ethics* (translation and notes) (Hackett), *Classical Thought*, and *The Development of Ethics*, 3 vols (Oxford University Press).

Susan James is a Professor of Philosophy at Birkbeck College. Her books include *Passion and Action: The Emotions in Seventeenth-Century Philosophy*, *The Political Writings of Margaret Cavendish*, and *Spinoza on Philosophy, Religion and Politics: The Theologico-Political Treatise*.

Anthony Kenny was a philosophy tutor, and then Master, at Balliol College, Oxford. He was later President of the British Academy and Chair of the British Library Board. He is the author of the four-volume *New History of Western Philosophy* for Oxford University Press.

Chandran Kukathas holds the Chair in Political Theory in the Department of Government at the London School of Economics. His books include *The Liberal Archipelago: A Theory of Diversity and Freedom*, and *Rawls: A Theory of Justice and Its Critics* (co-authored with Philip Pettit).

Melissa Lane is Professor of Politics at Princeton University and director of the Program in Values and Public Life at the University Center for Human Values. Her books include *Method and Politics in Plato's Statesman, Plato's Progeny: How Plato and Socrates Still Captivate the Modern Mind*, the Introduction to the 2007 Penguin edition of Plato's *Republic*, and *Eco-Republic*.

Mary Margaret McCabe is Professor of Ancient Philosophy at King's College London. She writes mostly on Plato and Aristotle; her books include *Plato's Individuals* and *Plato and his Predecessors: the Dramatization of Reason*.

Hugh Mellor is Emeritus Professor of Philosophy at Cambridge University. His books include *The Matter of Chance, Matters of Metaphysics, The Facts of Causation, Real Time II, Probability: A Philosophical Introduction*, and *Mind, Meaning and Reality*.

Peter Millican is Reader in Early Modern Philosophy at Oxford University, and Gilbert Ryle Fellow and Tutor in Philosophy at Hertford College. He is the editor of *Reading Hume on Human Understanding* (2002), and also the Oxford World's Classics edition of Hume's *Enquiry concerning Human Understanding*.

A.W. Moore is Professor of Philosophy at the University of Oxford. He is the author of four books: *The Infinite, Points of View, Noble in Reason, Infinite in Faculty: Themes and Variations in Kant's Moral and Religious Philosophy*, and *The Evolution of Modern Metaphysics: Making Sense of Things*.

Nick Phillipson taught at Edinburgh University until his retirement in 2004. He is now an Honorary Fellow in the School of History, Classics, and Archaeology at Edinburgh. He was a founder editor of *Modern Intellectual History* until 2011. His books include *Adam Smith, An Enlightened Life*, and *David Hume, The Philosopher as Historian*.

Richard Reeves is Director of Strategy to UK Deputy Prime Minister Nick Clegg and former director of the think tank *Demos*. His books include *Happy Mondays* and *John Stuart Mill: Victorian Firebrand*.

Aaron Ridley is Professor of Philosophy at the University of Southampton. He works primarily in aesthetics and on Nietzsche's philosophy, and his books include *The Philosophy of Music: Theme and Variations* and *Nietzsche's Conscience: Six Character Studies from the 'Genealogy'*.

Peter Singer is Professor of Bioethics at Princeton University and Laureate Professor at the University of Melbourne. His books include *Animal Liberation, Practical Ethics, The Expanding Circle*, and *The Life You Can Save*.

Quentin Skinner is Barber Beaumont Professor of the Humanities at Queen Mary, University of London. His books include *The Foundations of Modern Political Thought; Reason and Rhetoric in the Philosophy of Hobbes, Liberty before Liberalism, Visions of Politics*, and *Hobbes and Republican Liberty*.

Barry C. Smith is Director of the Institute of Philosophy at the University of London School of Advanced Studies. He is editor of *Questions of Taste—The philosophy of wine* and co-editor of *The Oxford Handbook of Philosophy of Language*.

Robert Rowland Smith is a writer, journalist, broadcaster, and consultant. His books include *Derrida and Autobiography, Breakfast with Socrates*, and *Death-Drive*.

Robert Stern is Professor of Philosophy at the University of Sheffield. His writings on Hegel include *Hegel and the* Phenomenology of Spirit, *Hegelian Metaphysics*, and *Understanding Moral Obligation: Kant, Hegel, Kierkegaard*.

Robert B. Talisse is Professor of Philosophy, Professor of Political Science, and Chair of the Philosophy Department at Vanderbilt University. His books include *Democracy and Moral Conflict, Pluralism and Liberal Politics*, and *A Pragmatist Philosophy of Democracy*.

Nigel Warburton is Senior Lecturer in Philosophy at the Open University. His books include *Philosophy: The Basics, Thinking from A to Z, Free Speech: A Very Short Introduction,* and *A Little History of Philosophy.* With David Edmonds he hosts the *Philosophy Bites* podcast.

Mary Warnock is a crossbench member of the House of Lords, a philosopher, and journalist. Her books include *The Philosophy of Jean-Paul Sartre, An Intelligent Person's Guide to Ethics,* and *Dishonest to God.*

Jonathan Wolff is Professor of Philosophy at University College London. He works in the area of applied political philosophy, and his books include *An Introduction to Political Philosophy, Why Read Marx Today?, Disadvantage* (with Avner de-Shalit), *Ethics and Public Policy: A Philosophical Inquiry,* and *The Human Right to Health.*

FURTHER READING

CHAPTER 1: SOCRATES
Plato, *Apology.*

Plato, *Euthyphro.*

Plato, *Charmides.*

These dialogues can be found in: Plato, *Essential Dialogues of Plato*, ed. Pedro de Blas, trans. Benjamin Jowett (New York: Barnes & Noble Classics, 2005).

CHAPTER 2: PLATO
Plato, *Symposium*, ed. C. J. Rowe (Warminster: Aris and Phillips Classical Texts, 1998). Contains the Greek as well as a translation and detailed notes.

J. Lesher, D. Nails, and F. Sheffield eds., *Plato's Symposium: Issues in Interpretation and Reception* (Cambridge, Mass.: Center for Hellenic Studies, Harvard University Press, 2006). Collection of articles.

Gerald A. Press ed., *The Continuum Companion to Plato* (New York: Continuum, 2012).

CHAPTER 3: ARISTOTLE
Aristotle, *Nicomachean Ethics*, trans. W. D. Ross, ed. L. Brown (Oxford: Oxford World's Classics, Oxford University Press, 2009). Especially useful for the beginner.

S. W. Broadie, *Ethics with Aristotle* (Oxford: Oxford University Press, 1991). For the more advanced student.

CHAPTER 4: THOMAS AQUINAS
Anthony Kenny, *A New History of Philosophy* (Oxford: Oxford University Press, 2010).

Aquinas, *Selected Philosophical Writings*, ed. & trans. Timothy McDermott (Oxford: Oxford World's Classics, Oxford University Press, 1993).

CHAPTER 5: MICHEL DE MONTAIGNE
Michel de Montaigne, *The Complete Works*, trans. Donald Frame (New York/London: Everyman's Library, 2005).

Terence Cave, *How to Read Montaigne* (London: Granta Books, 2007).

Sarah Bakewell, *How to Live: A Life of Montaigne in One Question and Twenty Attempts at an Answer* (London: Vintage/Other Press, 2011).

CHAPTER 6: NICCOLÒ MACHIAVELLI
Niccolò Machiavelli, *The Prince*, trans. & ed. Russell Price and Quentin Skinner (Cambridge: Cambridge Texts in the History of Political Thought, Cambridge University Press, 1988).

Felix Gilbert, *Machiavelli and Guicciardini: Politics and History in Sixteenth-Century Italy* (revised edn, New York: W. W. Norton and Co., 1984).

J. G. A. Pocock, *The Machiavellian Moment: Florentine Political Thought and the Atlantic Republican Tradition* (revised edn, Princeton, New Jersey: Princeton University Press, 2003).

Quentin Skinner, *Machiavelli: A Very Short Introduction* (Oxford: Oxford University Press, 2000).

CHAPTER 7: RENÉ DESCARTES
René Descartes, *Meditations and Other Metaphysical Writings*, trans. Desmond M. Clarke (London: Penguin Classics, 1998).

A. C. Grayling, *René Descartes: The Life and Times of a Genius* (London: Free Press, 2006).

CHAPTER 8: BARUCH DE SPINOZA
The Collected Works of Spinoza, vol. 1, ed. & trans. Edwin Curley (Princeton, New Jersey: Princeton University Press, 1985).

Michael Della Rocca, *Spinoza* (London/New York: Routledge, 2008).

Genevieve Lloyd and Moira Gatens, *Collective Imaginings. Spinoza Past and Present* (London/New York: Routledge, 1989).

Susan James, *Spinoza on Philosophy, Religion and Politics: The Theologico-Political Treatise* (Oxford: Oxford University Press, 2012).

CHAPTER 9: JOHN LOCKE

John Dunn, *Locke: A Very Short Introduction* (Oxford: Oxford University Press, 2003).

John Marshall, *John Locke, Toleration and Early Enlightenment Culture* (Cambridge: Cambridge University Press, 2006).

John Locke, *Letter on Toleration*, ed. Mark Goldie (Indianapolis, Ind.: Liberty Press, 2010).

CHAPTER 10: GEORGE BERKELEY

George Berkeley, *A Treatise Concerning the Principles of Human Knowledge* (1734), reprinted in M. R. Ayers ed., *Berkeley: Philosophical Works* (London: Everyman, 1975), pp. 62–127.

John Campbell and Quassim Cassam, *Berkeley's Puzzle* (forthcoming).

CHAPTER 11: DAVID HUME

David Hume, *Enquiry concerning Human Understanding*, edited by Peter Millican (Oxford: Oxford World's Classics, 2007)—includes also 'Of the Immortality of the Soul'.

David Hume, *Dialogues concerning Natural Religion* and *The Natural History of Religion*, edited by J. C. A. Gaskin (Oxford: Oxford World's Classics, 1998).

Simon Blackburn, *How to Read Hume* (London: Granta, 2008).

All of Hume's philosophical publications are to be found at <http://www.davidhume.org>, together with a variety of resources including images of the original handwritten manuscript of the *Dialogues*, and numerous papers (from introductory to specialist) on Hume and his works.

CHAPTER 12: ADAM SMITH
Adam Smith, *The Theory of Moral Sentiments* (London: Penguin Classics, 2010).

James Buchan, *Adam Smith and the Pursuit of Perfect Liberty* (London: Profile, 2006).

Fonna Forman-Barzilai, *Adam Smith and the Circles of Sympathy* (Cambridge: Cambridge University Press, 2010).

CHAPTER 13: JEAN-JACQUES ROUSSEAU
Joshua Cohen, *Rousseau: A Free Community of Equals* (Oxford: Oxford University Press, 2010).

Frederick Neuhouser, *Rousseau's Theodicy of Self-Love: Evil, Rationality, and the Drive for Recognition* (Oxford: Oxford University Press, 2008).

Jean-Jacques Rousseau, *'The Discourses' and Other Early Political Writings*, ed. Victor Gourevitch (Cambridge: Cambridge Texts in the History of Political Thought, Cambridge University Press, 1997).

CHAPTER 14: EDMUND BURKE
Richard Bourke, 'Edmund Burke and the Politics of Conquest', 4(3) *Modern Intellectual History* (2007), pp. 403–432.

Iain Hampsher-Monk, 'Edmund Burke', in Iain Hampsher-Monk, *Modern Political Thought: Major Political Thinkers from Hobbes to Marx* (New York: Wiley-Blackwell, 1992).

F. P. Lock, *Edmund Burke*, 2 vols (Oxford: Oxford University Press, 1998–2006).

J. G. A. Pocock, 'The Political Economy of Burke's Analysis of the Revolution', in J. G. A. Pocock, *Virtue, Commerce and History: Essays on Political Thought and History, chiefly in the Eighteenth Century* (Cambridge: Cambridge University Press, 1985).

CHAPTER 15: IMMANUEL KANT
Immanuel Kant, Prolegomena to Any Future Metaphysics, trans. L.W. Beck (Indianapolis: The Bobbs-Merrill Co, 1950).

Sebastian Gardner, Kant and the Critique of Pure Reason (London: Routledge, 1999).

Frederick Copleston, A History of Philosophy, Vol. 6, Pt II (New York: Doubleday, 1960).

CHAPTER 16: G.W.F. HEGEL
Stephen Houlgate (ed.), The Hegel Reader (Oxford: Blackwell, 1998).

Stephen Houlgate, An Introduction to Hegel (Oxford: Blackwell, 2005).

Robert Stern, Hegel and the 'Phenomenology of Spirit' (London: Routledge, 2002).

CHAPTER 17: JOHN STUART MILL
William Stafford, John Stuart Mill (New York: Macmillan, 1998).

Richard Reeves, John Stuart Mill: Victorian Firebrand (London: Atlantic Books, 2008).

John Stuart Mill, On Liberty and Other Essays (Oxford: Oxford World's Classics, Oxford University Press, 2008).

CHAPTER 18: SØREN KIERKEGAARD
Søren Kierkegaard, Fear and Trembling, eds C. Stephen Evans and Sylvia Walsh (Cambridge: Cambridge University Press, 2006).

John Lippitt, Routledge Philosophy Guidebook to Kierkegaard and Fear and Trembling (London/New York: Routledge, 2003).

Clare Carlisle, Kierkegaard's Fear and Trembling (New York: Continuum, 2010).

CHAPTER 19: FRIEDRICH NIETZSCHE
Daniel Came ed., Nietzsche on Art and Life (Oxford: Oxford University Press, 2012).

Aaron Ridley, Nietzsche on Art (London/New York: Routledge, 2007).

Julian Young, *Nietzsche's Philosophy of Art* (Cambridge: Cambridge University Press, 1992).

CHAPTER 20: HENRY SIDGWICK
Henry Sidgwick, *The Methods of Ethics*. 7th edn, available free online at http://www.laits.utexas.edu/poltheory/sidgwick/me/.

Mariko Nakano-Okuno, *Sidgwick and Contemporary Utilitarianism* (New York: Palgrave Macmillan, 2011).

David Phillips, *Sidgwickian Ethics* (Oxford: Oxford University Press, 2011).

CHAPTER 21: THE AMERICAN PRAGMATISTS
Robert Talisse and Scott Aikin eds., *The Pragmatism Reader* (Princeton, New Jersey: Princeton University Press, 2011).

Robert Talisse and Scott Aikin, *Pragmatism: A Guide for the Perplexed* (New York: Continuum, 2008).

Cheryl Misak, *The American Pragmatists* (forthcoming, Oxford: Oxford University Press, 2013).

CHAPTER 22: LUDWIG WITTGENSTEIN
Ludwig Wittgenstein, *Philosophical Investigations* (Oxford: Blackwell, 1953).

Malcolm Budd, *Wittgenstein's Philosophy of Psychology* (London: Routledge, 1991).

David Pears, *The False Prison: A Study in the Development of Wittgenstein's Philosophy*, Vol. 2 (Oxford: Oxford University Press, 1988).

CHAPTER 23: FRANK RAMSEY
Jérôme Dokic and Pascal Engel, *Frank Ramsey: Truth and Success* (London/New York: Routledge, 2002).

F. R. Ramsey, *Philosophical Papers*, ed. D. H. Mellor (Cambridge: Cambridge University Press, 1990).

CHAPTER 24: JEAN-PAUL SARTRE
Mary Warnock, *The Philosophy of Sartre* (London: Hutchinson, 1965).

Simone de Beauvoir, *The Prime of Life* (London: Penguin, 1965).

Andrew Dobson, *Jean-Paul Sartre and the Politics of Reason* (Cambridge: Cambridge University Press, 2009).

CHAPTER 25: F. A. HAYEK

F. A. Hayek, *The Constitution of Liberty* (Chicago: University of Chicago Press, 1960).

Chandran Kukathas, *Hayek and Modern Liberalism* (Oxford: Oxford University Press, 1989).

Edward Feser ed., *The Cambridge Companion to Hayek* (Cambridge: Cambridge University Press, 2006).

CHAPTER 26: JOHN RAWLS

John Rawls, *A Theory of Justice, revised edition* (Cambridge, MA: Harvard University Press, 1999).

Norman Daniels (ed.), *Reading Rawls* (California: Stanford University Press, 1989).

Samuel Freeman, *John Rawls* (London: Routledge, 2007).

CHAPTER 27: JACQUES DERRIDA

Jacques Derrida, *Points...: Interviews, 1974–1994*, ed. Elisabeth Weber, trans. Peggy Kamuf et al. (Stanford, Calif.: Stanford University Press, 1995).

Jacques Derrida, *Cosmopolitanism and Forgiveness*, trans. Mark Dooley and Michael Hughes (London/New York: Routledge, 2001).

WINNERS OF THE TWITTER COMPETITION: DEFINE 'PHILOSOPHY' IN 140 CHARACTERS OR FEWER

A message from David Edmonds and Nigel Warburton: *Thanks to all those who entered the competition. We had around 800 entries, the standard was incredibly high and narrowing them down to just ten was tough. There were insightful, poetic, and some very funny entries too. We're grateful to our distinguished panel of judges, Miranda Fricker, Tim Crane, Jo Wolff, and Barry Smith. And many congratulations to our winner.*

Top 10

WINNER @Matt0wen: Philosophy is a lot of locks and the occasional gilded key.

@twitkarl7777: Philosophy is a way to make complex things simple. And simple things complex.

@timjay: Doing the most one can with a language that is not quite fit for purpose.

@GlynREvans: Philosophy is loving the world by working out the right questions to ask it.

@Mark_A_Hooper: Philosophy is the search for truth. Or, (failing that): consistency. Or, (failing that): clarity.

@DanzieD: Philosophy is still asking those questions
                     you started asking as a child.

@nialv: Philosophy is hard-earned uncertainty.

@JoMarchant: Philosophy is.... climbing to the top of a
                     really really really tall tower. Then
                     looking up.

@adamjforster: Philosophy is trying to think outside the
                     box, whilst you're shackled to the inside.

@TomChatfield: Philosophy is the systematic conversion
                     of intuitions into doubts.